Sign Here

How to Understand Any Contract *Before* You Sign

Mari Privette Ulmer

Although the author and publisher have exhaustively researched all sources to ensure the accuracy and completeness of the information contained in this book, we assume no responsibility for errors, inaccuracies, omissions or any other inconsistency herein. Any slights against people or organizations are unintentional. Readers should consult an attorney for specific information in their own situations, as facts in every case may be different.

First printing 1998

Library of Congress Cataloging-in-Publication Data
Ulmer, Mari Privette.
    Sign here: how to understand any contract before you sign / Mari Privette Ulmer.
        p.   cm.
    Includes index.
    Originally published: Garden City, N.Y. : Doubleday, 1985
    ISBN 0-9643161-8-8 (trade pbk.)
    1. Contracts—United States—Popular works.   I. Title.
KF801.Z9U43   1998
346.7302—dc21   97-40028
                                                                    CIP

To my love and support, James Ulmer

Sign Here

How to Understand Any Contract *Before* You Sign

How To Use This Book

First, sit down, put your feet up, and get in the right frame of mind. You need to understand all those documents shoved at you throughout your life, all those times you're told, *Sign here*. So *think positive*. If this book does nothing more than convince you that you can read a contract with comprehension, that it need not turn into a blur of gobbledygook before your eyes, its purpose has been achieved. I also want you to enjoy it; untangling legal riddles can be as entertaining as reading a good mystery.

Next, read the first chapter, "Contract Basics." This chapter explains the elements of *any* contract regardless of the subject matter of the agreement; e.g., the same rules apply to an insurance policy and to buying a car.

The first chapter is also essential in acquainting you with the terminology and logical reasoning of contracts law so that later in the book you'll greet phrases such as "meeting of minds" as old friends.

Now, for your special area of interest, check the Contents. It lists the major headings for each chapter (more detailed outlines are at the beginning of the individual chapters). If the Contents doesn't give you the information you need, try the Index at the back of the book.

Since I want you to be able to translate legalese, words that have an odd or particular legal meaning are starred (*) and defined in the Glossary (unless they're rarely used and defined in the text itself).

Since this book is intended for the use of both men and women, and since judges, attorneys, businesspersons, and so on, may be male or female, you'll see that pronouns alternate between "he" and "she." Unless a point of law where men and women are treated differently is being discussed (for example, in the area of child custody and support), remember that the law will apply to all, whatever the sex of the person in the example.

Sign Here can't teach you all there is to know about contracts any more than law schools can teach students everything about the law. It can show you what to consider, where you might find unexpected rights or duties. The general basics of contract law are here but are not intended to substitute for the advice of your attorney. Each particular fact situation must be dealt with individually. Laws vary from state to state and change with the times. There remains one constant: the law makes sense. The purpose of this book is to give you the understanding to *make the law work for you.*

Enjoy!

Mari Privette Ulmer

Contents

Chapter I —Contract Basics

Chapter II—Insurance

Chapter III
Marriage and Divorce or Dissolution

Chapter IV
Things: Buying, Selling, and Leasing
Warranties & Guarantees

Chapter V
Real Estate: Buying and Selling, Leasing, Optioning, Mortgaging

Chapter VI—Credit

Chapter VII
Contracts with Doctors and Hospitals

Chapter VIII
Contracts with Attorneys
and Going to Court

Chapter IX—Authors and Artists
Contracts and Copyright

Chapter I

Contract Basics

Introduction/History

When the barons of England pinned down King John at Runnymede, the result was the Magna Carta, the forerunner of our Constitution. It is our most important contract: the consent to be governed.

We are involved with contracts from cradle to grave: an implied contract makes our parents responsible for necessities provided us as minors; the state is one of the contracting parties in our marriage and, therefore, divorce (now frequently referred to as "dissolution," a contract term); our jobs are based on contracts of employment; credit cards represent a credit agreement; buying or renting a home or apartment is accomplished by contract; insurance is a contract; and finally we may contract funeral plans. Even when we call in a pledge to a telethon, we're making a contract.

This chapter covers the generalities that are true of every contract. Whatever the label, it makes no difference whether the instrument is called a "credit agreement," "food plan," "book club," "property settlement," or "insurance policy," the rights and duties involved are contractual. Contract law lurks behind every subject discussed in this book.

Historically, contract law has no morality. There is no right or wrong, just or unjust. Contract law descends from the "law merchant," which was developed by traders sailing the seas. They didn't care what the law was so long as they could count on it remaining the same in all situations—stable. Custom was codified by the fourteenth century.

The rule of the marketplace was *caveat emptor** (Latin, meaning "let the buyer beware"). That meant "You took your chance," or "Tough luck if you got shafted." Too bad if that "gold" chalice you bought was only painted gold or if your new kettle had a hole in it.

It's only recently that the courts have begun to worry about the now familiar little old lady in tennis shoes and unequal bargaining power. This switch to a certain morality in contract law has made *caveat emptor* bite the dust, defeated by such phrases as "consumer protection" and by such actions as the courts allowing suits to be brought directly against manufacturers of defective products (see Chapter IV, page 143, under "Warranties and Guarantees": "Express" and "Implied").

Definition of Contract

Look up the definition of "contract" and you're likely to find something to the effect of: "A contract is an agreement that the courts will enforce." Great. A real non-answer. Just what *is* this agreement that has the honor of being enforced?

Starting backward, when a court "enforces" a contract, it does one of two things: it makes the person causing the breach (breaking the promise) either (a) pay the money damages he caused by his actions, or (b) do whatever he promised to do in the first place. Doing the deed—that last bit—is called "specific performance."*

Now we're back to the original question: What is a contract? It is a meeting of the minds that is clear enough about the rights and duties of each party—the "terms"— that a judge can tell who was supposed to do what. A contract meets the requirements set out below.

Contrary to what you've probably been told, a perfectly good contract may be oral—unless it comes under the "Statute of Frauds"* explained later. And a contract may be implied* (a fiction created for the sake of fairness) or express* (spelled out as you'd expect).

Elements of a Contract

Every contract—no matter what the parties are contracting about—has four basic parts: (1) offer and acceptance; (2) consideration; (3)

parties capable of contracting; and (4) a subject matter or purpose that is not illegal.

First: offer and acceptance. This is what the courts are fond of calling "a meeting of minds." You'd probably call it something like "striking a bargain" or "making a deal."

Offer equals: "I'll give you ten bucks for that rake."

Acceptance equals: "Okay."

Second: consideration, or "What's in it for me?"

In old English law, the courts said that consideration could be "a hawk, a rose, or a robe," meaning that consideration could be almost anything. For instance, in our rake-buying contract above, consideration was giving ten dollars on one side and handing over the rake on the other. Each party gets something. Or turn it inside out: each gives up something.

Consideration doesn't have to be money, and don't pay any attention when your brother-in-law says that you must put in the contract that you paid a dollar.

Consideration: (a) doing something you don't have to do; (b) not doing something you have a right to do; or (c) an exchange of promises.

(a) Doing something you don't have to do: "I'll wash the car if you . . ."

(b) Not doing something you have a right to do: "I won't sue you for the money you owe me in exchange for . . ."

(c) An exchange of promises: "I'll pay you $100 for that chair." (an offer); "I promise to sell you this chair for the $100 you offered." (acceptance).

Third: parties capable of contracting. The contract must be between those old friends, "consenting adults." (You could throw in nonpersons such as corporations, but I'm not going to here.) The parties to a contract must have the legal capacity to enter into a valid agreement. The parties cannot, therefore, be minors or persons not mentally competent, whether the disability is physiological or drug- or alcohol-induced.

Fourth: the purpose of the agreement must be legal. For example, the courts will say there's simply no contract at all if the agreement was to pay off a gambling debt or "I'll give you five big ones to kill my wife." That kind of contract is just plain void; others are "voidable,"* meaning the courts will set them aside and not order damages or performance for their breach if proceedings are brought. The voidable contracts often involve principles of fairness.

Contract law is, quite literally, neat. One principle dovetails nicely into the next in a tidy and logical manner. Contract law epitomizes my own credo: the law makes sense, and if it doesn't make sense, it's not the law.

PS: To read a contract, search out the subject, the verb that goes with that subject, and then find the object, ignoring all participles (dangling or not) and any other extraneous phrases. After you've figured out your subject, verb and object, go back and see what all the other junk applies to, paying particular attention to double negatives, of which lawyers seem to be particularly fond (as well as talking in triplicate). Remember a double negative cancels itself out and becomes a positive. (Sorry.)

Questions And Answers

Through the years I've not only drawn up many contracts, but have also advised clients in all sorts of situations on whether they were bound by a contract or, in turn, could hold someone else to an agreement. I've organized the most frequent questions, and my answers, according to this outline. Each chapter in this book follows this format—an introduction to the subject, an outline of the topics covered, and a discussion including the most often asked questions with their answers.

1. "Here's what I'm gonna do . . . " or making the offer
    a. Definition of offer
    b. Changing your mind
    c. Mistake
2. "Shake, you're on!" or acceptance
    a. Definition of acceptance
    b. Changing your mind
    c. Changing the terms
3. "What's in it for me?" or consideration

a. Definition of consideration
4. "We agreed . . ." or terms
5. Who can contract—competency
   a. Minors
   b. Incompetents—mental condition
6. Getting out of the contract (see also "Going to Court," in Chapter VIII)
   a. General
   b. Fraud
   c. Duress, coercion, and undue influence
7. Performance or breach
   a. Defined
   b. Has there been performance?
   c. Is there a breach?
      1.) Damages
      2.) Specific performance
8. Is this a contract?
   a. General
   b. "Yes, but . . ." or the Statute of Frauds
   c. "Surprise! It's a contract," or contracts implied by law
9. Sample contract—to be translated
10. Sample contract—being translated
11. Final translation of sample contract

"Here's what I'm gonna do . . ." or Making the Offer

Definition of offer

Although the word "offer" is a "word of art" (has a particular legal meaning) it's really the plain old word you'll find in Webster's, defined as "a presenting for acceptance."

An example of an offer is: "Here's what I'm gonna do. I'm gonna let you have this genuine leather album for only ten dollars down and a small monthly fee of . . ." An even more familiar offer is: "Four books for only one dollar! All you do is accept six books a year for the low price of . . ."

Q When you talk about a contract starting off with an offer, do you mean something like those ads that say: "Free offer! No obligation!"?

A Not really. Most offers that you'll run into aren't labeled "offer" and there *is* an obligation if you accept.

Often the kind of "offer" you see in ads is just to supply information—such as a pamphlet describing an insurance plan—and no contract is created. In other offers, the contract is completed before you ever know you had one. An example would be an offer to give you a toy when you buy a hamburger. The offer was that bonus for your purchase, which, of course, wasn't "free" at all. The acceptance was when you did buy the hamburger in expectation of getting that toy.

NOTE: The offer of the toy induced you to buy the hamburger: therefore, the outfit had better have one for you or else it has breached the contract.

Q We put our house on the market for $85,000 several months ago. Now some people have just offered us $70,000. Is their "offer" the one that starts the contracting, or are you talking about our original price?

A Both. Real estate language works better than many fields as to the legal meaning of words.

First, you did "Put your house on the market" with a legal "offer" to contract to sell it for $85,000. If someone had come along and said, "I accept," you would have had your contract.

Second, when your prospective buyers offered $70,000 they were, in effect, rejecting your offer and starting over, making an offer of their own. *If you accept,* that's a contract. If you come back proposing a higher figure, that's a counteroffer which they are free to accept or reject.

NOTE: A change in the terms of an offer begins the process again.

Q I just got back from an auction where I thought I'd bought myself a marvelous antique wardrobe because I had the highest bid, but the auctioneer said, "Sorry, we can't let it go for that," and took it away. Is this legal?

A No—unless the auction is advertised "with reserve." Every auction is an offer to sell for the highest bid; your bid forms the contract, since the auctioneer is bound to accept.

When the auction is "with reserve," it means the sellers are reserving the right to refuse a sale below a certain amount.

Changing your mind

Q I offered to sell my stamp collection to a dealer but then changed my mind. He said that once I'd made him the offer, I *couldn't* change my mind. Is that true?

A No—as long as the offer hasn't been accepted, you can change your mind and withdraw the offer. (The major exception to this is when a person has received consideration* to keep the offer open for a certain length of time.)

Q How much time do I have after I sign a contract to change my mind?

A None—in many circumstances. However there are important exceptions. These are mainly laws enacted to protect you from high pressure sales.

One example is in a credit situation, if you can show *within a reasonable time* that the item's value to you is not what it should be, and why. This "reasonable time" is also affected by the creditor's actions.

See also the following questions and comments.

Q I was watching my favorite TV show when a phone solicitor called. He was telling me what I'd save if I switched carriers and at no charge, jabbering on and on. I was in a hurry and don't even remember saying Yes. Now I've been switched over and my bill is much higher. Can I be held to that contract?

A I'd say, No. The law really is sensible and here it's obvious that you wouldn't have switched—*if* you did—without a benefit. None of the savings anticipated and the solicitor's hard sell add up to no meeting of the minds and no contract that a court would enforce.

If you've contracted away a "security interest" in your home, you basically have three days to cancel that contract. This is *not* the same as a mortgage, but applies to a variety of credit agreements, e.g., sale of goods, installment plans and so on.

Q We live out in a rural area. Yesterday a very likeable young man came around and said that his crew had done two driveways in our neighborhood. Because of left-over materials they could asphalt our dirt drive very cheaply. I said we didn't have the money and he said he'd do it on the installment plan so long as we showed our good faith by putting up the house. That was just to show we'd pay.

My wife and I read over the papers when he left and now we're frightened. We're scared he can take the house.

A No! Besides bearing all the earmarks of these traveling con men (driveways are popular) this comes under the law (Consumer Protection Law) giving you three days to renege, change your mind, on a credit agreement giving a security interest in your home.

Tell the man you don't want the driveway and are cancelling the contract. Write it down and date it. If he gives you any trouble, see a lawyer. You can also call the Attorney General toll free. Ask for the Consumer Protection section.

And back to your question of "How much time . . .?" you can agree with the creditor on how long you have to revoke or change your mind. If the creditor has pressured you into agreeing to an unreasonably short period, the courts won't hold you to it.

All this comes under federal laws designed to save you from yourself—the Uniform Commercial Code and the Federal Consumer Protection Law. See Credit, Chapter VI, page 210, for more information.

Q What about a "ten-day free trial offer"?

A Legally, any sort of acceptance from you would not take effect (bind you to the bargain) until that trial period is up.

NOTE: A "no obligation" offer means just what it sounds like, so don't' let anyone make you believe you've made some sort of contract when you act upon it.

Q I offered to baby-sit for a friend for a certain price per day. I've decided it's too low. Can I raise my rate?

A Yes. If there aren't more facts I should know about, there's no consideration to keep your offer open. In other words, if you were offering a daily rate, each day starts a new offer. I would prefer you give the friend reasonable notice, though, i.e., what an ordinary person would consider fair.

Q We want to sell our car and don't want to discourage buyers by setting the price too high. If we put an ad in the paper saying "Best offer," what happens if that offer is too low?

A Sell, if you want to stay legal. With that ad, you're agreeing to accept the best offer, just as stated.

Mistake

Q My brother-in-law says he really got to a guy. He saw in the contract to have his house painted that the painter wrote in the figure $120 as the price for his work when he meant $1,200. Can my brother-in-law hold the painter to that amount and really pay him only $120?

A No. When there's a "unilateral mistake"* (a mistake of one party), the one making the mistake can be held to the figure he recited *if* it's something like a mathematical error that's his fault but *not* when it is as far out of line as the example you gave and would be apparent to the other party. Such a gross mistake shows there was no "meeting of the minds."

Q There was a mistake over which lot of goods the dealer was buying from my company. We thought he wanted three-quarter inch fillings and it was one-quarter. What happens to that contract now?

A It just died. When there's a mistake on both sides (bilateral) as you describe, the courts say there never was that necessary "meeting of the minds," and, therefore, no contract.

"Shake, you're on!" or Acceptance

Definition of acceptance

If an acceptance taken with an offer is going to create a contract, the "acceptance" must be to the offer as it stands without any changes or conditions put on it; acceptance can't be "Yes, but . . ."

For instance:

Joe offers, "I'll sell you my bird dog for $250."

Sam answers, "I'll take her, *if* you throw in the litter."

This is *not* an acceptance. Instead, the person making the offer has changed places, and now it's Sam saying what amounts to the offer "I'll buy your bird dog and her litter for $250." There won't be any contract until Joe agrees. Sam can't hold him to the original offer of $250 because that was canceled out when Sam demanded the litter, too.

Caution: There is one little thing to worry about: sometimes the law says that silence—not speaking up with a "no"—is acceptance. This only happens when you've either specifically agreed that would be the case or where your past behavior has set this up. A common example is book clubs: you have agreed that if you do *not* send back the card rejecting the next selection, your silence means you've accepted it. Conversely, if a company sends you something out of the blue, you have *no duty* to do anything. You don't even have to return the item.

Q I thought I was accepting some machinery for my plant on a trial basis. It turned out I don't like it, but the manufacturer says we have a contract. Is there anything I can do?

A It depends.

1. If there was any mention of "trial" or anything else to indicate you were in agreement only in that you *might* contract in the future, you haven't accepted and there's no contract.

2. Without an indication that goods are being purchased "on trial," a business is not obliged to take them back unless they are defective or misrepresented.

Q I received a tie in the mail from some company I've never heard of. Now they keep billing me for the tie. Can I send it back?

A Yes, but you don't have to do anything at all, since it wasn't solicited. If the billing bothers you, write the company and ask them to send postage for you to return it.

*Caveat:** If you pay for this tie and the company sends you additional ones, you've created a different situation and could be held liable.

Q I sent in a coupon for a "diamond," for which the ad said I had to be "unconditionally pleased." Well, I'm not, but the company is billing me. Do I have to pay for it?

A No, but you do have to return it. That "unconditional" meant there wasn't acceptance to the company's offer unless you were in fact pleased.

Q The personnel manager of a big corporation said if I moved here he'd have a job for me. I did move, but he told me that the position was filled. My brother-in-law says I can't do anything about it because I never had a contract. Is that right?

A Wrong. This is one of those "If you . . . I will . . ." situations which are called "unilateral contracts.*" The offer was from the personnel man; your acceptance—making the move—created the contract and was also performance of your part of the contract.

In addition to "performance," which makes an oral contract enforceable, you relied on the promise to your detriment, or injury, in leaving your other job, cost of moving, etc. This is called "detrimental reliance,"* entitling a person to damages.

Changing your mind

Q We were offered some parts at a good price, but after I mailed the order, I found it wasn't such a good deal after all. Am I stuck?

A Probably. The contract was complete when you put your acceptance in the mail. That's according to the "common law,"* the old English rules of law on which our American case law has been based. All our transactions would be too insecure otherwise.

If more is involved than bad judgment on your part, see an attorney and ask if there has been a violation of the Uniform Commercial Code.*

Q A salesman came to the house last night and talked me into buying a freezer to go along with a food plan. When I told my wife, she showed me it wasn't a bargain at all. Is it too late to tell the people I contracted with that I've changed my mind?

A It depends. And, if it makes you feel better, you're not alone; for twenty years I've been trying to rescue clients from what seem to be the "big three": freezers and food plans; photographic portraits, usually with expensive albums; and encyclopedias (permanent awnings and vacuum cleaners are close also-rans).

Back to your case: you accepted the man's offer, normally creating a contract. However, a credit arrangement in your home is different. Nor will a court enforce what I've frequently seen: a form that rescinds your right to change your mind!

Changing the terms

Q This character offered to paint my house and I accepted. Now, halfway through, he says he has to have more money because prices have gone up and that otherwise he won't finish painting. Can I hold him to the original bargain?

A Yes. He took the risk and can't change terms in midstream (with few exceptions, see pages 9 & 10).

Incidentally, by saying he wouldn't finish without more money, your painter committed what's called an "anticipatory breach,"* which means that what he's saying ahead of time is such that you can treat the contract as broken (breached) now.

Q My car's in fair, not good, condition, so I offered to sell it to a guy at work for $1,000. He said, "No, but I'll give you $750." I refused. Later he came back with, "Okay, I'll give you your thousand." By then I'd decided not to sell, so he says he's going to sue for breach of contract. Should I let him have the car?

A You don't have to. When he changed the terms, that ended your being held to the first offer; he can't later accept and bind you to a contract.

Q Is there anything I can do about part of a contract I don't like?

A Yes. Remember, contracts and other documents aren't writ in stone; you can always negotiate changes and write them in to be initialed by both parties *before* you sign. For example, if you take out a mortgage that carries the standard clause that you will be forced to pay attorney's fees if the mortgage holder has to take legal action to collect, you can change that to read that the holder must pay your attorney's fees if you successfully defend.

Q They just shoved that contract at me and said, "Sign here," and I did. Now I don't want to go along with some of the terms they say are in the contract. Do I have to?

A Without more facts, I can't tell you, but it's presumed you read the contract. To say you didn't gets you nowhere unless, of course, some disability kept you from reading it. Assuming you weren't forced or tricked, the "shoving it at you" doesn't do away with the presumption that you knew what you were signing. If you're Mr. Joe Average and not a minor or incompetent by reason of drink, drugs, or mental condition, you're competent to sign.

There's another exception, of course: you won't be held to the contract if there is vastly unequal bargaining power. This is a relatively new idea or approach in contract law: fairness. An example is that famous little old lady who can't be held to a bargain struck with a shrewd businessman.

Caveat: The courts are not going to go about striking down contracts willy-nilly for slight unfairness.

Many callers have scolded me saying, "You tell us to read the contract, but what can I do when that salesman sits there drumming his fingers, waiting for me to sign here?" Don't be intimidated. Stick to your guns and say, "I'll just have to take this home to read it." Then he says that the offer is only good now and you'll have to make up your mind—and you say, "Bye."

Usually only the shady or questionable deals—those *not* in your favor—must be signed on the spot.

"What's in it for me?" or Consideration

Definition of consideration

Up until now I've been promising plain English meanings. I can't do that with "consideration" but it's still understandable, so don't panic.

According to Black's Law Dictionary, consideration is the "inducement to a contract," the "impelling influence which induces a contracting party to enter into a contract."

Consideration is the glue that binds the bargain. Consideration is the label for the answer to "What's in it for me?"

Consideration doesn't have anything to do with whether you made a good or bad bargain. It's the bargain itself that we're talking about: What did this one give up and that one receive? An example is: "If you'll agree not to sue me, I'll pay you a thousand dollars for your injuries." Agreeing not to sue is a detriment (giving up a legal right), while not being sued is a benefit. In comparison, if I just promise not to sue, that, by itself, won't get the job done; there's nothing in it for me and therefore no consideration. I'm not bound and there's no contract.

The main thing to keep in mind is that consideration can be almost anything and certainly does not have to be money or some tangible object. As discussed earlier, consideration can be: (1) an exchange of promises; or (2) doing something you're not obliged to do; or (3) not doing something you have a right to do.

Q My brother-in-law says that you have to put in something like "for one dollar" to hold somebody to a contract.

A Wrong. Phrases like "for the value of one dollar hereby acknowledged" or "in consideration of one dollar" aren't magic and don't by themselves make a contract valid.

Two points: (1) "consideration" does not have to be money, and you can "hold somebody"—make a binding contract—without an exchange of money; and (2) sticking in a phrase like that accomplishes nothing if there's a question raised as to whether there was valid consideration.

Q I promised to fix the car of a friend, but changed my mind. Now my ex-friend says he's going to hold me to my promise. Can he do that?

A Not on the facts as you tell them, because there's no consideration. Your promise is just floating about; to tie it down, your former buddy would have to put up something on his side, money or another promise.

Q My son just came into a good bit of money, and I figure I'm entitled to some of it for all the years I fed him and put a roof over his head. He says he won't give me any and I said I'd take him to court.

A Please don't. While he was a minor you owed him the duty of support. If he's older than that now and you're still feeding and housing him, the law considers you a volunteer.

Q I settled a fender-bender with the insurance company myself. They gave me a check with all sorts of printing on the back of it, which I signed, but I don't remember signing anything else. Now my back hurts. Can I go after them for more money?

A Probably not. It's unusual for the insurance company not to have you sign a release in which, for consideration, you contract not to sue. That printing on the back of the draft (the check) was almost certainly a release in itself, stating that when you endorsed the draft you were agreeing that your claim was paid off in full and that you gave up any right to bring suit. The draft was the consideration.

Q My former friend offered to pay me twenty bucks if I'd take my pickup out to where they had a country auction and pick up the furniture he bought. When I had already done that and unloaded the stuff at his house, he said he thought I was doing him a favor out of friendship. No money. Does he owe me the twenty?

A Yes. You had an oral contract where picking up the furniture was both acceptance and performance. The contract was complete. You're entitled to the twenty.

"We agreed to . . ." or Terms

Definition of terms

The "terms" of the contract are the reason the parties got involved with each other in the first place.

The "terms" of the contract are what the whole thing is about: What is the agreement?

When I promise to take out the trash if you wash the car, the terms are trash-taking-out on one side and car-washing on the other. That's the bargain. The mutual promises are also the consideration.

Frequently the "terms" of a contract are what the parties are fighting about. Examples of disputed terms would be:

"You promised to make a payment by the tenth of each month."

"I never agreed to stay late every night."

"You said this air conditioner was all I needed."

"I didn't promise to paint the whole thing for that much money."

When one party claims the other has not performed a contract, it's the "terms" that define the duties.

The important point to keep in mind when contracting is that the terms should be clear, precise, and without ambiguity. The main idea here is not the requirement that the terms be sufficiently specific for the court to enforce, but that they be sufficiently specific to keep you *out* of court.

I can't count the number of times over the years clients have said to me, "We're such good friends we don't need a contract." My answer is always, "You need a contract so you'll stay good friends." That's terms.

Q This fellow brought his car into my garage and we agreed on the price for me to put in a new transmission, but he keeps adding on to what I'm supposed to do for the same amount. Can I tell him I'm sticking to the original bargain?

A Yes. Of course, if it was only an oral agreement, you'll be into a swearing match about what work was agreed upon. It's better to get it in writing.

Q I signed a contract with a roofer to put a new roof on the house. The contract didn't say when the work would be completed, but three months have gone by and still no roof. He says that he'll do it when he's ready. Do I have to wait?

A No, usually a contract must be sufficiently specific in its terms for a court to enforce it, but when no time is stated, the court will read in (take it to mean) "reasonable time."

It's up to you to show the court by way of such arguments as custom, as well as the condition of your roof (leaks?) and weather (you're freezing?), that the man has taken an unreasonable time and, therefore, breached the contract. Then you get your money back, plus any damages caused by his unreasonable delay.

NOTE: This is one of a few examples when the court will add terms. It will *not* rewrite a contract.

Q When I took my franchise, I agreed to buy all my supplies from the company doing the franchising. Now I find I can get the paper products cheaper here in town. Do I have to keep that part of the agreement?

A Probably. Franchise law is growing into a whole new ball game of its own, but the underlying contract law is that one party cannot change the basic, or material,* terms of the contract. In your case, it sounds as if buying everything from the franchise company is that kind of basic term. Check with an attorney.

Q I sell homemade candy and use 100 pounds of sugar a week. My contract with the supplier calls for that much to be delivered weekly. The supplier just wrote me that he can't afford to deliver that often and that he will send the sugar every ten days. Can he do that to me?

A No. He's attempting to change a material (basic) term of the contract.

Q I just signed a contract and started a new job, but it turns out that the boss expects me to stay late every night, which wasn't mentioned when I was hired. She makes me feel like it's an "or else" situation. What can I do?

A See a lawyer to go over your contract with you. Normally, whether it says it or not, a written contract has in it all the terms of the agreement. That's so that the parties know where they stand and no one can come along and try to prove there's more to the contract. From what you tell me, it appears staying late is not part of the contract, but you want to make sure—and keep your job.

Q We hired an architect to design us a house. His plans turned out to be a place that we would never consider building. He says he'll take us to court if we don't pay him. Can he do that?

A He *can* take you to court: the question is whether he'll win or not.

You don't say whether the contract between you and the architect contains the *terms* that the plans must have your approval. If not, this is a case where the court might well add terms. In other words, the court might read into the agreement that the architect's work had to meet with your approval before he could demand payment.

NOTE: The court would hold that you could not unreasonably withhold approval.

Q Our landlord agreed that if we painted the apartment we could skip a month's rent. Now he is trying to evict us on the grounds that we didn't pay that month's rent, saying there wasn't anything about credit for painting in the lease. We can tell the judge about the painting agreement, can't we?

A The presumption is that the contract contains all the terms of the agreement. Therefore, normally, you can't bring in verbal or "parol"* evidence such as your agreement with the landlord. However, in your case you could probably show that you would not have painted the apartment unless the landlord had made some kind of agreement outside the terms of the written contract.

Q I had a contract to haul dirt to a building site. Now the owner won't pay me because he claims I have to spread it. That wasn't in the agreement and it would add a great deal to my costs. Do I have to have that dirt spread in order to get paid?

A No. If you go to court to collect what the owner owes you, your argument would be that the contract was clear and unambiguous and did not contain a provision that you were to spread the dirt.

Caveat*: A possible exception is if *all* the dirt haulers in your area spread the dirt, i.e., if this is the known custom of the community. If so, this is where a court breaks its own rule not to add terms to a contract and does just that by a fiction. It might say that because the contract is *silent* as to dirt spreading, the contract *included*, by implication, the custom of the community to spread the dirt.

Who Can Contract—Competency

Anyone can contract who's not under a legal disability, meaning a person who is incompetent in some way. The idea is that such a person cannot give legal consent. Since there must be that "meeting of the minds" to contract, an incompetent can't contract.

Historically, this included minors under the age of 18 who were not emancipated* (usually meaning married or living and working outside the parental home). All but three states have 18 as the age of majority (Alabama - 19; Mississippi - 21; Nebraska - 19), but the law has changed as to a minor's ability to contract. Varying among the states, the majority hold that minors *can* enter into contracts for: medical and related services, including giving consent to treatment for emergencies and drug/substance abuse; birth control; AIDS treatment and testing. Some allow consent to organ transplants and blood donation; permit a minor to contract for various types of insurance, such as life insurance; and, contract for an educational loan.

The same reasoning causes contracts to be set aside as invalid if one party wasn't competent at the time. Incompetency can be the result of a physical ailment or can be drug- or alcohol-induced (one rationale being that the person didn't have the sense to make a contract). There would have to be proof that the person's mind was affected to such an extent that he or she couldn't legally consent to the agreement.

Our legal system leans toward upholding contracts for the pragmatic reason that people need to keep their affairs in order. This, in turn, has to be balanced against today's notions of fair play, which say a person shouldn't be held to a contract if that person lacked the mental faculties to bargain.

Minors

Q Our daughter was injured in a motorcycle accident and was treated at a nearby emergency room. The hospital bill is too big for us to pay right now, but my barber says we don't have to pay it because she's a minor and couldn't contract for the treatment.

A Wrong. You are responsible for medical treatment and necessities furnished your minor child.

Q Our underage son bought a car from a used car dealer and has gotten behind on his payments. The dealer says he's going to go after *us* for those payments. Are we responsible?

A No. Your son cannot contract for this sort of thing while he's a minor. He will have to return the car, however.

Q What's an emancipated minor?

A A child who is under age but who either works and lives away from home or is married.

Incompetents—mental condition

Q My father is quite elderly and forgetful. He's been buying all sorts of things he doesn't need or even want. The doctor says he's suffering from Alzheimer's disease. Do we have to pay for all that merchandise?

A I would take care of those bills and plan for the future.

A contract can, of course, be set aside if one of the parties is incompetent—there would be none of that "meeting of minds" we talked about, *but* . . . The "but" is the practical matter of the expenses of court hearings to void the contracts those charge accounts represent, unless you're talking about such a large amount of money to make those proceedings worthwhile.

Now, as to the future: if your father appears really impaired, and your doctor agrees with you, hire a lawyer to set up a competency hearing and have a guardian appointed. He or she, in turn, can correct the charge accounts and take care of practical matters. This guardian remains responsible to the court for an accounting of expenditures.

Many people plan ahead and execute a "durable power of attorney"* which kicks in when one or more (depending on what the document says) doctors certify the person is incompetent. This way whether a loved one is mentally or physically unable to handle his/her affairs, the power of attorney provides a named person and successor to take over to do everything: cash checks, collect insurance, pay bills, bank, etc. The ones I draw up often contain the "right to die"/ "living will" as included on pages 250-251.

Q We have a relative who's really acting weird. It looks like she's going to give away her whole estate. My brother-in-law says she's not fit to contract. What should we do?

A See if she will agree to see a psychiatrist or psychologist, or she might have a family physician who is willing to discuss her condition with you.

You should be aware, however, that just acting "weird" is not sufficient reason to have someone declared incompetent. For instance, in a case involving a will the testimony was that, nightly, the testator had places laid and sat down to formal dinner with his numerous dogs. The court held that this was eccentric, but not proof of incompetency.

Getting Out of the Contract

General

The most clear-cut excuses for a party getting out of (avoiding) a contract are that the contract was induced by fraud, duress, coercion, or undue influence.

Fraud. When someone hollers, "That's a fraud!" they mean the same thing that the words stand for in law. The difference is that the legal meaning of the word "fraud" is more precise. To prove fraud, a person must show that, in order to get him to enter into the contract, the other party: (1) made an intentional misrepresentation which (2) he intended be acted upon, and (3) which was acted upon detrimentally. In other words, the party upon whom the fraud was practiced would not have entered into the contract if he had not been tricked into it.

Duress. A party is claiming duress when she says she was forced to enter a contract against her will.

Coercion. Coercion is close to the same thing as duress, but it conveys more connotation of physical threat.

Undue influence. When a claim of undue influence is made, the gist of it is psychological—a party is operating, not under his own will, but under that of another.

Q Is there any time when a person should break a contract on purpose?

A Yes. You might have made such a bad bargain that it would cost you less to breach it than to stick with the contract.

See your attorney! The law usually isn't absolutely black or white. It's always better to try for a compromise and settlement ahead of time than to anger the other party by failing to perform without notice.

Your lawyer will talk about "exposure"* and "liability,"* which, here, will mean what the other party might collect in court for your breach. She can also advise you of what she thinks it will cost you to get out of the contract without going to court by making a settlement.

There is also arbitration (both binding and not) which some jurisdictions require.

Q Can I break a contract?

A People "break" or "breach" contracts all the time. Sometimes they are made to pay money damages or perform the contract. Other times they have good defenses or reasons for the breach and therefore are not held accountable. If you're talking about being made to do what you promised, and it's a personal service—if, for example, you're reneging on a promise to sing a concert—the court won't order you to perform though you will be liable for damages. This is because of the difficulty of enforcing that order to sing.

There are only a few instances when a person is ordered to perform what was promised (as opposed to paying damages). The most common example is when a contract for the sale of real estate is breached: the seller may be ordered to convey the property (transfer the title) on the theory that damages in its place aren't adequate because each piece of property is unique. This is called "specific performance."*

Fraud

Q I bought a secondhand car from a dealer who assured me it had never been wrecked. I couldn't see any telltale signs on the car that would indicate he wasn't telling the truth. Now I've just discovered that not only was the car wrecked, but the front half and back half of two different cars have been welded together. Can I do anything?

A Yes. You had a fraud committed on you, which makes the contract void. This is because there never was consent to the true facts, and thus no "meeting of the minds." Fraud* is the intentional misrepresentation of a material fact (here the welded-together halves) with the intention it be acted upon.

Q We answered an ad and purchased sight-unseen one of those "ranchitos" in the West. When we made a trip out there to look at our new land, we found out it doesn't have any water available at all. Can we get our money back from the promoter?

A Take comfort in the fact that you're not alone! Many people have purchased dry ranchitos in the West and swampland in the South. Whether or not the buyers can get out of these contracts has been litigated, and the question is, as usual, reasonableness: here, the reasonableness of expecting water on a homesite.

First, did the advertisement explicitly promise water? If so, it's a clear case of fraud, which will cause the court to set aside the contract. (I don't think a court would say you should have investigated the truth or falsity of the assurance of water because of the reasonableness of your belief under the circumstances.) You'd get your money back and damages.

Second, if water wasn't expressly promised, is this a case where a court would find that silence constituted concealment or fraud?

I'd go for the argument that it's fraudulent not to reveal that land touted as a homesite is without water, or, saying it the other way around, it's reasonable to assume such land would have water.

Usually silence isn't fraud, but here it would be "concealment of a material fact" (no water).

NOTE: As to the second example above, a court might call the silence "misrepresentation," a milder word than "fraud." "Misrepresentation" is used when the false statement or concealment is only negligent or even innocent.

Q A character came to town and set up a showroom in a motel with all sorts of supposedly "fine jewelry" for sale at incredibly low prices. I bought my wife a "ruby," which we took for an appraisal. The jeweler said it's very nicely cut glass. Can I get my money back, or have I been had?

A The latter, probably. Legally, the deal appears fraudulent, but, in actuality, it's unlikely you'll catch up with the man or that he'd have your money available if you did. Usually a "con" can't take place without a little larceny in the heart of the victim. Were you told it was a ruby, and did you rely on that assurance when you bought it? And did you have a right to so rely, in the face of an inordinately low price? This is application of common sense to all the circumstances.

Duress, coercion, and undue influence

Q My partner said that unless I signed a paper agreeing to pay off all the company debts from my personal account, he would throw us into bankruptcy. I panicked and signed, but now I want to fight him. Can I get that agreement set aside?

A First, we need to examine that agreement you signed to see if there's a valid contract. There probably is because your partner's promise not to take bankruptcy would be the consideration. Second, as to duress and coercion: historically these defenses to breach of contract have been based on threatened or actual physical harm, but now what might be called psychological harm is often enough to get the contract set aside. It would be difficult to prove that you were coerced into signing rather than that you simply made a bad bargain and want to get out of it.

Q I'm my aunt's only heir, but now she's taken in a young man who's a phony and really playing up to her. She's falling for his flattery and talking about deeding him the farm. Could we have this deed set aside as being signed under duress or coercion or undue influence?

A You're talking about the last, and the answer is probably not. Usually a claim of undue influence based on flattery will get you nowhere in court. The courts have said that the most outrageous behavior leading a person to act—so long as it's affirmative and not based on fear—is seldom undue influence and certainly not duress or coercion. Those two words refer to behavior that causes one to act out of fear. Only negative behavior is restrained.

Here, to make a case for undue influence, you would have to show that your aunt is so under the man's spell that his will is substituted for hers.

Q A hard-sell salesman came to my house and somehow hypnotized me into buying a series of "portraits" of my baby along with a fancy album. We can't afford it at all. Can I claim I was forced into it?

A Not by duress or coercion, but if you signed a credit agreement, the law designed to protect people from this type of very hard-sell occurrence gives you a reasonable time to cancel. This is by statute (federal and often state) rather than the common law* we've mostly been talking about.

Performance or Breach

Defined

"Performance" is doing what you promised to do. "Breach" is breaking that promise. Although the meaning of "performance" and "breach" seem clear, the situation often becomes cloudy when one party argues he did perform and the other argues there was a breach.

Since the law is tailored to apply to innumerable sets of facts, qualifications are added to the definitions of performance and breach. For instance, if that broken promise is to be deemed a breach of contract, the failure to perform must be substantial and without legal excuse.

A legal excuse for failing to perform would be a defense such as: the party charged was actually prevented from performing by the party claiming a breach; consideration was lacking; the party's inability to contract (minors and incompetents, discussed earlier in this chapter); mistake; or the grounds of fraud, duress, coercion, or undue influence.

Failure to perform is *not* excused by unexpected expenses, difficulties, or other factors that remove the advantages of the bargain. However, if the unexpected expense, for instance, is enormous, then the court won't enforce the contract, reasoning that this factor was so crucial the parties never actually had a contract because there was no meeting of minds. In line with this new idea of fairness, more and more courts will refuse to enforce a contract that would mean catastrophe to the defaulting party.

When there is a breach of contract, there are, naturally, an injured party and a guilty party. In order to make up to the injured party for what was lost because of the actions of the guilty party, the injured party is awarded damages.* The purpose is not punishment of the guilty party, but an attempt to put the innocent party back in the condition he was in before the breach of contract. It follows that the innocent party can't get rich at the other's expense.

The rule of unjust enrichment is that when a party defaults because of circumstances beyond his control, and the supposedly injured party has already received more benefit by the bargain than he will be damaged by the breach, then the defaulting party may recover some compensation.

An example of the above would be: a contractor has substantially built the house contracted for by the owner, but is unable to finish the job because he can find no more of a certain floor tile with which he started. This excuse is not a legal defense that would get him out of the contract, but the owner, with the benefit of an almost finished house, has come out ahead of any damages caused by the contractor's breach. Therefore, if the owner sues for breach of contract or refuses to pay the contractor, a court would award financial compensation to the contractor to prevent the owner from being "unjustly enriched."

Flood, fire, and earthquake are called "Acts of God." These are usually, but not always, an excuse for nonperformance.

Has there been performance?

Q I contracted to make furniture for a fancy office furniture place, part of the agreement being that the store would supply the oak. Well, some of the wood was of such a low grade that I couldn't use it and some wasn't even oak. After a lot of argument I told them I just didn't want to make furniture for them at all. They're threatening to sue me. Don't I have a good defense to what they claim is my breach of contract?

A Yes. You have a "legal excuse," as discussed—failure to perform. When the furniture outfit claims that you breached the contract, your answer is that they performed in such a way as to prevent you from keeping your part of the bargain.

Is there a breach?

Q I contracted to pay a lot of money to have a new carpet installed in the living and dining rooms. Trouble is, the carpet man didn't make his workers put back the molding around the edges. When I called him we both got pretty angry. I told him I'm not paying one red cent the way it looks!

A Please do. The carpet man has done what's called "substantial performance."* A court won't let you be "unjustly enriched"* with a whole new carpet just because of the molding; it would order you to pay (plus court costs and perhaps attorney fees). You will probably be allowed to deduct the cost of having someone put the molding back on or the court might suggest that the carpet man do it.

Q We're in a rural area and I have a contract to have my trash picked up every Wednesday. Last Wednesday the trash man didn't come at all and dogs got into it, making a big mess. I figure that since he caused me all that grief I don't have to pay for the other days he came last month! Right?

A Wrong. Substantial performance again. I'm afraid you probably can't get anything for your "grief" but you can deduct the proportional amount of one missed day.

Q My aunt gave her daughter the family home and all its furnishings in exchange for the daughter's promising to support her for life. Now the daughter tells my poor aunt she's changed her mind and can't manage the support. Is there anything my aunt can do?

A Yes. In a similar case the judge decided that this was a breach of contract and the damages (to be paid by the daughter) would be what it cost the mother to be supported by someone else.

Q In my professional capacity as an architect, I drew up plans for a house for some people. After I had turned over the plans, they decided they couldn't build after all because of the cost. They don't want to pay me because they're not building a house, but I put in the work and think I should be paid. Who's right?

A You are. You performed. The law says that the people who contracted with you have breached the contract and owe you for services rendered. They would say that they had a "good excuse," but this is not the kind of excuse that lets a defaulting party off the hook legally.

Q My partner and I are contractors putting up a commercial building; we hired a subcontractor to furnish the trucks and do all the hauling from the excavation site. Now that the weather has gotten bad, the sub says he can't continue the hauling because in this wet weather he would have to use caterpillar trucks, which he doesn't have. We think he should have foreseen this and is liable to us.

A Right. In a similar case, the court said the subcontractor was obligated to do the hauling even though it turned out to involve equipment he did not possess.

Damages

Q I rented an apartment from the man who owned the building and paid him a deposit. When I tried to move in, the man said the apartment was taken. I had already hired a truck and a moving crew. Can I get back more than my deposit?

A Yes. If you've given me all the facts, you can recover damages—the amount you've had to pay out because of the breach of contract.

Q The bank verbally agreed to loan money to my husband and me, but when we went to pick up the check the loan officer told us they had changed their minds. In the meantime, interest rates have gone up. Can we sue for breach of contract, and, if so, what can we collect?

A If a *verbal* contract for a loan is okay in your state, then it does appear to be a breach of contract, and you would collect damages. Since damages are supposed to put you in the position you would be in if the other party hadn't broken the contract, you would be entitled to what you'd have to pay for the loan at those increased interest rates. For example, if the new interest rates increase your loan by $1,000, then you would be awarded $1,000 in damages, more if you suffered other losses as a direct result of not getting that loan.

Caveat: What I mentioned above about a verbal contract refers to your state's statutory version of the Statute of Frauds,* which demands certain contracts be in writing. (See Glossary and pages 33 & 34.) The federal version doesn't cover your loan agreement. But even if this law about an agreement being in writing did apply to your case, if you have any written, sufficiently specific memo from the bank, that will do it.

Of course, the bank isn't going to happily hand you the damages, but you may be able to stay out of court. If it looks like you can prove up a good enough case, the bank may settle with you to avoid going to court. They know banks aren't universally loved by juries.

Q I contracted with a company to add a room onto my house. They kept stalling and I finally gave up on them. The trouble is, I've checked around and can't get the job done for that price. Can I collect damages?

A Yes. The damages are the difference between the contract price and what it would cost you to have the job done by someone else. Of course, the "stalling" must have been for an unreasonable length of time.

Specific performance

Q After years of hunting, I finally found a carrousel horse in a man's barn. I paid him and he was to deliver it. The next day the man called and said he had decided not to sell the horse. Can I make him do it?

A Yes, you had a contract and performance on your side. You would get the carrousel horse instead of just money damages because it would come under the category of things (or land) that can't be replaced by money. Your carrousel horse, many antiques, paintings, and other items, are unique, and therefore the court orders specific performance* instead of damages. "Specific performance" means the person has to perform as agreed—in your case, handing over the carrousel horse.

Q Our club contracted with a big-name singer to come and entertain for a charity benefit. Now she says she can't come. We have all the advertising out, tickets sold, and other expenses. We want to take her to court and make her sing.

A A court won't order this sort of personal performance. Although money damages may not be adequate, it just isn't feasible to order someone to sing.

Q I ordered a sweater from a catalogue but it didn't come until it was too warm to wear it. I sent back the sweater and refused to pay. The company is threatening to sue and mess up my credit rating. Can they do this?

A Sure they *can* but you will win and you can make them straighten out your credit. When no time is stated, the courts write in "reasonable" time. Here you won't have the intended use of the sweater because it was not shipped to you in a reasonable time—a breach of contract on their part, a failure to perform an essential term even though it wasn't stated. (By the way, many contracts recite "time is of the essence" but that's not necessarily true.)

Is This a Contract?

General

Over the years, I've had many people come to me arguing both sides of the question: Is this a contract? In some cases, people want me to tell them they do have a contract; in others, they want me to make it go away. Basically, if you're trying to prove there is a contract, you must prove that big catch-all: that there was a meeting of minds. "Meeting of minds" takes in the offer and acceptance, consideration, sufficiently defined terms, and parties able to contract. Contracts may be oral or written. But in certain circumstances an oral contract won't be enforced: 1) contracts for the sale of goods valued over $5,000; 2) contracts for sales of securities; 3) contracts for security agreements, such as loans with collateral as security; and 4) certain manufactured goods. Our federal acts and state statutes on this come from the old English Statute of Frauds that I've mentioned earlier. Another contract that had to be in writing was to be responsible for someone else's debt.

On the other side, the reverse may happen and you may find "Surprise! It's a contract." Understandably, the rules of fairness sometimes lead a court to say there was an "implied contract." This means that although there wasn't any contract at all in actuality, the court believes justice demands it invent one. An example would be your visit to a doctor: even though there was no explicit agreement, the court says there was an "implied contract" to pay for the doctor's services.

Q My brother-in-law says that I can forget about a contract I just signed because it wasn't notarized.

A Wrong! (Unless the contract specifically called for notarization.)
Many people, like your brother-in-law, think notarizing is magic. It isn't. A notary has two functions: 1) to prove up a signature, i.e., witness that you're the person who signed in front of her; 2) to administer an oath to make the document one that's been sworn to, e.g., an affidavit. A document—such as a deed—must be notarized to be filed at the

courthouse. Also, many states now accept notarizing a will as part of the "proving it up" later without needing to find the witnesses.

Notarizing does not make anything "true."

Q The car park attendant damaged my car when he was bringing it down to me, but a friend says I can't recover because the ticket had on it: "Not responsible for loss, theft, or damage."

A This gets into a complex area. The basic law is that a person can't contract away his own negligence; the car park people can't say that when you accepted that stub you agreed to let them smash your car. Therefore, in your particular case, you could recover. On the other hand, the car park could avoid liability for loss, theft, or damage not attributable to its own fault. There are a lot of conditionals here; one of them is the question of whether a customer would be put on notice by that printed disclaimer and could expect the car park not to be responsible. This even gets into the size of the letters on the claim ticket.

NOTE: Compare signs in dry cleaners', etc. See your lawyer.

Q Do you need a witness for an oral contract?

A Assuming you don't get knocked out of the ring by the Statute of Frauds* because your contract isn't in writing, an oral contract doesn't demand a witness, but one is always helpful in what will turn into a swearing match if you end up in court.

Q My boyfriend promised to buy me a stereo for Christmas and didn't. Can I get him for breach of promise?

A No. First of all, the courts will no longer enforce breach of promise actions because they were too frequently used as blackmail. Second, what you are describing is not even what's known as "breach of promise," which relates to a promise to marry. Third, you're talking about a gift and not a contract. There wasn't any consideration, so your boyfriend isn't bound.

"Yes, but . . ." or the Statute of Frauds

Q When does an oral contract become binding?

A Immediately—if at all. You're making the assumption that it will eventually be binding, which isn't necessarily so.

Most of the states follow the Statute of Frauds* (see the introduction to this section: "Is This a Contract?-General"), which was enacted in England in 1677. It listed a variety of agreements that wouldn't be binding unless in writing and signed by the party against whom the agreement was to be enforced. The present-day statutory version in the Uniform Commercial Code (see page 145) hasn't changed the law all that much.

The most important points are that contracts for the sale of land, an agreement which can't be performed in less than a year, sale of goods in excess of a certain amount—all must be in writing. If such a contract is not in writing, this doesn't make it void; it just means the courts won't enforce it.

NOTE: Even in cases where an oral contract is normally invalid, there are a variety of exceptions. For instance, performance, in whole or in substantial part, may make the oral contract enforceable by the courts (see the next question for examples).

Q My aunt told me that if I moved to the farm and helped her with it, she'd leave the farm to me in her will. She didn't. What can I do?

A See a lawyer. This sort of situation has been taken to court many times and is complex. There are three main questions:

1. Your agreement was oral, and generally contracts for land must be in writing. One exception to this is when one party has performed his side of the bargain; in your case, this was moving to the farm.

2. Did you "suffer some detriment"—give up something, such as a job—relying on your aunt's promise?

3. Can the court enforce a promise to make a will? Since the breach of contract won't come up until your aunt is dead, the court could only do its enforcing against the estate (the property left, represented by the executor or personal representative).

"Surprise! It's a contract," or contracts implied by law

Q, My boat came loose from its moorings and was drifting out to sea when a fisherman came along, towed it in, and pulled it up on his dock to keep it from sinking, since it was damaged. I really appreciate what he did, but now he wants to charge me storage. Can he get away with that? Where's any contract?

A When someone, like your fisherman, provides a necessary service he's not obliged to perform, the law invents a contract—called a "quasi contract"—and you're responsible for a reasonable fee for the service.

The fisherman could have let your boat float merrily off.

Sample Contract—to Be Translated

Many people panic at the sight of a contract, especially with all the fine print, and assume that it won't make sense. If you keep your cool and convince yourself it's English, you probably can understand it. If you can't, make whoever is offering you that contract explain every word you're uncertain about. Embarrassment is a good deal cheaper than being held to a contract you didn't read.

Some states now have the "plain English" law. That means that documents such as insurance policies must be written in language the average person can understand. Here is a sample contract, which will then be translated:

KNOW ALL MEN BY THESE PRESENTS that:

WHEREAS, on this _____ day of_____ ,19___ , Gus Goodguy (hereinafter referred to as Party of the First Part) and John Jones (hereinafter referred to as Party of the Second Part) are desirous of entering into a contract, and

WHEREAS, for consideration received, the Party of the First Part and Party of the Second Part do grant, bargain, and agree

NOW THEREFORE, the agreement is as follows, to wit:

Party of the First Part, for and in consideration of the covenants and agreements herein contained to be kept and performed by Party of the Second Part, his heirs, executors, administrators, assigns, and successors in interest, and upon the terms and conditions herein contained, does hereby grant, bargain, and convey to Party of the Second Part one (1) milk cow by the name of Bossy (hereinafter referred to as "cow"), a legal description of which, including her milk-giving capacities, for which no warranty is made, and registration, is attached hereto labeled exhibit "A," and made a part hereof by reference, under the terms and conditions hereinafter set forth, and Party of the Second Part does hereby accept said "cow" and agree to the below provisions.

TERMS. The terms and conditions of this Agreement shall be the payment by the Party of the Second Part to the Party of the First Part of six (6) equal installments of one hundred dollars ($100.00) each installment, beginning on the _____ day of _____ , 19___ , and ending on the _____ day of_____,19___ , in the total amount of _____to be delivered to the residence of Party of the First Part.

Party of the Second Part, for and in consideration of this Covenant and Agreement, hereby agrees and covenants with Party of the First Part to pay for the aforesaid cow the above-described payments without notice or demand. All of the payments shall be paid by Party of the Second Part to Party of the First Part or Party of the First Part's order in lawful money of the United States at #1 Blueberry Lane, City of Kansas City, County of Jackson, State of Missouri, or such other place as Party of the First Part may designate from time to time for this purpose in writing to Party of the Second Part.

BANKRUPTCY AND INSOLVENCY CLAUSE. Default. Should Party of the Second Part take bankruptcy, become insolvent, or default in any one or more of the above-described payments it is covenanted and agreed by and between the parties hereto that the Party of the First Part may declare the full sum as due and payable and Party of the Second Part shall pay and discharge all costs, attorney's fees and expenses that shall arise from enforcing the covenants of this indenture by Party of the First Part, Party of the First Part's heirs, executors, administrators, assigns, or successors in interest.

BINDING. It is hereby covenanted and agreed by and between the parties hereto that the covenants and agreements herein contained shall extend to and be binding upon the heirs, executors, administrators, assigns, and successors in interest to the Parties to this Agreement.

ALL AGREEMENT. It is covenanted and agreed by and between the parties hereto that the Agreement incorporates all of the agreements, covenants, and undertakings between the parties hereto concerning the subject matter hereof, and that all such covenants, agreements, and undertakings have been merged into this written Agreement. No prior agreement or understanding, verbal or otherwise, of the parties or their agents or assigns shall be valid or enforceable unless embodied in this Agreement.

IN WITNESS WHEREOF, the parties have hereunto set their hands and seals the day and year first above written.

_____(SEAL)

_____(SEAL)

Sample Contract — Being Translated

Delete - excess verbiage

'KNOW ALL MEN BY THESE PRESENTS'that:

Delete

'WHEREAS,' on this _____ day of _____ ,19___ , Gus Goodguy '(here

Seller

inafter referred to as Party of the First Part)'and John Jones '(hereinafter

Buyer

referred to as Party of the Second Part)'are desirous of entering into a

contract, and

Delete - proves nothing   *Seller*

'WHEREAS, for consideration received,'the'Party of the First Part and'Party

Buyer   *Lawyers always talk in triplicate*

of the Second Part'do 'grant, bargain, and agree'

Delete - exess verbiage

'NOW THEREFORE,' the agreement is as follows, to wit:

Seller   *Delete*

'Party of the First Part,' for and'in consideration of the covenants and

Buyer's promise agreements herein contained to be kept and performed by 'Party of the

Buyer

Second Part,' his heirs, executors, administrators, assigns, and successors

in interest, and upon the terms and conditions herein contained, does

unnecessary triplicate again   *Buyer*

Means: didn't want to bother identifying Bossy in contract hereby 'grant, bargain, and convey'to'Party of the Second Part'one (1) milk

cow by the name of Bossy (hereinafter referred to as "cow"), a legal

description of which, including her milk-giving capacities, for which no

warranty is made, and registration, is attached hereto labeled exhibit "A,"

Just means "terms as follows"

and made a part hereof by reference, 'under the terms and conditions

Buyer

hereinafter set forth,' and'Party of the Second Part'does hereby accept said

"cow" and agree to the below provisions.

TERMS. The terms and conditions of this Agreement shall be the payment

Buyer   *Seller*

by the'Party of the Second Part'to the'Party of the First Part'of six (6) equal installments of one hundred dollars ($100.00) each installment, beginning

on the _____ day of _____ , 19___ , and ending on the _____ day

of_____,19___ , in the total amount of _____to be delivered

Seller
to the residence of Party of the First Part.

Buyer
Party of the Second Part, for and in consideration of this Covenant and

Seller
Agreement, hereby agrees and covenants with Party of the First Part to

pay for the aforesaid cow the above-described payments without notice or

Buyer
demand. All of the payments shall be paid by Party of the Second Part to

Seller   *Seller's*
Party of the First Part or Party of the First Part's order in lawful money of

the United States at #1 Blueberry Lane, City of Kansas City, County of

Seller
Jackson, State of Missouri, or such other place as Party of the First Part

may designate from time to time for this purpose in writing to Party of the

Buyer
Second Part.

BANKRUPTCY AND INSOLVENCY CLAUSE. Default. Should Party of the

Buyer
Second Part take bankruptcy, become insolvent, or default in any one or

more of the above-described payments it is covenanted and agreed by and

Seller
between the parties hereto that the Party of the First Part may declare the

Buyer
full sum as due and payable and Party of the Second Part shall pay and

discharge all costs, attorney's fees and expenses that shall arise from

Seller
enforcing the covenants of this indenture by Party of the First Part, Party

Seller's
of the First Part's heirs, executors, administrators, assigns, or successors

in interest.

Margin notes:

buyer to pay seller

Buyer agrees to make the payments without being told

Translates: buyer will make cash payments to seller at his home

Means: If buyer goes bankrupt or simply misses a payment seller can demand the full amount owing and buyer has to pay any costs of collection

Translates:
if either
party
dies,
his heirs
are still
stuck
with this
contract

BINDING. It is hereby covenanted and agreed by and between the parties

hereto that the covenants and agreements herein contained shall extend

to and be binding upon the heirs, executors, administrators, assigns, and

successors in interest to the Parties to this Agreement.

ALL AGREEMENT. It is covenanted and agreed by and between the parties

hereto that the Agreement incorporates all of the agreements, covenants,

Translates: and undertakings between the parties hereto concerning the subject matter
this
written hereof, and that all such covenants, agreements, and undertakings have
contract
is the been merged into this written Agreement. No prior agreement or under-
entire
agreement standing, verbal or otherwise, of the parties or their agents or assigns shall

be valid or enforceable unless embodied in this Agreement.

IN WITNESS WHEREOF, the parties have hereunto set their hands and
out of date
Translates: seals the day and year first above written.
contract
okayed
and
signed

_____(SEAL)

_____(SEAL)

Final Translation of Sample Contract

How the original could have been written in the first place:

On the _____ day of _____ , 19___ , Gus Goodguy (Seller) and John Jones (Buyer) enter into the following agreement. Seller agrees to sell Buyer one milk cow named Bossy (description attached) for $600 to be paid in 6 monthly installments of $100 each for six months, beginning on the _____ day of _____ , 19___ , and ending on the _____ day of _____, 19__.

No warranty is made as to the continued volume of milk produced.

The payments are to be made to Seller at his home address, #1 Blueberry Lane, Kansas City, Missouri.

If Buyer should become bankrupt or miss a payment, Seller has the right to declare the entire amount due and Buyer shall be responsible for any cost of collection.

The parties both agree that the contract shall continue in force although one or the other party may die or assign it.

This written contract represents the entire agreement between the parties.

To signify their agreement to the terms of this contract, the parties have signed below.

_____

_____

The essential, standard parts of a contract are the identification of the two parties to the contract; the terms (which must be clear enough for a court to enforce); the consideration; and the execution (the signing).

This disclaimer in re* the milk is for the protection of the Seller and is not one of the essential terms.

CHAPTER II

Insurance

INTRODUCTION/HISTORY

Insurance is a contract between the insurer* and the insured,* and is a contract on a legally recognized gamble. The insurer carefully assesses the odds on the risk that the insured will indeed suffer the loss to be insured against, and charges a premium, a monetary consideration, based on those odds. The insured contracts to pay that premium in exchange for the promise of the insurer to reimburse should the insured incur the insured loss.

Apparently the earliest insurance contracts were entered into in the ancient Middle East, and are known to have existed among the Babylonians before 2000 B. C. It was marine insurance—in the sense that the moneylender would provide funds to a trader with the understanding that if his ship were sunk, the loan was canceled out. The interest was set to make the risk worthwhile to the lender.

Marine insurance can be traced from ancient Babylon to Greece and Rome, right on through to the most famous gambler in today's world, Lloyd's of London.

Lloyd's began in a coffeehouse in the late 1600s. Mr. Lloyd, the owner, would post lists of the sailing ships being readied for ocean voyages, and his prosperous customers would sign their names and the amount of risk they were willing to take under the ship's name. Thus, the familiar term "underwriter" was coined.

Lloyd's is now known as the place where insurance can be obtained on almost anything imaginable. In one of these cases, some years ago, a well-known American surgeon insured, not just his hands, but his *limbs* for the then enormous amount of $100,000. Subsequently the surgeon happened to shoot off his big toe as he walked down the stairs of his home with a gun in his hand. Lloyd's disputed paying off, but eventually the surgeon with his insured limbs won.

Since insurance is a contract, it has the same four elements of all contracts discussed in Chapter I: (1) offer and acceptance, that meeting of minds, as to the subject matter which, in insurance contracts, includes the risk insured against, its duration, and the promise to pay in either a specific or an ascertainable amount; (2) consideration; (3) parties with a legal capacity to contract; and, (4) a legal purpose, which includes the special insurance point that the person purchasing the insurance must have an "insurable interest"* in the risk insured against.

Following the logical rules of contract law, this chapter on insurance is set up as follows:

1. Basic insurance contract—the rules applying, whatever type of insurance is involved
    a. General—elements
    b. Offer and acceptance
        1) Representations by insured (avoidance)
        2) Acceptance and execution by insurer—issuance of policy
    c. Payment of premiums—consideration
        1) General
    d. Terms: Who must do what when
        1) General
        2) What must be done *before* the policy takes effect (conditions precedent)
        3) What voids the contract *after* the policy takes effect (conditions subsequent)
    e. Subject matter—insurable interest—risk
        1) General
2. Kinds of insurance
    a. General
    b. Auto
        1) General
        2) Liability
        3) Collision
        4) Medical pay

      5) Uninsured or underinsured motorists

      6) Theft

    c. Workmen's compensation—different in every state

    d. Homeowner's or tenant's

      1) General

      2) Fire, theft, storm, and other hazards

      3) Liability—duty to public

    e. Health and accident

    f. Life

    g. Title

3. Causes of loss (along with notice and proof of loss)

    a. General

    b. Specific risk—general

      1) Auto

      2) Workmen's compensation

      3) Homeowner's

      4) Life

      5) Health and accident

      6) Title

    c. Notice and proofs of loss

4. Collecting on your loss

    a. General

    b. Appraisals, estimates, "adjusters"

    c. Particular insurance

      1) Auto

      2) Workmen's compensation

      3) Homeowner's

      4) Health and accident

      5) Life

      6) Title

5. Defenses by insurer (arguing why they shouldn't have to pay off)

    a. General

    b. Misrepresentation, fraud, breach of warranty

    c. Breach by insured (conditions subsequent)

6. Standard auto policy and its translation

Basic Insurance Contract

General—elements

Generally, the application for the insurance is the offer (to buy) and there is no contract until that offer is accepted by the insurance company. Sometimes, the parties having agreed upon the terms and the essential elements of a contract being present, an agent can orally bind an insurance company if he has real or apparent authority* to do so.

The contract can be complete without the actual policy being issued, unless there is a state law to the contrary. However, it is safest to assume that there is no insurance coverage until the policy (which represents the contract) is signed in the home office. Unfortunately, group insurance often only supplies you with a card or some little short thing and leaves you in the dark as to exactly what is covered and what are the exemptions. Get a full policy if you can.

NOTE: Laws are being passed in a growing number of states to the effect that insurance and other contracts must be written in language understandable to a layperson. Called the "plain English" law, it's long overdue. For example, I had a case where it took two senior partners, myself, and an appeal to the state supreme court to interpret a contractor's policy. That's silly.

The reason insurance policies have become so involved is that when an insurance company loses a lawsuit, it frequently adds a new paragraph to make sure it won't happen again. And, as to those paragraphs, rather than have an important clause decided against it, an insurance company will often settle a case out of court. This is to avoid what they call "making bad law."

PS: Always read the pages in different parts of the policy headed "Exemptions" or "Exceptions" or "We do not cover." Those list where your insurance does *not* protect or cover you. (The same page in front that breaks down your premiums contains what *is* covered.)

Offer and acceptance

Application
Representations by insured (avoidance)

Q I told an agent just what kind of insurance I needed for my contracting business and she said "Fine" and that she'd issue a binder. Am I just applying or what?

A You made an application and the agent accepted, making it a contract. Despite what I said about the home office okay, the courts have held that an agent "appears" to represent the company and be able to contract for it—even if the agent actually does not have that authority.

Q This company sent me a bunch of advertising saying, "no one refused!" along with a list of rates for each $5,000 worth of accident insurance and a card to fill out and send in. Well, I had exactly the kind of accident their advertising described—cut off the end of one finger with my power saw. I thought I'd hit the jackpot, but now that outfit says the card was just an application for insurance and I get zero, zip. Can they do this to me?

A Nope. This is the reverse of the usual in that I think all that stuff the company sent you constituted an *offer* with sufficient particularity that when you filled in the card that was an *acceptance* and there was a contract. Unless there's some fine print you aren't telling me about, they owe you! Get a lawyer.

Q I was afraid if I put on the application that the doctor was going to do a biopsy I couldn't get the major medical insurance. It turns out I do have breast cancer, but since I didn't know for sure at the time, I think the insurance people have to pay my bills. Please tell me I'm right.

A I understand your reasoning but know the company will say that you misrepresented your health and claim "avoidance." They can say a "reasonable" person would know your condition was something that should be revealed and your cancer is a "prior existing condition." Don't give up hope, though! Maybe with more details and a careful analysis of the policy and the law defining "prior existing," an attorney can find you're covered.

Q My health insurance policy has in it something to the effect that I swear I'm in good health on the date of application. Well, it so happens on that day I was sick in bed with the flu. Can they get me for this?

A First, nobody is going to "get you," and second, when a policy stipulates that the insured must be in good health, that simply means not suffering any serious or chronic ailments; you're allowed to have the flu.

Acceptance and execution by insurer—

issuance of policy

Q Last night a life insurance agent came to see my husband and me and said that a policy on my life would be effective as soon as we paid the premium. Since I still have to have a medical examination by their doctor, the agent telling me I would be covered now doesn't make sense to me.

A You're right to be confused. There have been cases holding that the agent can't bind the company as to when a life insurance policy goes into effect, and certainly not when a physical remains to be done.

NOTE: You would be considered to have been put on notice that the agent didn't have authority to contract by the fact that the insurance company did require a medical examination.

In a similar case, the court held that the applicant was put on notice as to the effective date by means of a provision to that effect both in the application and also on the receipt for the premium. Yet in this case, too, the agent had said that the insurance would be effective at once.

Q I'm executrix of my grandmother's estate. In checking her books, I've found that she had paid the premium on a new insurance policy, but the insurance company claims it never accepted her application. My brother-in-law says the company has to pay off because it kept the premium. Is he right?

A No. See an attorney! There have been cases holding that the insurance company may have accepted the premium without having accepted the application, and there was, therefore, no contract.

NOTE: One factor that would be in your favor in court would be if you could show that the delay in keeping the premium without acceptance was unreasonable. Then you win.

Q When does my insurance become effective?

A When the policy is signed by the company doing the insuring.

Remember, when dealing with a contract of insurance, your application is the offer and there is no contract until there's acceptance by the insurance company (with the exceptions explained above).

NOTE: You can almost always get a "binder"* so that you're covered in the interim between application and execution. A binder means that the insurance company will cover you for any loss in that period before the company has executed the policy. This is done simply by asking your agent or broker to issue one.

Q When am I covered?

A Basically, from the time of the "effective date" listed in your policy.

Court decisions don't always line up neatly in agreement. In a disputed case, lawyers on each side would have a good argument if the application didn't set out when the policy would be effective. In one point of view, if the agent *seems* to have the power to give the insured an oral "binder" (see Question 1, above) and/or take a written application along with the premium, the apparent majority of the courts say that the company is bound and must pay off if the insured has a loss. Other courts disagree.

Caveat:* Be sure to look at every scrap of writing, because if it anywhere states the date, such as "Date effective _____ ," or "Date of issuance," or anything having to do with "acceptance" or "execution," the policy will not be in force until that date.

Many policies provide that they are not in force, or effective, until accepted by the home office. This acceptance means the policy must have been signed by the individual having the power to do so in the home office.

Q When we moved here, I bought a homeowner's policy from a local agent. The agent took down all the information, filled out forms, and asked me for the premium. I thought everything was all settled. Now, having reported my stereo and TV stolen, I have received a letter from the company telling me it never accepted my application. Can it do that to me?

A Probably not. The agent had what's known as "apparent authority." This means that when an insurance company allows an agent to sell insurance, furnishes him with forms, and otherwise makes it appear he has authority to contract, then the court holds he does have that authority whether or not the company says he does.

NOTE: Some other courts have held the opposite way on this point, finding that the insurance company was not bound by these actions of the agent.

Payment of premiums—consideration

General

Q The insurance agent gave me a binder on the car, I promised to pay the premium, but had a wreck before I got around to paying it. Am I insured?

A The odds are in your favor. Courts have held that a promise to pay the premium is sufficient consideration to hold the insurance company to its contract.

See a lawyer! He will need to examine the facts more closely to make sure you are covered.

Q I've paid on a home fire insurance policy for many years. Wouldn't you know that I missed a premium for the first time, and by only three days, just before my house burned! Can the insurance company get out of paying me?

A Probably not. A court would likely look at the unfairness of allowing the insurance company to say that you had forfeited your policy under these conditions.

The question is whether your policy makes payment of the premium an essential term of the agreement. Nevertheless, a court might refuse to enforce the provision in your particular case. See a lawyer!

Q I don't have the money to make this year's life insurance payment, but I don't want to lose the policy because the premiums on a new one would be much higher. Is it true that if I just pay part of the premium, they can't cancel on me?

A Probably not. Usually a partial payment is about the same as no payment and doesn't affect whether or not the company must continue your policy. If the policy itself or the state statutes demand you be given a grace period,* you're allowed that additional time to make payment without regard to whether you have made a partial payment.

Ask your insurance company whether it will accept a partial payment and get the answer in writing.

Q I had an accident the day after I was supposed to have paid the premium. The insurance company says I was canceled out because I was late, but I thought I had thirty days to get the premium paid. What should I do?

A See an attorney! Depending on both your insurance policy and the statutes of your state, the law as to whether the insurance company could legally cancel you could go either way.

1. If the policy does not say failure to make a payment on time results in forfeiture, the court is likely to decide in your favor. In most states it *is* allowed for the insurer to make timely payment a condition of coverage, however.

2. Statutes in your state may demand that the insurer give the grace period you mentioned and/or that you be notified before the policy is canceled.

Q My uncle was in excellent health when he died . . . My family's in
a hassle with the insurance company because my uncle had taken
and passed the physical exam for life insurance, so we all contend the
company should pay.

A You may be right, but I'd need considerably more facts before telling
you your chances of collecting on your uncle's life insurance policy.
I *can* tell you that there have been cases which held that taking the
medical exam was sufficient consideration to hold the insurance company to its promise to insure even though no policy had yet been issued.

Caveat: This is dangerous ground, and both the facts and/or the
cases in your state might prevent recovery from the insurance company.

Q I got my premium payment to the insurance agent the day it was
due, but of course the company didn't have it at the home office then.
Am I covered?

A Probably. If your agent had authority (or apparent authority*) to
accept a payment, it's the same as if you had paid it to the insurance
company itself. See page 44 and the other questions above, in this
chapter.

Terms: who must do what when

General

"Terms"* have the same meaning when dealing with insurance as
with any other contract. (See Chapter I, "Contract Basics: Definition of
Terms," page 16.)

The terms of an insurance contract are what the parties have each
agreed to do—the bargain.

In general, the insurer promises to reimburse the insured upon the
occurrence of a specific risk. The terms set out in what manner this risk
must happen and to what extent the insurer will indemnify the insured.
On the other hand, the terms also place certain duties on the insured,
such as paying premiums in a set amount and notifying the insurer
within a certain time that the event insured against has indeed occurred.

NOTE: A growing body of law holds that whatever may be written in the policy, the insurer will be held to what the insured can *reasonably* believe was covered—or what the agent promised.

What must be done before the policy takes effect (conditions precedent)*

Sometimes a court will hold that there never was a contract, that the policy never took effect, because the insured didn't do his part—most frequently by failing to make the original payment. Another, as in the case of health and life insurance, would be the insured's failure to take and pass a required physical examination.

What voids the contract after the policy takes effect (conditions subsequent)*

Sometimes an insured loses out because she did not perform one of the terms after the policy was in force. The most common of these is the insured's failure to give the insurance company notice of her loss. (This is discussed in more detail below, under "Causes of Loss: Notice and proofs of loss," on page 72.)

Subject matter—insurable interest—risk

General

As with any contract, the subject matter of an insurance policy must be legal. The person taking out the insurance must have what's called "an insurable interest,"* and the risk insured against must operate by the odds of chance, beyond the control of the insured.

These latter rules follow common sense. Without them, so many uncertainties would exist that no premium could be set because no one could accurately figure the odds in any one instance. It would also be against public policy for the insured to have any control, tempting the insured to cheat.

What "insurable interest" amounts to is that, to buy insurance, you must have more than a simple interest in the outcome of a gamble between you and the insurance company. Normally, the event insured against must affect your pocketbook.

"Insurable interest" can be either positive or negative—you can insure that which will benefit you by continued existence, and you can also insure against the happening of an event that will bring you a loss.

A financial interest is sufficient to insure against casualty; a pecuniary interest, blood ties, or marriage is sufficient in the field of life insurance; and a possible loss of money in the form of damages is sufficient to insure against liability.

The courts will take a liberal rather than a strict view when interpreting whether or not a person has an "insurable interest."

Q Could I insure a building and then collect if it burned down?

A Not just any old building. In order to be entitled to insure a building and collect the insurance if it burned, you would have to have an "insurable interest" in that building—a legitimate interest such as ownership, lease, or mortgage. (See above discussion.)

Q When my husband and I got a divorce, part of the property agreement was that he would carry life insurance making the children beneficiaries. Now he tells me he has dropped it. When I said that I would buy some on him myself, he said that was against the law. What can I do?

A First, if maintaining insurance was part of the property agreement, you can go back to court to have that provision enforced against your ex-husband.

Second, it is not against the law for you to insure his life. If your ex-husband owes child support or maintenance, you have what is known as an "insurable interest." Here, that means that because of your ex-husband's continuing duties to you and/or the children, you have a right to take out insurance on his life.

(Public policy prevents a person from insuring the life of a stranger or someone in whom he does not have an insurable interest.)

Q When my former wife and I were first married, we each took out a life insurance policy on the other. Now that I'm divorced, is that policy automatically canceled out?

A Not according to some cases. You had an insurable interest in your wife's life while you were married and, in the case of life insurance, once a person has an insurable interest in the life of another, it continues. Therefore, the policy on your wife's life does not end with divorce and if you wish, you can keep it up.

Q If insurance is a matter of playing the odds, can I insure anything I want to gamble on?

A No. Since insurance is a contract, the subject cannot be illegal. In addition to that rule, there are also rules that come under the heading of public policy: you cannot insure the happening of an event that would allow you to act against the best interests of the public.

Q I thought a person could take out life insurance only on himself, so I want to know how business partners can take out insurance on each other.

A You're mistaken about the first part. The answer to the second part is that partners can take out insurance on the life of one another because they are held to have an "insurable interest," which is the importance to each partner that the other continue to live and contribute to the business. This is true not only of partnerships but also of corporations and other organizations. It is frequently known as "key man or key woman insurance."

Q The people who have the mortgage on our house said that we had to have fire insurance payable to them—what about our losses?

A You can insure your interest. It sounds very technical, but with fire insurance you are not actually insuring the house; you are insuring the risk to your financial interest in it. For this reason, the mortgage holder could insure its interest in the house to the extent of its financial involvement, and at the same time you could insure what you have invested in the house.

Q Can I insure the life of someone I'm living with, even though I'm not married to her?

A Probably. In light of the awards for "palimony," there is precedent
for your having an insurable interest in the person you live with.

Historically, if you benefited financially from a person's continued
life, you could insure it. You could *now* make an argument of benefits
from cohabitation.

Kinds of Insurance

General

Most insurance falls into one of two categories: (1) indemnification,
in a specified amount, for you or your beneficiaries, against financial
loss from the occurrence of an event over which you have no control;
or (2) payment up to a specified amount to a third person for injuries
and/or damages for which you are legally responsible.

Auto

General

Almost all standard automobile policies have a piece of paper
attached to the front of the policy. READ THIS! It's usually labeled
"Declarations" and will have several lines on it listing such coverages*
as liability, collision, and uninsured motorist. If there is a dollar amount
for the premium charged on the same line as the kind of coverage, you
know you have that coverage. The opposite is, of course, true; if no
premium amount is listed, you do not have the coverage on that line.

There are four major kinds of auto insurance coverage. First, and
required in most states, is liability insurance; your insurance company
is agreeing to pay for that for which you are liable. This means that your
insurance company would pay for the damages you caused to the other
driver, his passengers, and property if you were the one responsible
(liable) for the wreck.

Caveat: Your insurance policy will recite the "limits of liability."
The "limits of liability" are the amounts your insurance company will
pay for *each* injury and for the *total of all injuries*. If the other person
can prove more damages than your policy provides, you are responsible
for the excess amounts. Exceptions to your personal liability basically

depend on your company's good-faith attempts to settle the matter. Its actions can make it liable for the whole enchilada.

Second is collision coverage. Your insurance company pays you when no other car is involved in your wreck. A premium for collision coverage usually also pays for theft of your automobile and damage from such things as hail. In some policies these are separate.

Third is uninsured* motorists coverage. This one is tricky. Basically, your insurance company pays you what you would have collected from the other driver's insurance company if she'd had insurance, but doesn't. In many areas you are now covered if the other driver is "underinsured."*

Finally, there is "medical pay."* Almost every policy has a basic "medical pay" provision (commonly referred to as med. pay), which takes care of medical costs resulting from the accident no matter who is at fault. (In the sample policy at the end of this chapter, the med. pay is limited, but often the med. pay will cover all injuries.) This coverage is usually not expensive and, therefore, you would be wise to have a substantial amount of it.

NOTE: All of these points are discussed in more detail on pages 91-109, where the insurance policy is analyzed.

Q If I have a wreck, I don't understand whose insurance pays for what.
A Usually the insurance company of the driver at fault is the one that does the paying. This is not simple because frequently "fault" is hotly disputed. This is why you hire an attorney. (Note: if the other driver is at fault but has no insurance—or too little—*your* insurance pays under the "Uninsured or Underinsured Motorist Coverage."

Once there's some agreement as to fault, the tough next step is to determine damages—the extent of the bodily and property harm. Usually the amount paid shows a balancing of fault, or liability, with the damages. For instance, an insurance company will pay more for the actual injuries when it is quite clear that its insured caused the accident. On the other hand, in some instances, an insurance company will pay what is called a "nuisance claim," which means it's cheaper for the company to settle a small claim for which it doesn't believe it is responsible than to fight the claim in court.

NOTE: To the dismay of some but usually to the joy of the parties involved in an auto accident, an increasing number of states are adopting "no-fault" insurance. It's called "no-fault" because blame is not attached to either party to the accident; instead, each party's insurer pays for its insured's medical and property damage expenses. (There is no joy among those seeking punitive damages.*)

One circumstance that brought about "no-fault" insurance was the strangulation of our court system by the myriad lawsuits filed on account of auto accidents.

Q When I wrecked my car, my insurance company wouldn't give me a loaner. My brother-in-law says I should sue them because when he had a wreck, he got the use of another car until his was fixed.

A Your brother-in-law is probably wrong again. Whether the insurance company must provide a loaner depends on the coverage you purchased, which is shown in your insurance policy. It's unlikely that your insurance company would refuse to provide you with a loaner if you did have that coverage.

Liability

Liability insurance is designed to protect you against claims by third parties for damages you have caused to their persons (personal injury) or their property. This protection takes the form of the insurance company paying in settlement of the claim or furnishing you with an attorney to defend the claim(s) in court, and paying the judgment against you, if you lose, up to the amount of coverage you have purchased. The company is obligated to pay only what you legally owe (with exceptions based on "bad faith"*).

Liability insurance does *not* pay for or cover injuries to yourself or your own property.

Q I'm worried because I'm being sued over a car wreck and I can't get my insurance company to settle. I'm afraid the case is going to go to court and I'll be stuck with a big judgment. Is there anything I can do?

A Yes. Remind the insurance company that unless it makes a good-faith attempt to settle, it is the insurance company, not you, that is stuck with the full amount of judgment. This is true no matter how much the judgment exceeds your coverage.

I suggest you hire an attorney to press this point for you.

NOTE: Since the terms of your policy probably state that the insurance company will defend all suits on your behalf, if it's acting in bad faith it will have to pay the fee of that attorney I told you to hire.

Q A friend says that because I was the one who got a ticket, and not the other driver involved in the accident, my insurance won't cover me. Is that true?

A No. If you are being sued and are, therefore, talking about your liability insurance, it protects you against the claims of third persons whom you become legally obligated to pay. You're legally obligated only if you were at fault. By the way, the citation is only part of the case: additional investigation may prove that you're not at fault—though it would be nice if you weren't the one with the ticket.

Q I got into a big pileup on the freeway. The man who caused it all says he doesn't have any insurance. Will my own insurance cover it where it says "Liability"?

A Not there. "Liability" has to do with the claims of third persons against you, not the other way around. You want "uninsured motorists coverage" which is not normally found under "liability coverage." It usually has a separate heading by itself, labeled simply "Uninsured motorists."

See a lawyer to untangle your policy for you.

Collision

Collision coverage is the opposite of liability coverage—it is designed to reimburse you for damages to your own vehicle.

Collision coverage will always include the damage to your automobile when it comes into violent contact with another object.

Sometimes a particular policy will include such things as hail damage or malicious mischief under the collision provisions. In other cases those other types of loss will be separately listed and require an additional premium.

Collision, theft, and other risk coverages often have a "deductible."* (See next question.)

Q Why do some people say that it isn't worth it to buy collision coverage?

A Because collision coverage applies only to damage to your own car, sometimes the premium for this kind of coverage is more expensive than the replacement value of the car involved. Also, there's usually a "deductible," an initial amount you pay toward the loss that might be more than you'd want to spend on that car.

Medical pay

The "medical pay" coverage takes care of your own medical expenses without regard to "fault," and is often vitally important, such as when you are waiting to recover damages from the other side. It's usually inexpensive for what you get.

Depending on the wording of your med. pay, as we discussed, you may be able to offer to pay medical expenses (up to the limit of coverage*) to those in the other car and avoid suit. The reverse would also be true.

Uninsured and underinsured motorists

Basically, "uninsured motorists" coverage means that your own insurance company will reimburse you for the same amount you would have recovered from the other driver if he had had insurance. This includes your personal injuries and property damages if you have a collision with a person who does not have any insurance, and if the accident was caused by that other driver. The same now frequently applies to the "underinsured" driver.

Theft

Remember there is an enormous difference between theft *of* your vehicle and theft *from* your vehicle. The two points I've had to explain to clients most often are: (1) if your car is stolen, you recover only the amount a comparable auto was worth at the time it was stolen; and (2) many policies require that you show signs of forcible entry for the theft *from* your car to be covered. (I don't know of any policy that reimburses you for a claim that cash was stolen from your car.)

Q My brother-in-law says that he always leaves the ignition keys in his car in hopes it will get stolen. It's such an old clunker. Does he get a new car if someone really does steal it?

A No. Quite a few people are shocked with this when they hope to collect on a theft. (Insurance companies are also suspicious of fire insurance claims on an old car.) Normally the insurer only has to replace the auto with one in the same condition or reimburse the insured with the replacement cost. Usually the insurance company is the one that gets to make the choice.

NOTE: The insurance company ordinarily goes by the "Blue Book" evaluation, and it doesn't do any good to tell the insurer that your particular car had been beautifully kept up and was a veritable cream puff. However, most people don't realize that if their car is totaled, they can buy back the salvage from the insurer. ("Totaled" means the insurer decides it's cheaper to replace the car with a like model than to repair it.)

Q I left my purse in my car and forgot to lock it. It had all my credit cards and $100 in it. Will my insurance company reimburse me?

A You're asking three questions. 1) some policies would demand "forced entry," but many would pay for theft from the car even if not locked. 2) Your contract with the credit card company requires you notify the company as soon as possible. But what most people do not know is that your liability is limited to $50 under federal law. Since any loss here is provable, I think the insurance company should pay that, but they'll fight you. 3) The $100 cash is your loss because you can't prove it—and because many policies specifically do not cover cash.

NOTE: check both your auto and home insurance. Either or both may cover this theft from the car.

NOTE ALSO: Some companies either raise your rates or cancel you after one claim.

Workers' compensation

Workers' compensation is a contractual trade-off. The employer furnishes insurance to the worker to cover job-related injury or disease and therefore secures the right not to be sued for negligence in a court of law. The worker, for his part of the bargain, gets the security of being paid for that job-related injury or disease, without regard to fault, in exchange for giving up his right to sue and, perhaps, collect much greater damages than workers' compensation will pay.

Workers' compensation is created by statute in each state—and is thus different in each. It will provide that an employer of a certain number of employees in all but a few specifically exempted fields must either buy workers' compensation insurance or qualify as a self-insurer.

An employee receives workers' compensation benefits for lost wages and reimbursements for doctor and hospital bills. He is not compensated for "pain or suffering," as he would be in a negligence suit. In the latter, damages include not only out-of-pocket expenses, but also a monetary award to pay for pain and suffering from one's injuries. There is also the chance of suing and collecting for punitive* damages if the negligence is wanton, willful, gross and/or malicious. Work comp does not pay this either.

Workers' compensation awards are classified later in this chapter.

Q Why is workers' compensation listed under insurance? I thought it was something the state did.

A Workers' compensation is listed under insurance because the proper full name is "Workers' Compensation Insurance." And no, workers' compensation doesn't come from the government but from private insurance carriers paid for by the employer. (Some employers are their own workers' compensation carrier. If that is the case, the employer is called "self-insured.")

It is a contract with each party giving up something as the consideration.

Q I don't understand the difference between workers' compensation paying for my injury and my collecting from the government.

A Workers' compensation is demanded by statute, but is private insurance for which the employer is responsible. This insurance is paid to the employee for job-related injury. On the other hand, the payment (if any) received from the federal government is Supplemental Security Income, SSI, and is for disability without reference to where or how it was incurred.

Q I'm covered by workers' compensation, but my uncle says I would collect a lot more money if I would just sue my employer for getting my leg broken on the job.

A You might, but you cannot. When you took your job, accepting workers' compensation coverage, you in effect contracted not to sue if you were injured on the job.

NOTE: You can have a workers' compensation hearing if your attorney is unable to come to a satisfactory settlement. You should have an attorney in order to reach the best possible settlement of your claim with the workers' compensation insurer.

Q My attorney said I probably had a "permanent partial" for my workers' compensation claim. I hated to ask, but what does "permanent partial" mean?

A "Permanent partial" means that your injury is lasting, but that you will still be able to work although you are limited in the types of work you can do.

The awards for workers' compensation are divided into: (1) temporary partial, (2) temporary total, (3) permanent partial, and (4) permanent total. "Temporary partial" means the worker is only partially disabled temporarily, as for example, with a sprained ankle. "Temporary total" means the worker is totally disabled and unable to work temporarily, but will recover, e.g., with a broken hip. "Permanent total" means the worker will not ever be able to work again, an extreme example being a brain injury causing lasting coma. There are also categories for which a specific amount is paid, e.g., loss of one or both eyes, or loss of a limb, etc.

Homeowner's or tenant's

General

Insurance for homeowners and that for tenants is combined in this category because it is much the same for both, with the exception, of course, that the tenant does not have the same interest in the structure.

A "Homeowner's Comprehensive Policy" normally covers the insured's financial interest in the structure and its contents, and also the risk that he/she may be held answerable to others for violating his/her duties resulting from ownership.

You will need to weigh the deductible against the reduction in premium to determine how high you want your deductible to be.

Fire, theft, storm, and other hazards

Fire

Q I've heard that often the worst damage when a home burns is not from the fire but water damage from the fire fighting. Will my homeowner's policy cover this?

A Almost always.

Q I left a cigarette burning in an ashtray and it fell out and burned an antique end table, destroying its value. Will my fire insurance take care of this even though it's my fault?

A You should have made sure of this at the time you were taking out the policy. The fact that the damage was caused by your negligence usually does not matter; your negligence would have to approach the intentional before the insurer could deny coverage for that reason. Also check if your company is one that pays replacement value or only a proportionate depreciated amount. In addition to that, you should have that table and any other antiques appraised and so listed in the policy—in a fine arts rider*. It will cover both the damage and loss.

Theft

Q We were really ripped off! Now we're getting ripped off all over again with our insurance company saying they won't pay for anything that's not "documented." Naturally we don't have receipts for things bought years ago—or gifts. Can they pull this on us?

A Afraid so, but see an attorney. Your state may have cases where an insurance company has been taken to court on the grounds this is an unreasonable demand. Otherwise, several companies have gotten together and agreed they won't pay for theft without that documentation. Too late now, but for the future make a video or photo record of *everything* in your house.

NOTE: And remember I told you to get a "fine arts rider" for all jewelry, art, silver, and antiques. It doesn't cost that much comparatively and is what you need to get full value for these objects. It will require an appraisal which will go with this rider* or endorsement* on the policy.

Storm

Q We had a big hail and wind storm a few weeks ago. Our insurance company sent a man out to check our roof and then paid us a few hundred dollars to have it patched. Now we see that all the neighbors seem to be having their entire roofs replaced. How come we didn't get that much for our roof?

A Your neighbors probably hired attorneys; an insurance company will always be more generous when an attorney is in the picture. The insurance carrier also makes a big difference; some nationally advertised companies pay out far less and with much more reluctance than others. Finally, it could have been that the man who appraised your house was honest, and your roof really did not need replacing.

Other hazards

Q I'm sure my homeowner's policy has in it about water damage, but when I told the company my basement was leaking, they said they were sorry, but I didn't have coverage for that.

A Most policies that cover water damage relate only to storms and/or flooding, not seepage caused by underground waters. Check the page relating to what is "Not covered" or "exceptions," as well as "water damage" under "Definitions."

NOTE: You do not have to accept that your leaky basement is the result of underground waters, or that, whatever the cause, your policy does not cover it. See an attorney to interpret the references to water in your policy.

Storm

Q How come people who live in parts of the country that keep having disasters don't get insurance to protect their property?

A Because usually one of the policy exceptions is for the type of disaster expected in that area. For instance, along the southeast coast, many policies have in them that "wind-driven water," is not covered; this is taken to mean damage from the hurricanes that frequently occur.

Vandalism or Malicious mischief

Q What I hate is that besides burglarizing us, the creeps did disgusting things all over the house besides slashing upholstery and messing up other surfaces with flour and syrup. I can understand stealing but not this wanton destruction. The insurance adjuster said my policy won't pay for anything but the theft. Tell me she's wrong!

A Probably. If you have theft coverage, you most likely have "vandalism or malicious mischief" which this is. See a lawyer. Done more often in auto policies than homeowner's, you can bring suit for "bad faith refusal to pay" and even for unreasonable or "bad faith *delay*" in attempting to settle.

Q A delivery man fell in the snow on our front steps. Is this the sort of thing that comes under the liability section of my homeowner's policy?

A Yes. As a homeowner, you have certain duties to the public, and the sort of accident you describe is exactly what is covered in a comprehensive policy. You have a duty of reasonable care not to negligently cause injury to those on your premises. The extent of the duty varies according to whether the person is an invitee or trespasser, with more care owed the former. (Basically, a trespasser is entitled only that you not set traps—such as a hole covered with a rotten board.)

Q We had a big party going on and a bunch of guests were out on our back deck that's sort of a balcony projecting over a ravine. It collapsed and a lot of people were hurt. Surely something like that isn't our fault, is it?

A Afraid so. It may not seem like "fault" but you would be liable— failure to properly construct, failure to warn, allowing too many people to occupy the deck, etc. This is paid under your liability coverage, but *note:* your coverage will have a limit per person *and* a total limit for the one occurrence. The insurance company will defend but in your case I'd hire my own lawyer, too, to be sure my interests were protected. You have what's called a lot of "exposure." If that "bad faith refusal to pay" comes into it, the insurer will owe the whole amount no matter what the policy limits are.

Q When we had a small fire at our house, a fireman fell through a rotten place on the front porch and was injured pretty badly. Now he's going to sue. I say he was on the job and we don't owe him a thing!

A Your insurance company may try to say the same thing rather than pay out under the liability section of your homeowner's but the company is wrong. The old law used to be that a fireman takes the premises as he finds them: more recent law is that a duty of care is owed the fireman.

Again, you may need your own attorney. Remember that "bad faith" I told you about.

Health and accident

NOTE: HMOs, health management plans, vary so much and are the subject of so much constantly changing legislation, as well as litigation, that generalities cannot be or remain accurate.

Managed Care got its start as a form of insurance, cooperative health care organized by Oklahoma farmers in 1929. Next Kaiser came into the market. It jogged along for a while and then in the last decade Health Maintenance Organizations have blossomed and multiplied. Health is a business with a bottom line.

Today, more than 80% of all doctors are connected to HMOs in one manner or another; and over 75% of patients are under some type of managed care. The numbers continue to grow.

The *staffed* HMOs are the largest. They employ the health care providers, own or lease the facilities, and demand the patient use physicians within their system. The fact that referrals to outside specialists is discouraged leads to lawsuits as does the discouraging of expensive tests. In fact, the areas which could put the patient at risk are too numerous to handle here.

The *independent practice* HMO is a legal entity but one in which the physicians maintain independent practices to some degree.

Traditionally, there are so many types of health insurance policies, which have not become standardized, that space prohibits an analysis of all of them. However, health policies can be separated into five major areas of protection: those that cover medical generally; those referred to as "major medical"; hospitalization; surgical; and disability (and/or accident).

You should go over your own policy carefully before you need it to understand both what is covered and the extent to which the policy will pay.

Medical. These policies frequently do not cover visits to the doctor's office and, whatever they cover, often pay only a percentage of the cost. Check carefully to see that yours does cover office visits if that is where you anticipate most expenditures. Also check to see if prescription medicines are covered, as well as any special services you might need. Dental would normally not be covered under your medical policy, but under separate Dental Insurance. However, sometimes dental work is covered if you require hospitalization or if your health is affected.

Major medical. This policy usually has a deductible amount, a sum you are responsible for before the policy starts paying. Its name, "major medical," indicates it is for the more disastrous types of illness or injury, as opposed to normal doctor's visits. Check to see how much you would be responsible for in initial outlay or in percentage cost of a continuing illness. Check also to see if there is a limit to the amount of money the insurance company will pay.

Hospitalization. Check for any limitation on the types of disease or injury for which you might be treated in the hospital and also whether it includes surgical procedures. Often a semiprivate (not private) room is required, and such things as special nursing care are limited or even excluded. The daily amount and the number of days are limited. You'll also want to know about later care, such as in a nursing facility, and medications.

Caveat: If you buy a cancer policy as Major Medical go over it carefully! This is another that sounds good but is often severely restricted as to when it will pay and in what amount.

Surgical. Sometimes these policies list only the types of surgical procedure that will be covered and the amount the surgery can cost. These policies are tricky in that, for instance, one type of eye surgery might be covered and another not.

Disability and/or accident. These are discussed together because the advertised "deal" often lumps them together. The cautionary note here is that the come-ons to some of these policies make it appear that you (or your heirs) will collect a mint of money but fail to clarify under what circumstances. Don't buy one unless the company will supply you with a real policy and then check carefully before paying! Often these policies are *very narrow* as to what accident or disability is covered—

such as, you must have your left arm amputated as a result of a collision with a freight train.

"Disability" is usually very restrictively defined in the fine print and will often require hospitalization and proof of disability in the sense that you're totally disabled.

"Accident or Accidental Death" follows the same pattern, delineating what constitutes an "accident"; the "Accidental Death" policies usually limit the coverage to death resulting directly from listed factors such as an auto accident.

There are so many names given these types of policy that my caveat is: whatever the headline in the advertising, read the fine print to see if the offer is actually for one of the above "Disability and/or Accident" types—and how much you'll be paid under what circumstances.

Life

General

The two major distinctions between life insurance policies are whole life and term.

Whole life is usually written to pay a set amount when you die that remains constant from the time you purchase the policy. Because it can be borrowed against and develops a cash value, many people use it like a savings account and also think it's a good investment—often on the advice of the company. At risk of stone-throwing at my head, I'll duck and say, "I don't." Think of the interest you could be getting on that money elsewhere.

Term is for a set period of time, the amount and the premiums reducing as the years pass. For instance, you might take it out on your own life to protect the children if you should die but have it reduce as they age and become better able to care for themselves. You normally have nothing to borrow against or a cash value. It's good.

There are, of course, many variations on these two basic types.

Q Do I say who's going to get my insurance in my will?

A I can't really answer that with a yes or a no. When you buy life insurance, you list the beneficiary or beneficiaries and how they shall be paid. The insurance company will pay according to this and does not look to your will. The exception is when the insurance is payable to your estate. Then the insurance will go to whomever you have named to receive it in your will. If no one is named where the insurance is payable to the estate, then the proceeds will pass to the person or persons named in what's called the "residuary clause" of your will, which distributes all assets not specifically given out.

I usually do mention the insurance when drawing up a will so that there is no opportunity for confusion; i.e., the will and the policy are made to correspond.

NOTE: For the purpose of federal estate taxes, if you pay the premiums on a policy, your estate is taxed. (This can be avoided.) There are no estate taxes owed on estates worth less than $600,000 but the insurance proceeds *are* included in adding it up.

Q The other night an insurance man was making notes on the kinds of life insurance I needed, and he asked me if I wanted "double indemnity." I've read that phrase in murder mysteries, but I don't know what it really means.

A "Double indemnity" is the term used for life insurance that pays double the amount stated if the person is killed accidentally. Probably you've read about double indemnity in those mysteries because the killer tries to make Aunt Agnes's death appear to be an accident in order to collect that larger amount.

Q What's to prevent me from insuring the life of Joe Schmo, like the guy upstairs that I know's in a bad way, then collecting when they die?

A The law that you must have an "insurable interest"*—that the insured person's death would directly affect you financially or is of such blood or affinity to expect some benefit from the continued life of the insured. It's against public policy for you to be able to make the life of another a gamble.

Title

When a house is being sold, the seller is usually required to furnish either a title insurance policy or an "abstract" showing good title to the property. An "abstract" is an instrument that traces your title back through all the buyers and sellers to the original land grant, for example, from the King. In most states a title policy is given far more frequently than an abstract.

NOTE: The average policy contains so many exceptions that, if you should get into a dispute later with your seller, you are likely to find your title insurance does not cover the problem.

Among the exceptions will be anything you might have seen while walking over the property, such as neighbors using a part of your land as their garden or a path across your property. Another uncovered exception would be "easements,"* which allow a third party the right to pass over your land, for instance, with telephone lines, electricity wires, or pay TV cables.

In addition, a straight title policy does not guarantee that your property is free of liens and encumbrances.

With title insurance, you certainly need an attorney to tell you if, once you get past the exceptions, you are left with any kind of insurance at all. The terms of the policy can often be negotiated before it's purchased.

Q We're selling our house and were told that part of the closing costs would be title insurance. First of all, I don't understand what title insurance is. Second, it doesn't sound like something we should have to pay for.

A Title insurance substitutes for an abstract* in that part of the contract where you promise to furnish "good and marketable title," meaning you are guaranteeing to the buyer that no one else has any valid claim to the property and that you have the power to pass to the buyer full rights of possession and enjoyment.

In title insurance an insurance company is promising that the title is clear and will make good if it isn't. The seller pays for it because it is his duty to guarantee good title.

Q Even though I read all of the things the policy said it didn't cover on my title insurance, I'm still not sure if I have insurance against squatters.

A Probably not, for three different reasons. (1) The policy is likely to state that your title, possession, and enjoyment are only insured as to "matters of record"* (such things as liens* and other matters that are filed in the courthouse). (2) The list of "exclusions" (matters that the policy does not cover) is likely to list squatters under phrases such as "adverse possession"*—matters you could have seen had you physically viewed your property. (3) Finally, you'd likely lose out in court on the basis that it was your duty, not the insurance company's, to check for squatters.

Q Everybody and his brother is cutting across my lawn and have been ever since I bought this place. The title company won't do a thing about it!

A All you get is my sympathy. If the people have been using your land as a shortcut for a sufficient length of time (varies among the states), in most jurisdictions they have established a public easement and can keep on truckin'. Your title policy does not cover this.

Causes of Loss (Along with Notice and Proof of Loss)

General

The "risk insured against" is the event you're taking out insurance to cover. For you to collect, this must be the cause of your loss. The "extent of risk" is how much the insurance company will pay you upon the happening of that event.

Therefore, it's your own job to decide exactly where you need protection. Examples of the questions you must ask yourself are:

Risk

In re* your auto policy: Is your car worth enough to justify paying premiums on collision insurance? In re your homeowner's policy: Is your furniture of such quality, e.g., antiques, that you need to list it separately with an appraisal, and/or insure against damage as well as total destruction? In re health: Do you need protection to cover those individual visits to the doctor's office, or can you save money by getting major medical? In re life: compare the cost of whole life to decreasing term and ask yourself what kind of life insurance you really need for your family; in re whole life bought as an investment, is this the best bang for your buck?

As to the extent of risk for which the insurance company is responsible, here you need to ask yourself whether you have enough insurance coverage. For example, most people seem to have too little fire insurance and even less as to contents coverage for their homes.

A point under auto is the consideration of today's high verdicts in auto accident suits. You can buy relatively low-cost "excess coverage," which takes over where your regular insurance leaves off; e.g., you might have $100,000 on your standard coverage and buy fairly inexpensive excess coverage insurance of $1 million.

Specific risk—general

Auto

Q My car was vandalized last night, and I don't know if my insurance policy covers this or not.

A I don't either, without seeing the policy, but I can tell you this: if your policy says "vandalism," okay; if it does not use the word "vandalism" but does contain the phrase "malicious mischief," you're covered under the latter. If neither term is used, you might still be protected under the collision coverage, dependent on the interpretation of the language. NOTE: If your policy has the provisions dealing with collision coverage separately from those for vandalism or malicious mischief, the collision coverage alone is not sufficient and you must have paid additional premiums for the vandalism or malicious mischief coverage.

Q While I was walking toward my car in the shopping center lot, I saw some man back into it and then drive off. Which part of my insurance policy would cover that?

A In some policies, it would be a separate provision under your uninsured motorists coverage, the clause dealing with hit-and-run under the property damage section. In other policies, this type of collision with a motor vehicle is separate from the uninsured motorists coverage, and it would then be covered under "Collision."

Q The agent told me I was buying "comprehensive coverage." Does that take care of my hitting a telephone pole?

A It should, but you can never count on collision coverage being automatically included in your insurance. Check the "Declarations" page in the front of your policy (see page 55) and see if you paid a premium for what would probably be called "collision" coverage or "property damage" (but not "property damage" in the "liability" portion of your policy because that relates to claims from another driver).

Q I was a passenger in a car my wife was driving when we ran into a wall. Can I get at the liability insurance by suing her?

A Maybe. Historically, one spouse could not sue another on the basis that it was against public policy; suits might be manufactured, collusion. Then suits between spouses were allowed in the cases of intentional tort,* a wrong done on purpose, such as assault. Now, in an increasing number of states, negligence suits are allowed between spouses. If the lawsuit would be allowed at all in your state, the next question is whether or not the insurance policy prohibits suits among family members. The courts assume the spouses remain happily married.

Q I never would have thought my auto insurance would cover hail damage but my neighbor collected quite a sum on his new car. Mine's all pitted, too. What do I look for to see if I've got that kind of insurance?

A Start with the word "hail." Policies vary as to putting this kind of damage under "Collision" or "Storm"—or, bad luck, might list it under the "exclusions." You may not have paid for that comprehensive coverage. If you think maybe yes, but aren't sure, see a lawyer.

Q Why do people talk about a whiplash injury as if it were a joke?

A Because a whiplash—which derives its name from the way a person's head snaps back and forth when a car is hit from the rear—can't be proved objectively. The result is very painful, but the injury normally does not show up on X rays, and so there is no proof except the testimony of the person injured. A number of unscrupulous attorneys and people in the medical profession have fraudulently claimed their client had a whiplash injury.

Several insurance companies have agreed never to settle a whiplash injury but will insist on having it tried in court. On the other hand, new tests such as the MRI are able to discern this soft tissue injury and other new techniques demonstrate the violent forward acceleration and backward halt. This can be a serious and lasting injury, so don't sell yourself short.

NOTE: The damage to your vehicle can be quite *slight* and the injury to you *severe* as the force travels to your body.

Workers' compensation

Q I had a heart attack at work. There wasn't any accident involved, so this would not come under my workers' compensation coverage, would it?

A Yes, it would if it was work-related. Workers' compensation coverage is not restricted to accidents. Another instance would be lung disease from working with hazardous material and the infamous "black lung" suffered by coal miners.

Q When I was working, a little piece of metal hit my eye and did some damage. The boss says I didn't have on my safety goggles so no work comp for me.

A Wrong! When you give up the right to sue for negligence in exchange for work comp, your employer gives up the defense that you were negligent. You win.

Homeowner's

Theft

Q I left my watch in the ladies' room, and when I came back it was gone. I told my insurance company I had lost the watch, and they said it was not covered under the insurance policy. But the same thing happened to a friend of mine and she recovered from the company.

A It's because you used the wrong word. You said you "lost" your watch; your friend probably said she had her watch "stolen." Your theft insurance will cover the latter but not the former, so long as it included theft away from home.

Q My sister says that since I left the door unlocked, my homeowner's policy won't cover the theft of all my jewelry. That isn't right, is it?

A Unfortunately, it might be.

See an attorney. You might very possibly be covered even though the language indicates you aren't. Does the policy demand that there be "forcible entry"? Also, is there a clause about your "negligence" that might prevent recovery?

An attorney can translate the policy for you to see if the insurance company is still on the hook despite your having made it easier for the theft to occur.

The courts have given a broad interpretation to the word "theft" in insurance policies, and have held it does not need to be as strict as the criminal-law definitions of burglary or larceny.

Fire

Q We had what I would call a fire last night, but actually all it did was smolder and fill the house with smoke. Is this covered by my fire insurance?

A I would argue "yes" for you, although there have been many cases in which the parties were fighting over whether this sort of thing comes within the meaning of "fire." And your policy might specifically *exclude* it.

See a lawyer; your policy most likely has the definition of "fire," and she can tell you whether or not there's a way to make your smoldering come within it.

Q My house had some damage but was not destroyed by a fire. The trouble is, I think it's a total loss because it smells so awful from the smoke that nobody could live there. The insurance company refuses to pay me for a total loss. Who wins?

A You don't, most likely. In similar cases, the courts have held that when the actual damage is not total, you can't just walk away and thereby make it a total loss. However, you can make a good argument with your set of facts, and I don't think those other decisions are good law in your fact situation.

The insurance usually *will* pay for the cost of cleaning. You might find a thorough professional job makes your place liveable.

Q Our cabin at the lake burned down, but when we put in a claim, the insurance company pointed to the fine print, which had a little provision saying that the insurance was void if the place had been vacant for the last six months, which it was. Can they do that to us?

A I'm afraid so. See an attorney to make sure there isn't any ambiguity.

Life

Q My wife died of cancer, but the insurer refuses to pay on her life insurance policy because it says her cause of death was not covered.

A They're probably talking about a "preexisting condition." Whether or not you can recover depends on whether your wife knew she had cancer at the time she took out the policy and whether cancer was queried if she had to fill out a set of questions. The latter is to determine if the company can argue "concealment."

See an attorney! Don't just give up. If the condition was either unknown or not asked about when the policy was purchased, you should recover.

To understand what the attorney will be looking for, see the discussion of "Defenses by Insurer" starting on page 88.

Q If someone jumps off the Empire State Building, does the insurance company pay out on the life insurance?

A It depends on the policy. Some policies cover any cause of death; others specifically state that suicide is not covered; still others include suicide if it occurs after a named period of time.

Q I always lie about my age—and I cut off a few years when I filled out the form for life insurance. The teeny little lie doesn't matter, does it?

A Afraid so. Unless it really was "teeny," putting down a younger age is a material fact that can void the policy. The premiums are based on actuarial tables, which tell the insurer how long you're expected to live. Therefore, no cheating.

Health and accident

Q I have an accident policy that would provide me with ample compensation for total disability, but the company says it won't pay me for my back injury because a doctor said surgery might remedy it. I don't want to have the surgery because I have seen what can happen if anything goes wrong. Does this mean I have to do without my benefits?

A No. In a case very much like yours, the court said that the insurance company must pay the benefits and could not force the insured to have the surgery.

Q I had a dizzy spell and fell off a ladder. The insurance company says my accident policy doesn't cover this because the cause of injury was whatever made me get dizzy in the first place, not the fall. Are they right?

A No. In a similar case the court found that the injury was caused by the fall and that it was an "accident" regardless of what made the plaintiff fall.

Q I saw an ad in a magazine for cheap accident insurance that appeared to pay off really big. What would the policy cover?

A It's unclear, because the courts are in a hassle over the definition of the words "accident" and "accidental death." Basically, the insurance would cover injuries resulting from a "fortuitous event beyond the insured's control." (You get sick accidentally, maybe, but an illness is still not an accident.)

An interesting point is that courts have found that accident insurance covers injuries *intentionally* inflicted by another. However, I don't think you would be covered if you started the fight yourself.

Also interesting is that if the court decides the insured was insane when she committed suicide, then suicide is considered an accidental death. *Caveat*: Beware of all those hard-sell accident policies; they are usually *very* limited.

Title

Q My neighbor has put up a fence and is planting a garden in a strip of land that the survey clearly shows is my property. The neighbor says he's been planting there for years. I called my title company and they won't do anything! Can I sue them?

A You *can*, but you won't win. This is a *risk* that is usually not covered—and in explicit terms. When you purchase title insurance you are responsible for checking out anything visible on the ground—and air. That would include people making adverse use of your property and the wires of utilities, for example.

To make you even more unhappy I'll add: that neighbor may have been using your property—fence and planting both important—for long enough to acquire a right to it!

Notice and proofs of loss

When contracting for insurance, you agree to certain duties to the insurance contract. These must be performed if you are going to recover your loss from the insurance company. They are the obligations to furnish notice, proofs of loss, and to cooperate.

"Notice" is exactly what it sounds like: you must notify the insurance company, within the time set by the agreement, that you have suffered the loss insured against. An automobile accident, a theft in your home, and your need for surgery, are examples of events demanding notice be given your insurer.

"Proofs of loss" are what you must supply to the insurance company to prove that the loss has occurred and to what extent. For instance, in the event of a theft, you would need to supply a police report along with a list of the things stolen and their value. (In the case of theft, a company may require that you go as far as furnishing original purchase receipts for the missing articles.)

A company can insert a provision in the policy saying that you lose all rights under the policy unless you furnish proofs of loss as it demands. However, the courts aren't fond of this provision and won't enforce it unless the provision is quite clear and definite, while other courts won't preclude recovery, whatever the provision.

As to both notice and proofs of loss, some courts have been quick to find that the insured has had an excuse for not supplying them to the company, such as injury or absence, e.g., on an extended business trip, and the insured has, therefore, recovered. Other courts have disagreed with this position: no recovery.

Q Everything in my house was ripped off and I thought I had insurance, but now the insurance people say they'll only pay for the things I have receipts for.

A First, we have to go over your policy to see what it says you must do in case of loss, as to proofs of loss. A court would do a balancing act here: the insurance company's right to demand reasonable proof of loss versus the unreasonable burden on the insured, you.

NOTE: The insurance companies are tightening up on payments for theft, and most now say they will demand receipts. Do you have pictures of the articles stolen, or an inventory, or is there someone who will testify that you did own what was stolen? From now on, keep an inventory supported by photographs and a date. Going from room to room taking a video of *everything* is a good idea.

Collecting on Your Loss

General

We've already discussed notice and proof of loss, which vary with the type of insurance and I've often advised you to get an attorney. If the prospects look good and the amount to be recovered is attractive (liability and exposure of the other side), an attorney will probably take your case on a "contingency."* That means the attorney will not charge you an hourly rate but take a percentage of what she recovers for you. Check your community for the standard percentage, i.e., one fourth if settled, one third if tried. Often it's higher and often the attorney will want an "upfront fee," money to pay for out-of-pocket expenses. You'll also have to pay for filing a suit and for things like depositions (questions under oath in front of a court reporter). Shop around. And *caveat*: do *not* agree to a big percentage of the settlement if this is going to be a "bait and switch" where the attorney settles the case with one phone call.

Remember, you have rights against your own insurance company. The newer thinking is that you have the insurance the agent promised and that you have the insurance you could reasonably expect. For instance, in one case a reasonable expectation and interpretation of the insurance policy in light of the cold winters where the insured lived meant coverage of the damage resulting from burst pipes. In court the insurer argued that a Florida court had held no coverage because it wasn't spelled out. The judge said to the company lawyer, "Too bad you're not in Florida!"

Other rights against your company are that it's obliged to defend you and to make a good faith effort to settle. If it doesn't and you lose in court, you can collect the entire amount of the verdict against you;

this is true no matter how much larger it is than the actual policy coverage.

A side point is that you *can* cancel your insurance. An elderly friend of mine was pressured by a salesman in her home to buy overlapping policies for health, long-term nursing care, and major medical, in addition to what she already had. When I explained the policies to her, she wrote and cancelled. The company then frightened her by sending increasingly threatening letters telling her she had to pay late premiums. Wrong!

Q Do I owe taxes on the money the insurance paid me for my injuries in an auto accident?

A No. That is considered reimbursement, not income.

Q Whose business is it to say whether I'm hurt or not?

A Everyone gets into the act. To prove almost any injury, a doctor's report describing the nature and extent of your injuries is required. (Your attorney won't tell you you're not hurt, but he *will* tell you if the insurance company is likely to pay for your injury.) Your attorney will then contact the insurance adjuster, who will be limited in the amount she can offer to settle. She needs home office approval for more. If the adjuster will not—or cannot—settle the claim for the amount your attorney is willing to accept for you, a lawsuit is usually filed at this point. Then the attorney representing the insurance company gets involved. If your attorney can't settle with the defense lawyer, it is the judge and jury (if you request a jury trial) who will decide whether you are hurt and to what extent.

Q A friend of mine was injured in a wreck I had when he was a passenger in my car. He says he's going to sue but that I shouldn't get angry because he isn't suing me but the insurance company. Is that right?

A Yes and no. The petition will name you as defendant and you will be the one actually in court. However, your defense will be handled by your insurance company, and it's the insurance company that will pay if your friend wins his case and is awarded damages (unless the damages are in excess of the amount for which you are insured).

Caveat: Your liability insurance may not cover suit by a passenger in your car. If this is the case, the insurance company is out of the picture and you're on your own as to the lawsuit. *His insurance* probably covers him as a passenger.

Q Can I sue my own insurance company?

A Yes.

Q My barber says that in collecting damages it's really cheaper for me to deal with the insurance company myself than to pay a lawyer and have him take a cut.

A Wrong. Besides the fact that an attorney will know what your injury's worth, the insurance company will have one figure in mind to settle with you, and a different—and higher—figure to settle with an attorney on your behalf.

Q Is it against the law for me to take the check the insurance company gave me to have my car fixed and just spend it? I mean without having any work done on the car?

A No. You have still suffered the damage, and so there is nothing wrong with deciding to take a monetary reimbursement instead of having the automobile repaired. But NOTE: many companies are now paying the repairman directly, so you won't ever see that check.

Q I put in my claim with the insurance company months ago! Can they just drag their heels forever?

A No. Write to the claims manager, give the date the claim was filed and for what, and say that you will be forced to seek legal counsel if you do not receive action within, say, seven days of the date of your letter. Then, if you don't receive action, do contact an attorney.

An insurance company does not like to be sued because of the reaction of a jury to one lone individual against that great big company.

Appraisals, estimates, "adjusters"

Q I had a wreck and the insurance company adjuster said my car was "totaled," but I'm really angry over the amount the company wants me to accept for my car as a total loss instead of repairing it. Is there anything I can do?

A One thing you can do on your own, without hiring a lawyer, is to tell the insurance company you would accept the payment for your car as a total loss, but want to know how much they would charge for the salvage. That is often quite low (sometimes $50 or $60), so you can have both the insurance proceeds and buy back your car as salvage yourself.

Q When I wrecked my car, I heard I'd better get estimates on how much it would cost to have it fixed, but the insurance company sent out an adjuster and nothing was said about an estimate. I don't understand.

A The ways of handling a loss vary from company to company and also with the type of loss. In some situations an insurance company will ask for from one to three estimates; in other cases a claims adjuster will decide the amount of damage. If the company uses an adjuster, it would still be wise for you to have an estimate in order to know if you can actually have your car fixed for the amount of money offered by the adjuster.

Q My partner and I are in the construction business and we told our insurance agent to give us a policy that covered us from liability. Well, a revolving door we installed in a building folded up and squashed a woman. She is suing us, but the insurance company says our policy does not cover it. What can we do?

A Hire an attorney! There are two important points involved in that question. First, an interpretation of the policy. Second, a fairly recent approach by the courts, which is basically that people have the insurance they reasonably believe they do have, whatever the policy says.

On the first point, your attorney will read the policy to see if the "risks insured" appear to include a collapsing revolving door. This probably will not be spelled out but will depend on language having to do with defective construction or installation. If the language is ambiguous, the rule is that it is resolved against the insurance company.

The second point is that more and more courts have been holding the insurance company liable although the policy actually did not cover this particular risk. This applies if you, the insured, can show that you left it up to your agent to provide you with the right kind of insurance, you reasonably believed the agent did so, and this risk itself was reasonable to anticipate.

Particular insurance

Auto

Q I was injured so badly in an automobile accident that I ended up losing my job. Can I collect for that?

A Yes. Assuming the other driver was liable,* responsible for the wreck, the loss of your job would be part of your damages and called "special damages." This means, basically, that the other driver's negligence caused you to lose your job as part of the chain of circumstances, which were foreseeable but not expected.

Q I had a fender-bender that was the other driver's fault, but since it occurred in the shopping center parking lot, I'm told I can't collect. Is this true?

A No. Many people are confused on this point because usually the police do not have any jurisdiction over a private parking lot.

If your insurance would cover this situation had it happened on a public road, your insurance would cover the same accident in a parking lot.

Q When I reported to the insurance company that I had wrecked my car, they said I didn't have collision coverage. I don't see where they get off, because I have read the policy and it has a whole lot in it about collisions.

A You were probably given an auto form policy that includes every type of coverage which that insurance company offers. This does not mean it all applies in your case. You have only the insurance you've paid for. Therefore, check the "Declarations" page to see if there is a dollar amount stated as the premium on the same line where it says "Collision." If so, you win.

Workers' compensation

Q The workers' compensation adjuster came out to my house and told me if I didn't settle the claim for the amount he was offering, I would be out of luck. Is this true?

A No. See an attorney! First, there's quite a bit of leeway as to how much a workers' compensation claim is worth, depending on whether the injury is temporary or permanent, and whether the injury makes you only partly disabled or completely unable to work. (See page 62.)

Second, the claim can go on up the ladder from the adjuster for the company carrying the workers' compensation insurance on through various hearings and appeals. It's not until the last appeal available that you must accept the amount offered.

Homeowner's

Q What's to prevent someone from insuring their house for a quarter of a million dollars and then burning it down?

A First, I hope, the thought of a felony conviction for arson! Second, the insurance company is not going to issue a quarter-of-a-million-dollar policy unless the house is worth it, meaning there'll be no profit from the loss.

Health

Q I'm so afraid I won't be covered for something I carry several health insurance policies. Well, I had to have angioplasty—big bill!—and my daughter-in-law says I can collect from two different insurers so I actually make a profit. This isn't true, is it? Wouldn't I go to jail?

A No, you're not going to jail and you *can* collect from both insurers. Health insurance is one of the few types of insurance where it's possible to collect on more than one policy. The reason this is allowed, and is not considered against public policy, is because people would not intentionally make themselves sick to collect on the insurance.

Life

Q Can I change the beneficiary on my life insurance?

A Yes. The only qualification I have to add is that not if it's part of the terms of a divorce decree or some contractual agreement such as "key man/woman" insurance for the business.

Title

Q A woman is suing us. She claims that her father should have inherited our property two owners back and that the record books show the purchasers at that time didn't have good title. They're trying to get our place and we're very upset. Will our Title Insurance policy protect us?

A Yes. They owe you a defense in court and, even more importantly, when the policy was issued the insurer agreed to protect you against loss or damage due to defects in title—which is what the plaintiff is claiming against you. The plaintiff is also alleging that the record shows what's called a "cloud on the title."

If the title insurer is saying your policy doesn't cover this, it would be very unusual because this type of attack is at the heart of your basic Title Insurance.

Defenses by Insurer

(Arguing Why They Shouldn't Have to Pay Off)

General

The most common defense by an insurer is simply that the policy does not cover the loss. But just because the company says so doesn't make it so; the courts will always construe or interpret an insurance policy in favor of the insured and against the insurance company where there's any doubt or ambiguity.

Attorneys are generally in agreement that two of the largest nationally advertised insurance companies are extremely difficult to work with and will drag their heels to avoid paying off a loss. Therefore, ask around before you buy insurance.

Q When we sent the insurance company notice of loss on our fire insurance, they said the agent had never informed them that he had sold us a policy, and therefore they don't have to pay us. What happens?

A You win. But see an attorney to do so. In a similar case the court held that the insured did have his rights under the fire insurance policy even though the agent had not reported to the company that he had issued the policy.

Misrepresentation, fraud, breach of warranty

The insurance company can get out of the insurance contract if it can show it was led to contract through the fraud of the insured. To prove fraud in court, the company must show that not only was there misrepresentation, but the insurer believed the false statements, relied on them, and would not have issued the policy if it had known the truth of the matter.

Fraud requires that the insured actually make a false statement. Concealment is a different matter and even harder to prove. If the company is saying the insured concealed a fact but there was no question concerning it on the application, then a court is likely to say that since the company didn't ask about it, it was not a material fact*; i.e., it was not of sufficient importance to void the policy.

Another defense is called "breach of warranty." This is just another way of saying that in your application you have "warranted" that certain facts are true and it turns out they are not. A common example of this would be on a health or life insurance policy where you falsely "warrant" that you are in good health or don't have some particular ailment set out in the application.

Q My brother-in-law says that since I lied about my age on my life insurance policy, they won't ever have to pay off. Is that true?

A I don't like agreeing with your brother-in-law, but this time he's probably right. When an insurance company contends that it can get out of the contract—avoid payment on the policy or deny coverage—for misrepresentation or fraud on the part of the insured, the question is always whether or not the insured's false statement would have kept the insurance company from contracting as it did if it had known the truth.

As to your case, it seems to me that an insurance company could successfully defend its not paying on a life insurance policy on the grounds that, given the true age of the insured, a different policy would have been issued, or one would not have been contracted for at all. That's what they hire actuaries for.

One note of hope: Was it a very small lie? Whatever, please correct this now.

Breach by insured (conditions subsequent)

Another common defense would be the claim that the insured has breached a condition subsequent,* which, most likely, would be either failure to pay the premium or failure to file notice of loss.

A court doesn't take kindly to either of these defenses. It probably wouldn't let the insurance company off the hook for the insured's failure to pay one premium in an "unfair" situation unless the policy clearly makes it a condition of coverage. The same is true of failure to file notice of loss. Even then, if it was a purely technical failure, I don't think a court would allow a company to refuse to pay; the insurer would have to show that the failure to give notice of loss had a direct effect on the company's liability.

Cancellation by Insured

General

There may be third party reasons why you're obligated to *not* cancel your insurance, but as *between you and your insurer* in every circumstance I can think of, you *can* cancel.

This right to cancel may seem too elemental to be mentioned here, but I've had clients whose insurance companies made them believe they were obligated to keep the insurance and keep paying the premiums.

The insurer can cancel you quickly enough and a rule of contract law that applies to *every contract* is that: if one party is not bound by the contract, neither party is.

Some third party instances I referred to (above) which might make it your obligation to *keep* insurance are: your mortgage holder's requirement that you keep your house insured; or, your divorce decree orders you to keep a certain amount of life insurance to benefit your children.

Q I'm eighty-five years old and found I had overlapping health insurance policies because the agent told me I needed them in case I had to have home nursing or went into a care facility. I wrote the company cancelling all these different policies, but they've been sending me bills for premiums due. I'm frightened because the letters are starting to sound threatening. What should I do?

A Ignore them! Also see a lawyer. That company is misbehaving. Your lawyer might find you have a case wherein you can get your earlier premiums back! But if you don't want to go into all that, be assured you do *not* have to pay any more premiums.

Q My car's so old I told the insurance company I wanted to cancel the collision coverage and get my premiums lowered. The agent says I can't. Is this true?

A No. If that particular company won't cooperate, saying it's some kind of company rule, just cancel the whole thing and get another insurer.

Standard Policies and the Translation into English

Actually, I'm going to provide you only with the translation of a standard family automobile insurance policy for a number of reasons, including: (1) you'll probably find yourself on your own more often with this one, trying to decipher language that seems more confusing than that of other types of insurance; (2) the text and questions and answers can more easily flag the major problem areas for you that apply to the other types; and (3) if you approach any insurance policy with the same principles of analysis used for the following auto translation, you'll at least begin to know what and where to question.

On the front of the policy is the statement:

This policy is completed by a Declarations page inserted herein. The Declarations designate the policy term and coverages applicable to the automobiles insured.

Translation: This means, first, you don't have a contract unless the printed policy issued to you has what the company refers to as a "Declarations" page. Second, it's the "Declarations" page, and only that page, which sets out the time period in which your policy is in effect and what coverages you have purchased for your automobile(s). This statement also puts you on notice that you must have a "Declarations" page and also what that page itself says.

PART I—LIABILITY

COVERAGE A BODILY INJURY LIABILITY
COVERAGE B PROPERTY DAMAGE LIABILITY
To pay on behalf of the insured all sums which the insured shall become legally obligated to pay as damages because of:

A bodily injury, sickness or disease, including death resulting therefrom, hereinafter called "bodily injury," sustained by any person;

B. injury to or destruction of property, including loss of use thereof, hereinafter called "property damage"; arising out of the ownership, maintenance or use of the owned automobile or any non-owned automobile, and the company shall defend any suit alleging such bodily injury or property damage and seeking damages which are payable under the terms of this policy, even if any of the allegations of the suit are groundless, false or fraudulent; but the company may make such investigation and settlement of any claim or suit as it deems expedient.

SUPPLEMENTARY PAYMENTS To pay, in addition to the applicable limits of liability:

(a) all expenses incurred by the company, all costs taxed against the insured in any such suit and all interest on the entire amount of any judgment therein which accrues after entry of the judgment and before the company has paid or tendered or deposited in court that part of the judgment which does not exceed the limit of the company's liability thereon;

(b) premiums on appeal bonds required in any such suit, premiums on bonds to release attachments for an amount not in excess of the applicable limit of liability of this policy, and the cost of bail bonds required of the insured because of accident or traffic law violation arising out of the use of an automobile insured hereunder, not to exceed $100 per bail bond, but without any obligation to apply for or furnish any such bonds;

(c) expenses incurred by the insured for such immediate medical and surgical relief to others as shall be imperative at the time of an accident involving an automobile insured hereunder and not due to war;

(d) all reasonable expenses, other than loss of earnings, incurred by the insured at the company's request.

Since this portion of the policy is labeled "Liability," it's limited to what the company will be responsible for *to others* making a claim against you for negligent use of your automobile, except for med pay which is available regardless of negligence. It will *not* have anything in it relating to *your own* personal injury or property damage.

Note particularly that this section begins with bold-faced type reciting "Coverage A—Bodily Injury Liability" and "Coverage B-Property Damage Liability." Since most states now require that you have both of these coverages before you can register your car, it's unlikely that you would have one without the other. However, be sure to check that "Declarations" page to see that there is a premium in a dollar amount on the same line as "Coverage A" and on the same line as "Coverage B." These are two different things.

The first sentence, immediately after the bold-faced type, means that the company is only agreeing to pay out, on your behalf, what a court has said you must pay. In other words, even though by far the most claims resulting from an auto accident are settled without ever going to court, the insurer doesn't have to pay off until there is a judgment against you. (But see discussion of bad faith, failure to settle on page 64.)

"A" translates as: If you hurt or kill a *person*, or even if that person has an illness, as contrasted to an injury, that results from . . . (NOTE: In the policy, this sentence is not going to end until we jump down after "B.")

"B" translates: The insurer will pay on your behalf for any damages you do to *property*, as contrasted to damages to a person, above; and this includes when your actions caused someone to lose the use of their property . . .

With the fine print beginning with the words "arising out of" we finally come to the end of the sentence and the answer to *when* the company is going to pay for "A—bodily injury" and "B—property damage." It's *when* you have been held legally responsible for that injury or damage arising out of either your *ownership* or your *use* of the car in question. The car involved does not have to be your own. (The policy uses the words "non-owned automobile" and takes three lines later on, under "Definitions," to describe what that means. I'll translate when we get to it.)

Still on the section beginning with "arising out of" that ownership or use, the insurer gets around to liability.* They will defend you in a suit where the plaintiff claims to have personal injuries or property damages (or both) with some provisos. One is the sneaky "payable under the terms of this policy." That means the insurance company can decide *if* you get a defense based on *if* it thinks the claimed damages come under the terms of the policy. If it decides in the affirmative, the insurer will defend you even if the plaintiff's allegations are full of hot air. It also reserves the right to investigate and settle any claim or suit that it wants to: you don't get to stand on principle.

And remember, this whole incredibly long sentence started way back up there with the words "To pay . . " Therefore, if *you* are *legally obligated to pay*, the company will pay for you *if* you and the suit or claim against you meet all these conditions we've been discussing.

NOTE: The insurance company cannot arbitrarily decide that the suit or claim against you doesn't come under the terms of the policy. There are rules developed from many law suits by the insured against its own insurer: the company must conduct a full and reasonable investigation, and do so promptly. If the insurer acts in an arbitrary, unreasonable manner, you can sue *it* for bad faith refusal to settle or defend. If you win, your damages will include the amount that the plaintiff is entitled to from you—even if they exceed the amount of insurance you've paid for.

Caveat: In the above lines, throughout the policy, and on the "Declarations" page, the insurance company is contracting only to pay the amount of liability insurance you purchased; the reference above to "all sums" doesn't really mean that at all.

The bold-face "**Supplementary Payments**" (still under "Liability") means that, besides paying up to the amount of coverage you purchased, the insurer agrees to pay:

(a) its own expenses and court costs, plus any interest tacked onto a judgment against you that accrues before the company pays its part;

(b) appeal bonds (usually required when you lose in trial court and are appealing to guarantee that you'll have the money to pay the judgment); the premiums due to get the other side to release an attachment of your property; and bail bonds, if resulting from the use of the insured car but not over $100 and with no responsibility to get the bond for you;

(c) emergency medical care without regard to negligence, but that's for others, not for you; and

(d) any expenses you incur because of doing what the company asks you to do, but any loss of salary doesn't count.

PERSONS INSURED The following are insureds* (persons covered by the policy) under Part I:

(a) with respect to the owned automobile,

(1) the named insured and any resident of the same household,

(2) any other person using such automobile with the permission of the named insured, provided his actual operation or (if he is not operating) his other actual use thereof is within the scope of such permission, and

(3) any other person or organization but only with respect to his or its liability because of acts or omissions of an insured under (a) (1) or (2) above;

(b) with respect to a non-owned automobile,

(1) the named insured,

(2) any relative, but only with respect to a private passenger automobile or trailer, provided his [either (1) or (2)] actual operation or (if he is not operating) the other actual use thereof is with the permission, or reasonably believed to be with the permission, of the owner and is within the scope of such permission, and

(3) any other person or organization not owning or hiring the automobile, but only with respect to his or its liability because of acts or omissions of an insured under (b) (1) or (2) above.

The insurance afforded under Part I applies separately to each insured against whom claim is made or suit is brought, but the inclusion herein of more than one insured shall not operate to increase the limits of the company's liability.

After liability, we found out what was insured and when it was insured—now we go to *who* is insured. NOTE: There are two categories of persons insured, those in sections (a) and (b) in the above fine print; (a) tells you who is insured if it's your own car that is involved, and (b) lists who is insured if the car involved is not one that you own.

The translation is:

(a) Owned automobile

(1) You, as the person who owns the policy, and anyone who lives with you are covered. (There are innumerable court decisions interpreting who comes within the meaning of the word "resident" and also the meaning of "same household.") NOTE ALSO: In this section, where we're talking about the *automobile you own*, a person can qualify as an insured if he or she lives with you, while below, under (b), that person has to be a relative, using a non-commercial auto.

(2) Also covered is anyone to whom you have given permission to use the car, but if that person isn't driving the car, you must have also given permission for whatever he or she is doing with it.

(3) Finally, in this section relating to the car you own, the policy also covers anyone who is liable because of something you, or those other fellows above, did or failed to do.

Section (b) of "Persons Insured" has to do with that car you do not own. This is so ambiguous that it practically invites a law suit if the insurer refuses to pay.

(1) You're insured as the "named insured."

(2) This time that "resident" is out and, instead, the other person insured must be your "relative," and, instead of anybody and their brother having permission, it's only that relative who gets covered and who also must have permission. NOTE: Now that required permission is expanded to include what amounts to "no permission but the person's reasonable belief that she *did* have permission."

(3) The same as (3) above.

Finally, under this section, the last lines simply tell you that the company may let you include all those folks above, but that's not going to boost the amount it pays out; that amount still has the same ceiling on it, which is simply how much coverage you bought.

Caveat: Practically every one of these words has been litigated—each side offering a different meaning. Therefore, I don't guarantee to have explored every possible meaning, e.g., exactly what is meant by the word "permission"? By "reasonably believed"?

DEFINITIONS Under Part I:
"named insured" means the individual named in Item 1 of the declarations and also includes his spouse, if a resident of the same household;

Your name on the policy equals "named insured," and if your spouse lives with you, he/she gets to be "named insured," too.

"insured" means a person or organization described under "Persons Insured";

If the person *is* covered but *is not* a "named insured," then the person is an "insured." The insured doesn't have to be a real person but can be an organization.

"relative" means a relative of the named insured who is a resident of the same household;

After all those lawsuits fighting over the meaning of the word, the company has decided to tell us that "relative" must also be one of those "residents of the same household."

"private passenger automobile" means a four wheel private passenger, station wagon or jeep type automobile;

Okay.

"farm automobile" means an automobile of the pickup body, sedan delivery, panel truck or van type used for farming or ranching but not customarily used for business or commercial purposes other than farming or ranching;

The body style of the "farm automobile" is described and also, naturally, its main purpose needs to be on the farm, since it's a "farm automobile."

"utility automobile" means an automobile, other than a farm automobile, of the pickup body, sedan delivery, panel truck or van type not customarily used for business or commercial purposes;

This "utility automobile" can*not* be a farm auto but *can* be all those other things so long as they're only occasionally used for business or commercial purposes—another of their ambiguous sentences just begging for court interpretation.

"trailer" means a trailer designed for use with a private passenger automobile, if not being used for business or commercial purposes with other than a private passenger, farm or utility automobile, or a farm wagon or farm implement while used with a farm automobile;

Okay, I throw up my hands. There's no punctuation where I think it should be so you're on your own if your trailer is anything other than one "designed for use with a private passenger automobile."
See my comment above as to law suits and ambiguity.

"owned automobile" means

(a) a private passenger, farm or utility automobile described in this policy for which a specific premium charge indicates that coverage is afforded,

(b) a trailer owned by the named insured,

(c) a private passenger, farm or utility automobile ownership of which is acquired by the named insured during the policy period provided (1) it replaces an owned automobile as defined in (a) above, or (2) the company insures all private passenger, farm and utility automobiles owned by the named insured on the date of such acquisition and the named insured notifies the company during the policy period or within 30 days after the date of such acquisition of his election to make this and no other policy issued by the company applicable to such automobile, or

(d) a temporary substitute automobile;

Sections (a), (b), and (c) mean that if you've paid the premium, your vehicle can be any of the ones we just finished describing, along with the trailer, and whatever you get to replace one of those during the policy period. [Don't worry about (c 2), which just gives you a break of 30 days extra if they've got all of your insurance coverage.] (d)—your "owned automobile" can also be a "temporary substitute automobile" which is the company's next definition.

"temporary substitute automobile" means any automobile or trailer, not owned by the named insured, while temporarily used with the permission of the owner as a substitute for the owned automobile or trailer when withdrawn from normal use because of its breakdown, repair, servicing, loss or destruction;

Pay attention to this one because you might find yourself involved in whether or not a "temporary substitute automobile" is covered. That substitute car—which is borrowed with the permission of the owner—can't be just any old automobile, but must be one you're using because your own has broken down or is otherwise unavailable.

"non-owned automobile" means an automobile or trailer not owned by or furnished for the regular use of either the named insured or any relative, other than a temporary substitute automobile;

This "non-owned automobile" is not a "temporary substitute automobile."

"automobile business" means the business or occupation of selling, repairing, servicing, storing or parking automobiles;

"use" of an automobile includes the loading and unloading thereof;

"war" means war, whether or not declared, civil war, insurrection, rebellion or revolution, or any act or condition incident to any of the foregoing.

The above three definitions are actually clear. I like the fact that "war means war."

ASSISTANCE AND COOPERATION OF THE INSURED The insured shall cooperate with the company and, upon the company's request, assist in making settlements, in the conduct of suits and in enforcing any right of contribution or indemnity against any person or organization who may be liable to the insured because of bodily injury, property damage or loss with respect to which insurance is afforded under this policy; and the insured shall attend hearings and trials and assist in securing and giving evidence and obtaining the attendance of witnesses. The insured shall not, except at his own cost, voluntarily make any payment, assume any obligation or incur any expense other than for such immediate medical and surgical relief to others as shall be imperative at the time of accident.

This might be called the company's fall-back paragraph because it lists everything that you are supposed to do to help out but that it's unlikely you would ever have to do. The company wants it in there so that it could always claim you breached the contract by failing to comply as set forth therein.

The "cooperation" paragraph includes your agreement to go after anybody who has caused the loss that your company must pay. You're also supposed to show up at the trial. *Caveat*: It's at your own cost if you go out and make any payments or incur expenses other than emergency medical, as, for example, paying the other driver's hospital bill.

LIMITS OF LIABILITY The limit of bodily injury liability stated in the declarations as applicable to "each person" is the limit of the company's liability for all damages, including damages for care and loss of services, arising out of bodily injury sustained by one person as the result of any one occurrence; the limit of such liability stated in the declarations as applicable to "each occurrence" is, subject to the above provision respecting each person, the total limit of the company's liability for all such damages arising out of bodily injury sustained by two or more persons as the result of any one occurrence.

The limit of property damage liability stated in the declarations as applicable to "each occurrence" is the total limit of the company's liability for all damages arising out of injury to or destruction of all property of one or more persons or organizations, including the loss of use thereof, as the result of any one occurrence.

Limits of liability for bodily injury to each person. The first paragraph simply says that the amount of money the company will pay out for injury you caused to any *one* person is the top dollar for *all* damages to that one person. NOTE: This first paragraph is talking about a real live person—the property damage limit can include property damage suffered by a non-person and is discussed in the next paragraph. It also limits the company's liability for "each occurrence."

Together, the two above simply mean that you are buying X number of dollars' coverage for a single person you injure in any one accident, and another amount that puts the lid on all the personal injury damages added together in that accident. Example: If you run a stoplight and hit another car with two people in it, this section means that if you, for instance, have 10-20 coverage ($10,000 and $20,000), the company will not pay out more than $10,000 for each of these two people, even if one has medical expenses far in excess of $10,000, and for the entire wreck with both people taken together, will only pay out a top figure of $20,000. To find out exactly the amount for which you are covered, look at the dollar figure on your "Declarations" page where it says: "Limits of Liability—Bodily Injury."

NOTE: If the attorney for those two people offers to settle within the policy limits and your insurer *unreasonably* refuses, the company will then owe the whole amount of the judgment even in *excess* of policy limits.

The second paragraph above under "Limits of Liability" pertains only to *property* damage and simply states that the coverage you purchased is the limit the company will pay for property damage caused by any one occurrence. Again, to find out your exact amount of property damage coverage, look on the "Declarations" page where it says "Limits of Liability—Property Damage."

TWO OR MORE AUTOMOBILES When two or more automobiles are insured hereunder, the terms of this policy shall apply separately to each, but an automobile and a trailer attached thereto shall be held to be one automobile as respects limits of liability.

OTHER INSURANCE If the insured has other insurance against a loss covered by Part I of this policy the company shall not be liable under this policy for a greater proportion of such loss than the applicable limit of liability stated in the declarations bears to the total applicable limit of liability of all valid and collectible insurance against such loss; provided, however, the insurance with respect to a temporary substitute automobile or non-owned automobile shall be excess insurance over any other valid and collectible insurance.

ACTION AGAINST COMPANY No action shall lie against the company unless, as a condition precedent thereto, the insured shall have fully complied with all the terms of this policy, nor until the amount of the insured's obligation to pay shall have been finally determined either by judgment against the insured after actual trial or by written agreement of the insured, claimant and company.

Any person or organization or the legal representative thereof who has secured such judgment or written agreement shall thereafter be entitled to recover under this policy to the extent of the insurance afforded by this policy. No person or organization shall have any right under this policy to join the company as a party to any action against the insured to determine the insured's liability, nor shall the company be impleaded by the insured or his legal representative. Bankruptcy or insolvency of the insured or of the insured's estate shall not relieve the company of any of its obligations hereunder.

"Two or More Automobiles": the coverage applies as if you had two separate policies. "Other Insurance": if you have other insurance that you think would cover the same accident or occurrence, see an attorney. This one is just too technical.

The same goes with "Action Against Company." If you suspect you have a reason to sue these folks, you do not want to proceed without a lawyer. This section mainly means you have to have done your part and the other side has obtained a judgment against you before your insured must pay. But remember, your company cannot legally jeopardize you by "unreasonable failure" to settle.

SUBROGATION In the event of any payment under this policy, the company shall be subrogated to all the insured's rights of recovery therefor against any person or organization and the insured shall execute and deliver instruments and papers and do whatever else is necessary to secure such rights. The insured shall do nothing after loss to prejudice such rights.

The translation of "Subrogation" is that by agreeing to this insurance contract, you are also agreeing to do all necessary to help your insurance company get back what it has paid out. In other words, if you yourself could have collected damages from the other party, then your own insurance company also has that right and you better not mess it up.

EXCLUSIONS This policy does *not* apply under Part I:

(a) to any automobile while used as a public or livery conveyance, but this exclusion does not apply to the named insured with respect to bodily injury or property damage which results from the named insured's occupancy of a non-owned automobile other than as the operator thereof;

NOTE: (a) above and the following provisions under "EXCLUSIONS" refer to "Part I" and, therefore, relate to your "Liability" coverage.

All these negatives sort out to state that you're *not* covered for liability incurred while using an automobile as a commercial conveyance but *are covered* if the damage results from your occupancy. It boggles the mind to figure out what you're going to do that gets you sued while you're not operating but simply occupying a non-owned automobile!

Also, because of the position of "but this exclusion does not apply" we have an ambiguity of whether you're covered while occupying the otherwise excluded "public or livery conveyance"!

NOTE: "Occupancy" is distinguished from "operating/operator" and is another little quirk to watch out for throughout the policy.

(b) to bodily injury or property damage caused intentionally by or at the direction of the insured;

They won't pay if you intentionally cause the damage—or tell somebody else to do it.

(c) to bodily injury or property damage with respect to which an insured under the policy is also an insured under a nuclear energy liability policy issued by Nuclear Energy Liability Insurance Association, Mutual Atomic Energy Liability Underwriters or Nuclear Insurance Association of CanadA or would be an insured under any such policy but for its termination upon exhaustion of its limit of liability;

Okay.

(d) to bodily injury or property damage arising out of the operation of farm machinery;

Too bad if you hurt someone while driving a tractor.

The "Exclusions" (e) through (h) become so involved with the insured's employees, workers' compensation, fellow employees, use of owned and non-owned autos in business—and the exceptions to the "Exceptions"—that any translation would be too confusing itself. Therefore, if those circumstances arise and you're threatened with liability, see your own attorney to find out if you're covered.

The company won't pay for liability expenses relating:

(i) to injury to or destruction of
(1) property owned or transported by the insured or
(2) property rented to or in charge of the insured other than a residence or private garage;

Okay.

(j) to the ownership, maintenance, operation, use, loading or unloading of an automobile ownership of which is acquired by the named insured during the policy period or any temporary substitute automobile therefor, if the named insured has purchased other automobile liability insurance applicable to such automobile for which a specific premium charge has been made.

Nor for new car or substitute if you've purchased separate insurance on it.

NOTE: All the above relates *only* to your liability coverage.

PART II—EXPENSES FOR MEDICAL SERVICES

COVERAGE C MEDICAL PAYMENTS To pay all reasonable expenses incurred within one year from the date of accident for necessary medical, surgical, X-ray and dental services, including prosthetic devices, and necessary ambulance, hospital, professional nursing and funeral services:

DIVISION 1. To or for the named insured and each relative who sustains bodily injury, sickness or disease, including death resulting therefrom, hereinafter called "bodily injury," caused by accident,

(a) while occupying the owned automobile,

(b) while occupying a non-owned automobile, but only if such person has, or reasonably believes he has, the permission of the owner to use the automobile and the use is within the scope of such permission, or

(c) through being struck by an automobile or by a trailer of any type;

DIVISION 2. To or for any other person who sustains bodily injury, caused by accident, while occupying

(a) the owned automobile, while being used by the named insured, by any resident of the same household or by any other person with the permission of the named insured; or

(b) a non-owned automobile, if the bodily injury results from

(1) its operation or occupancy by the named insured or its operation on his behalf by his private chauffeur or domestic servant, or

(2) its operation or occupancy by a relative, provided it is a private passenger automobile or trailer, but only if such operator or occupant [either of whom are defined in (1) or (2)] has, or reasonably believes he has, the permission of the owner to use the automobile and the use is within the scope of such permission.

DEFINITIONS The definitions under Part I apply to Part II, and under Part II:

"occupying" means in or upon or entering into or alighting from.

LIMIT OF LIABILITY The limit of liability for medical payments stated in the declarations as applicable to "each person" is the limit of the company's liability for all expenses incurred by or on behalf of each person who sustains bodily injury as the result of any one accident.

NOTE: Part II without regard to liability closely parallels the language in "Part I—Liability"; the main thing here is to know that you and those folks described in Part I are covered for your medical expenses, ambulances, etc. straight through the funeral, if resulting from occupying the owned automobile or occupying or operating a non-owned automobile under certain conditions. In addition, both the named insured and relatives are covered if they are struck by any type of automobile or trailer.

Therefore, if you or your relatives are injured by any vehicle, see an attorney to find out your full coverage for all resulting expenses.

"Division 2" provides medical pay to others than those defined above dependent upon who is using the owned auto (a) or operating or occupying a non-owned auto (b).

NOTE: In the above definitions, "occupying" means in or on (?) the auto and getting in and out of it.

This type of coverage, as mentioned earlier, is relatively inexpensive and you should have a good deal of it.

PART III-PROTECTION AGAINST UNINSURED MOTORISTS

COVERAGE D UNINSURED MOTORISTS
(DAMAGES FOR BODILY INJURY)

To pay all sums which the insured or his legal representative shall be legally entitled to recover as damages from the owner or operator of an uninsured motor vehicle because of bodily injury, sickness or disease, including death resulting therefrom, hereinafter called "bodily injury," sustained by the insured, caused by accident and arising out of the ownership, maintenance or use of such uninsured motor vehicle; provided, for the purposes of this coverage, determination as to whether the insured or such representative is legally entitled to recover such damages, and if so the amount thereof, may be made by agreement between the insured or such representative and the company or, if they fail to agree, by arbitration in accordance with the arbitration provision of this policy, or by judicial determination.

No judgment against any person or organization alleged to be legally responsible for the bodily injury shall be conclusive, as between the insured and the company, of the issues of liability of such person or organization or of the amount of damages to which the insured is legally entitled unless such judgment is entered pursuant to an action prosecuted by the insured with the written consent of the company.

DEFINITIONS The definitions under Part I, except the definition of "insured," apply to Part III, and under Part III:

  "insured" means:

  (a) the named insured and any relative;

  (b) any other person while occupying an insured automobile; and

  (c) any person, with respect to damages he is entitled to recover because of bodily injury to which this Part applies sustained by an insured under (a) or (b) above.

The insurance afforded under Part III applies separately to each insured, but the inclusion herein of more than one insured shall not operate to increase the limits of the company's liability;

"occupying" means in or upon or entering into or alighting from;

"insured automobile" means:

(a) an automobile described in the policy for which a specific premium charge indicates that coverage is afforded,

(b) a private passenger, farm or utility automobile, ownership of which is acquired by the named insured during the policy period, provided (1) it replaces an insured automobile as defined in (a) above, or (2) the company insures all private passenger, farm and utility automobiles owned by the named insured on the date of such acquisition and the named insured notifies the company during the policy period or within 30 days after the date of such acquisition of his election to make this and no other policy issued by the company applicable to such automobile, or

(c) a temporary substitute automobile for an insured automobile as defined in (a) or (b) above, and

(d) a non-owned automobile while being operated by the named insured; and the term "insured automobile" includes a trailer while being used with an automobile described in (a), (b), (c) or (d) above, but shall not include:

(1) any automobile or trailer owned by a resident of the same household as the named insured,

(2) any automobile while used as a public or lively conveyance, or

(3) any automobile while being used without the permission of the owner;

"uninsured motor vehicle" includes a trailer of any type and means:

(a) an automobile or trailer with respect to the ownership, maintenance or use of which there is, in at least the amounts specified by the financial responsibility law of the state in which the insured automobile is principally garaged, no bodily injury liability bond or insurance policy applicable at the time of the accident with respect to any person or organization legally responsible for the use of such automobile, or with respect to which there is a bodily injury liability bond or insurance policy applicable at the time of the accident but the company writing the same denies coverage thereunder, or with respect to which there is a bodily injury liability insurance policy applicable at the time of the accident but the company writing the same is or becomes insolvent, or

(b) a hit-and-run automobile;

but the term "uninsured motor vehicle" shall not include:

(1) an insured automobile or an automobile furnished for the regular use of the named insured or a relative,

(2) an automobile or trailer owned or operated by a self-insurer within the meaning of any motor vehicle financial responsibility law, motor carrier law or any similar law,

(3) an automobile or trailer owned by the United States of America Canada a state, a political subdivision of any such government or an agency of any of the foregoing,

(4) a land motor vehicle or trailer if operated on rails or crawler-treads or while located for use as a residence or premises and not as a vehicle, or

(5) a farm type tractor or equipment designed for use principally off public roads, except while actually upon public roads;

"state" includes the District of Columbia a territory or possession of the United States, and a province of Canada;

"hit-and-run automobile" means an automobile which causes bodily injury to an insured arising out of physical contact of such automobile with the insured or with an automobile which the insured is occupying at the time of the accident, provided:

(a) there cannot be ascertained the identity of either the operator or the owner of such "hit-and-run automobile";

(b) the insured or someone on his behalf shall have reported the accident within 24 hours to a police, peace or judicial officer or to the Commissioner of Motor Vehicles, and shall have filed with the company within 30 days thereafter a statement under oath that the insured or his legal representative has a cause or causes of action arising out of such accident for damages against a person or persons whose identity is unascertainable, and setting forth the facts in support thereof; and

(c) at company's request, the insured or his legal representative makes available for inspection the automobile which the insured was occupying at time of accident.

This is the reverse of your liability coverage because this time your own insurance company agrees to pay you (or your representative if you're dead) what you are *legally entitled* to recover from a third person, the uninsured motorist.

NOTE Several important points:

1) The accident must be the result of that uninsured motorist's ownership or use of his car; if it is, there's *no limit* to the amount payable to you (and certain defined others) by the company for your injury, sickness, disease, or death resulting therefrom.

2) You and the company must first agree if you are legally entitled to recover from that uninsured motorist and, if so, how much. If you can't agree, you have contracted to go along with arbitration.

3) A real biggie: under the terms of this policy, you have agreed that a judgment in court is not conclusive. The only time a court judgment is conclusive is if you have brought suit with the written consent of the company.

NOTE: I am not going to translate all of the provisions under uninsured motorists because it is something your attorney will need to pursue for you. However, I do want you to be aware of the basic coverage you have purchased, as I've outlined above. One other point: this uninsured motorist coverage also includes a hit-and-run clause.

"Underinsured" as compared to "uninsured" has become a recovery issue here, also.

PART IV—PHYSICAL DAMAGE

COVERAGE E (1) COMPREHENSIVE (EXCLUDING COLLISION)
(2) PERSONAL EFFECTS

(1) To pay for loss, but only for the amount of each such loss in excess of the deductible amount stated in the declarations as applicable, caused other than by collision to the owned automobile or to a non-owned automobile. For the purpose of this coverage, breakage of glass and loss caused by missiles, falling objects, fire, theft or larceny, explosion, earthquake, windstorm, hail, water, flood, malicious mischief or vandalism, riot or civil commotion, or colliding with a bird or animal, shall not be deemed to be loss caused by collision;
(2) To pay for loss caused by fire or lightning to robes, wearing apparel and other personal effects which are the property of the named insured or a relative, while such effects are in or upon the owned automobile.

Note that this policy separates comprehensive coverage and personal effects. Also, in this section collision is not covered, but when you sort out all of the negatives, every other kind of cause of loss to your automobile is covered. This includes fire and theft and vandalism. (I like the fact that "colliding with a bird or animal" is defined as *not* a collision.) It's good to know that your "robes" are covered if they are damaged by fire or lightning! However, note this (2) is quite restricted as to causes of loss.

COVERAGE F - COLLISION To pay for loss caused by collision to the owned automobile or to a non-owned automobile but only for the amount of each such loss in excess of the deductible amount stated in the declarations as applicable hereto. The deductible amount shall not apply to loss caused by a collision with another automobile insured by the company.

This one seems to be written in English and it's the one that covers collision itself. NOTE: If you're told it's not a "collision," see a lawyer to carry on the argument as to the meaning of "collision."

SUBROGATION In the event of any payment under this policy, the company shall be subrogated to all the insured's rights of recovery therefor against any person or organization and the insured shall execute and deliver instruments and papers and do whatever else is necessary to secure such rights. The insured shall do nothing after loss to prejudice such rights.

If the company wants to go after a third person as the cause of the loss, you must cooperate. "Subrogation"* means that if you have a right, the company does; the insurer stands in your place.

Q My own insurance company has paid off my personal injury claim, but now they say that I have to sue the other driver. Can they make me do that?

A They can "make you" in the sense that under your policy the insurance company has what is known as a "right of subrogation." This means that when you signed the insurance papers, you, at the same time, consented to bring suit in your name to recover moneys paid out to you. This will be handled by the insurance company's attorneys.

Postscript
There are, of course, many other coverages relating to your ownership and use of an automobile. These include the cost of towing and labor, a "loaner," theft of personal goods, and special additional payments for death and disability.

The point of the translation is to make you aware of what you are buying—or not buying—under the main areas of liability, collision, medical pay, and uninsured and underinsured motorists.

Plain English Policies

Now you tell me! Yep, after all that work I offer light at the end of the tunnel. Twenty-nine states now demand that insurance policies be written in "plain English" rather than that mess we just waded through. Twelve others allow the insurance commissioner to disapprove forms which are misleading, ambiguous or deceptive. Vermont statutes allow the insurance commissioner to require a clear and concise statement of the coverage contracted for.

So that you can check you own, as of this writing, the states are:

States with "plain English" laws: Arizona, Arkansas, Connecticut, Delaware, Florida, Georgia, Hawaii, Indiana, Kentucky, Maine, Massachusetts, Michigan, Minnesota, Missouri, Montana, Nebraska, Nevada, New Jersey, New Mexico, New York, North Carolina, North Dakota, Ohio, Oklahoma, Oregon, South Carolina, South Dakota, Tennessee, and West Virginia.

States that allow the insurance commissioner to disapprove forms which are misleading, ambiguous or deceptive: Alabama, Alaska, Idaho, Illinois, Maryland, Rhode Island, Texas, Utah, Virginia, Washington, Wisconsin, and Wyoming.

CHAPTER III

Marriage and Divorce or Dissolution

INTRODUCTION/HISTORY

Marriage is a contract and the state is a party to that contract. Historically, all countries have had formalities of some sort to bind a couple together and formalities to sever that relationship—if that was allowed. In some places all that was required was for the husband (of course) to walk around the tent three times, saying, "I divorce you." Many countries have demanded a purely business/legal civil contract establishing property and other rights before any kind of religious ceremony could take place. Under the old English common law*, the source of our laws, the wife was part of the property included in the contract. She was a "chattel,"* a thing, who came equipped with a dowry and whose property became her husband's property. Because she owned nothing, "dower rights"* were established for the wife who became widowed.

The concept of the wife-as-property wasn't only some ancient English common law,* but was followed in this country. In one of the states in which I've practiced, a wife had only recently gained the right to make a will. This was because it had remained the rule that she had no property of her own to leave.

The justification of wife-as-property was that she and her property were protected by the husband. The courts included in that "protection" the rule that the husband could beat his wife with a stick no larger than his thumb!

Naturally, there was no divorce under these laws. When divorce was finally allowed, it was an adversarial proceeding. Early on, adultery was the only ground for divorce. Later on additional, but still grave, grounds were accepted. Now we have developed the concept of "no fault" divorce and refer to that proceeding as a "dissolution."*

Marriage is a contract by which a man and woman reciprocally promise to live with each other during their joint lives and fulfill the duties imposed by law on the relationship of husband and wife. Since marriage is based on a contract, each party must be capable of contracting and performing the duties undertaken by the contract.

The state is considered a party in interest* to the marriage contract or status, together with the husband and wife. Court decisions have added to the rules of law favoring marriage and the public policy to foster and protect marriage.

The legislature of each state has the power to control and regulate marriages within its jurisdiction.

The general rule is that the validity of a marriage is determined by the law of the place where it was contracted; if valid there, it will be held valid everywhere. There are, of course, some exceptions.

Divorce or dissolution must, therefore, legally undo all that the marriage contract has established. In line with this, a divorce suit is brought by a plaintiff against a defendant because it is actually a breach of contract suit by the supposedly injured party. (This is changed now in states with "no fault" and dissolution.)

Annulment follows this contract law concept: when there has been no "meeting of minds" because of fraud or a party incapable of contracting, the marriage is set aside as void from its inception, i.e., "annulled."

Since marriage and divorce or dissolution (the newer version of divorce) are inextricably entangled, the questions on both are considered together in this chapter, as follows:

1. Antenuptial Agreements
2. Marriage
    a. Validity determined by state
        1) Age
        2) Other requirements: licensing, solemnizing
        3) Foreign
        4) Common-law
    b. Meeting of minds—no valid consent equals annulment
        1) Minors
        2) Fraud
    c. Consideration
        1) Exchange of promises (marriage "vows")
        2) Property
    d. Property rights of husband and wife
        1) Joint and "entirety" and "community"
        2) Disinherit?—wills and dower rights
        3) Duty to support spouse and child
        4) Consortium
        5) Wrongful death
    e. Children
        1) Duties toward children (support and custody)
        2) Adoption
3. Separation, legal and otherwise (as distinguished from divorce)
4. Divorce and dissolution
    a. Injunctions
    b. Divorce/dissolution basics
    c. Custody and child support
        1) Custody
        2) Child support
    d. Property
5. Inter-spousal torts (wrongs actionable in court)

Antenuptial Agreements

An antenuptial (not *anti*-nuptial) agreement is a contract entered into *before* the marriage contract to establish rights pertaining to assets and debts, to protect either or both parties by stating how the property is to be divided—and not divided—in case of a subsequent divorce and/or upon death. An antenuptial agreement is very carefully drawn. It details, for example, what property will not become marital property, the purpose being that in case of divorce, the spouse who originally owned the property named in the agreement would keep it all.

Since an antenuptial agreement is a kind of contract, it will normally stand up in court like any contract. The proviso is that this agreement must, of course, be such that the court can enforce.

Q I'm in a community-property state, but my fiancé and I want to each have our own income and debts. Is there any way we can work this out?

A Yes, by antenuptial agreement.* (I've drawn up a few anti-nuptials, too, for those agreeing *not* to marry.)

I'll explain the jargon.

First, only a minority of the states are what are called "community-property"* states. In these, all the property, including income and objects, acquired during the marriage belongs equally to the marriage partners. Debts, too. With some exceptions, this does not include property owned before the marriage. Two other common exclusions are gifts to one spouse and inheritances. An antenuptial agreement means an "agreement before marriage," and you and your fiancé can make any agreement you wish as to what property will be separate and what joint, or community.

Q I don't want to worry that my fiancé is marrying me for my money. Can you fix it?

A I can't keep you from worrying but I *can* shield your property. That should demonstrate if love alone is enough. We can draw up an antenuptial agreement, a contract which your fiancé must be aware of and sign. It may not make him happy. He will be waiving certain property rights in the event of divorce or dissolution.

Q Before we were married, I signed an antenuptial agreement that says I will claim nothing from my husband's estate in case of divorce. Well, guess what? Divorce. And I don't think that antenuptial thing's fair. I've helped him acquire a lot of property in the years we've been together.

A I don't think it's fair either. See a lawyer. There's a good possibility that the antenuptial agreement doesn't cut you off like you think. Most of them preserve the status quo at the time of marriage as well as protect rights of inheritance; they usually don't affect after-acquired property.

Another point: if the document actually does state you will claim nothing from your husband's estate, you can argue you are not claiming from *his* estate but from the *marital estate.*

Marriage

Validity determined by state

Since the state is a party to this Contract of Marriage, it can make rules about it. These are set out in the following text and questions:

Age

The state can dictate the required minimum age for contracting. The age differs from state to state (with distinctions made as to with or without parental consent) and from male to female. It isn't necessarily the same as the particular state's age of majority.

Other requirements: licensing, solemnizing

The state also sets other requirements of this marriage contract, such as blood tests and waiting periods. The "license" signifies the state's approval of the contract; and the state regulates who "witnesses" execution of the contract by way of public official or recognized clergy, as well as whether an additional witness is required.

Foreign

Q My husband and I didn't want to wait for blood tests, so we got married in Mexico. Now I don't feel like we're legal; are we?

A You're probably okay. Mexican and other foreign marriages often come within the rule that a marriage which is valid where it's entered into is valid in the United States. This is a practical matter because the government can't go around checking out the validity of every foreign marriage.

The cautionary note is that if its validity were attacked (which isn't likely), your marriage might not stand up. An attack could come from anyone questioning your marital status, such as someone contesting who had a right to inherit property. For this reason, I'd advise you to tidy things up and remarry your present husband.

Common-law

Each state has a right to rule on whether or not a marriage is valid. In this capacity, more and more states are saying that there is no such thing as a common-law marriage (co-habiting without any legal formalities). In the states that do allow such a marriage, a living-together relationship must meet certain requirements before it is recognized. These include: the parties must have held themselves out to the world as husband and wife and for a particular period of time.

If a state declares that you have a common-law marriage, then you have a marriage no matter what its label and you would have to take legal steps to dissolve it.

Washington is one jurisdiction that holds marriage can *only* be created by compliance with statutory standards. Colorado, New York, Pennsylvania, Texas, Alabama and Utah are among those recognizing common law marriage so long as certain requirements are met: by mutual agreement to live as man and wife and to consummate the marriage or to hold themselves out as married. Some states warn the arrangement will be closely scrutinized.

Q I'm so distressed! We moved here from a state where our common-law marriage was legal. Now I find out that this state says a common-law marriage is not legal. Does this make all my children bastards?

A No. Common-law marriages come within the same rule as foreign marriages: a marriage, if valid where entered into, is valid in the rest of the United States. Since the state you lived in when you established a common-law marriage rules that your marriage was a lawful one, it doesn't matter that the state you are in now would have originally disagreed—you were married there, so you're married here.

Q I've never cared about a stupid piece of paper saying I'm married! What does it matter if what *we* call our common law marriage is recognized or not?

A I could recite a long list of why it matters—and still not be done. Property rights. The rights of children to inherit. Governmental and employment benefits to "spouses" and children. Insurance. Taxes. You hear what I'm saying?

Meeting of minds

— no valid consent equals annulment

There must be a "meeting of minds" for there to be a valid marriage contract, as in any other kind of contract. Therefore, this contract is set aside as void if the parties are incapable of contracting because they can't give legal consent, or if some sort of fraud has been perpetrated that would have prevented the other party from contracting if the truth had been known. When a marriage contract is involved, the particular process is called "annulment."*

Minors

Q Our minor daughter ran off with a boy and got married. We're going to have it annulled!

A No you're not. If your daughter is under the age of consent, she can have the marriage set aside, voided, anytime before she reaches that age, but she is the only one who can do it. However, I'm being too technical with you. Since your daughter couldn't contract, being under the legal age to do so, there is no legal marriage.

Annulment for fraud, etc. (impotency)

The grounds for annulment all go to that lack of true consent or meeting of the minds: physical disease or incapacity; mistake; pregnancy; undissolved prior marriage; fraud; misrepresentation; imprisonment; and various kinds of concealment of material facts.

The parties to an annulled marriage can marry again if it has been held void rather than voidable.

Q I married my wife because she could support me in the style to which I wish to become accustomed. Instead, it turns out that she doesn't have any money at all. I want to get that marriage annulled.

A I'm afraid you're out of luck as to annulment and would have to go the divorce route. As a general rule, deception as to wealth or social position isn't considered as going to the very fundamentals of the marriage relationship and therefore isn't a legal fraud sufficient for annulment. On the other hand, an annulment can be had for such fraud as when a foreigner marries an American for the sole purpose of getting into the United States without any intention of assuming the marital duties.

Q I married my wife because she said she was pregnant by me. Now she tells me the baby is not mine. Can I get the marriage annulled?

A Probably. This gets very tricky, but with the facts as you gave them to me, you could have the marriage set aside for fraud.

Q My marriage was never consummated because my husband is impotent. Can I have the marriage annulled?

A Yes.

Consideration

Exchange of promises (marriage "vows") or property

Most frequently, the consideration* that supports the marriage contract (binds the bargain) is the exchange of promises, which are commonly called the marriage "vows." Sometimes—always, in olden days—it is the property which the parties bring to the marriage (sounds silly but that's how lawyers talk). Historically, as previously mentioned, the wife brought her dowry and herself; on the other side of the exchange, the husband furnished his protection. A holdover of this today is what is known as "dower rights."* These are usually only heard of in laws that allow a wife the right to "take against the will," meaning she can choose a set statutory percentage rather than what her husband left her in his will. The fairness of this comes from the tradition that because the wife has given a dowry, she has some rights if the husband dies first. Now the courts are giving the husband the same rights, even though he doesn't have that historical tradition.

Property rights of husband and wife

Community, entirety, and joint

This marriage contract creates a multitude of property rights between the spouses. These include the rights to hold property—real and personal, tangible and intangible; to support and maintenance during the marriage; to consortium;* and to inherit, among others.

In some of the states, mostly those with a Spanish heritage, the property brought to the marriage, becomes "community property"* unless it's distinguished as "separate." Community property is a concept of the civil law of continental Europe as contrasted to the common law of England, from which we inherit most of our laws.

Community property is a different way of looking at marital property; it's a kind of marital partnership and pertains to any property or moneys coming into the marriage. It gets quite sticky as to what is separate property and what is community property. The general rule is that property you own before the marriage stays separate property, but you must be very careful to meet the particular rules of the state where you reside.

Some jurisdictions refer to a husband and wife "holding property by the entirety."* This phrase has almost the same meaning as "jointly held property."

In legal jargon, property in which you have a joint interest means property in which you have an "undivided interest in the whole with right of survivorship." The idea of "undivided interest"* is that neither party can point to one part of the entire piece of land and say, "That's mine." Instead, each party has an equal interest in the whole.

The "right of survivorship" part of jointly held property is that one joint tenant automatically inherits the whole thing when the other joint tenant dies. In the old days the courts made quite a fuss about tacking on the phrase "with right of survivorship" to the description of ownership. Now right of survivorship is assumed in almost all cases.

Disinherit—wills and dower rights

Based on the old ideas of dower, a spouse had a right to inherit. Now, if the deceased dies without a will, state statutes set up what percentage of the estate must go to the surviving wife or husband. NOTE: If there are children, they get a percentage, too; the entire estate does *not* pass to the spouse.

The same reasoning that makes one spouse the statutory heir of the other makes it impossible, in most states, to completely disinherit one's spouse by one's will. As mentioned earlier, if the husband or wife leaves too little to the surviving spouse, that spouse normally doesn't have to accept this but can get a statutory percentage. This is called "taking against the will."

Q My barber says that a person can't cut his wife and children out of the will and that you have to leave them at least a dollar.

A Wrong. You don't have to leave anyone anything and that famous dollar has nothing to do with it. As we've discussed, the surviving spouse can claim a statutory percentage if he or she is disinherited.

The children can be completely disinherited, which brings in an odd bit of law: if the children are not specifically disinherited and are simply not mentioned, a number of courts will hold that the testator "forgot them." This is called the "doctrine of pretermitted heirs," which then allows the child to inherit. To circumvent this and show intent, the testator simply includes in the will the statement "I specifically disinherit any heirs whether known to me or not." (That takes care of any illegitimate offspring, too.)

Duty to support spouse and child

Historically, the husband has had a duty to support his wife and children. This is why desertion was grounds for divorce even in the strict days of divorce. By deserting, the husband was breaching this contractual duty. Today the law is in a state of flux about when the husband might be allowed to claim that his wife owed *him* the duty of support. His duty to pay support to the children changes only if he has taken on their custody and care in the traditional role of the wife, and if she is the spouse working outside the home or with adequate independent income.

Consortium*

Historically, this legalese, "consortium," was based on the husband's right to his wife's "services." These included her sexual services as well as housecleaning, etc. Now, if either party is injured, the other has the right to sue the third person doing the injury for loss of "consortium" and the damages do *not* have anything to do with household services. It's the emotional distress suffered by one spouse who loses the normal company of his or her mate when the mate is physically injured due to the wrongful conduct of another. It's "derivative" in that one spouse must be injured and because of that the other is *presumed* to have suffered damages by loss of consortium.

Q My husband was injured in an automobile wreck and is suing the other driver for damages. My attorney says that I have a separate suit for "loss of consortium." Why?

A Because the law says that when your spouse was injured, you were, too. Your claim is separate and compares to his for "pain and suffering."

Q You've been talking about a separate suit for loss of consortium, but something's wrong. My wife was hurt at work and collected work comp. So why can't I get that consortium?

A Apparently the Worker's Compensation statutes in your state are written to bar a claim of loss of consortium. Check with a lawyer. Those work comp laws differ from state to state, but you're probably out of luck.

Wrongful death

Because of the financial and emotional support received by a spouse, if one spouse is killed through the negligence or other wrong of a third person, the surviving spouse and/or children can bring a suit for this "wrongful death."* In some states the amount of damages is limited by a statute; in others the spouse and/or children can ask unlimited damages for the loss of that spouse's or parent's income in the years ahead, and loss of his or her companionship as well.

Children

The state takes the role of paterfamilias (Latin for "father of a family," or "head of a household") toward the children throughout the marriage. There is scarcely ever a court decision involving children where the court does not say that the interest of the child comes first. The state supervises the support of children, the welfare of children, their pecuniary interests, and their adoption.

NOTE: Child custody, as involved in the whole process of divorce or dissolution, is discussed later in this chapter under "Divorce and Dissolution."

Duties toward children (support and custody)

A parent—traditionally the father—owes a duty of support to his child. This is an innate duty without reference to any court proceeding, such as an award of child support during a divorce or dissolution proceeding. In many states, if the father fails to support the child, who must therefore be supported by a governmental agency such as a welfare department, the state can proceed against the father for reimbursement of these funds. The state regards this duty of support so seriously that, upon desertion and failure to support, the state will sometimes go to the extreme measure of allowing that man's child to be adopted without the customary requirement of the father's consent to adoption. There is no more drastic a measure than severing, by decree, the father's ties with his child. Many states enforce child support duties through the Attorneys General, one to another. The federal government is involved, too.

Q My daughter is only sixteen, but she has gotten married. Do I still have to pay child support?

A No. A child who marries is considered an "emancipated minor,"* no longer a minor child.

Q I have remarried, and my new wife has three children living with her from a prior marriage and we have one together. I just can't make ends meet trying to support two families, my children from my first marriage and my new family. When does child support ever stop?

A Normally child support does not stop until the child is eighteen or over, or an emancipated minor (living on his or her own and working, or married). Too many fathers only care about the new family. And, P.S. You should have thought of this earlier.

Q Can they take away my children because my husband molested our little girl?

A Your child welfare agency is likely to do so until there is a juvenile court hearing. In most of these cases, the child is removed from the home by the agency—as are, sometimes, any other children. They are placed in a foster home until the juvenile court can decide what should be done about the situation. Normally, if you did not know of the molestation and the court believes that you were not just shutting your eyes to it, you will be able to get the children back. Sometimes the offending father must leave the home, but too often this was not required. There's now a backlash against agencies endangering the child or children in their attempts to keep the family unit intact.

Of course, every one of these situations is different, and the first thing you need to do is see an attorney.

Q Our minor daughter was slightly injured in an accident. We've settled the claim with an insurance company, but our attorney tells us that before we can accept the check we have to have a "guardian ad litem"* appointed. What does he mean? We're obviously our daughter's guardians!

A In order to protect the interest of a minor child, a general rule of law is that when a child has a claim against a third party or is bringing a suit, even the natural parents are not automatically guardians; to protect the child's interests, the court appoints either a "guardian ad litem" or a "next friend."* In many states the natural parents can qualify.

Q I don't think my wife's last child is mine. What happens if I refuse to support him?

A A lot! Because you're married, the legal presumption is that the child is yours. Under old English law, you had to have been gone across the seven seas for two years prior to the child's birth before you could overcome that presumption. Don't do anything hasty until your attorney can advise you about your state law on disproving paternity.

NOTE: In the past, a blood test showed only who could *not* be the father because of a different blood type; it did not prove who was. Now there are more sophisticated procedures such as DNA testing, which *can* prove who the father is.

Adoption

An adopted child becomes "of the blood," an historic legal phrase that means that once legally adopted, the child (or adult) has the same rights—including rights in inheritance—as a child born to the adoptive parent(s). Usually the birth certificate is changed to show this.

And, yes, an adult can be adopted but that adoption requires his/her consent.

Q Can my husband adopt my child by a former marriage without the consent of the natural father?

A Probably not. In most states the consent of the natural parent is required, although many do have the exception that if the parent has deserted or abandoned the child and has made no support payments for a defined period of time, consent of that parent is not necessary. But watch out for the new court decisions that go to any length to protect the rights of the birth parent, father or mother.

Q If my wife adopts my daughter by another marriage, is it true that we'll have to go through the whole process of being checked out as if we were adopting a baby we had never seen?

A I'm afraid so. When you start the adoption proceedings with your new wife, for instance, the entire statutory adoption procedure is followed; e.g., even though you are the child's natural father, the social worker will still make periodic visits to check out the house to see if it's the proper place to raise the child, and there will probably be a court hearing to determine your wife's fitness as a parent.

Q What's this new "open adoption" I've been hearing about?

A In total contrast to the old rules of extreme secrecy in re the birth parents, the "open adoption" is just that: the birth parents (or parent) are completely acquainted with the adoptive parents. In fact, they have often selected the adoptive parents from among others applying to adopt.

Separation, Legal and Otherwise

(as Distinguished from Divorce)

When a person refers to being separated from his or her mate, this may only mean that they are living apart; on the other hand, a *legal* separation is a specific state of affairs with rights and duties; it is quite distinct from divorce and leaves the marriage intact, but suspends and/or modifies some of the duties and obligations. On the other hand, divorce or dissolution *severs* the marital relationship.

Historically, a separation was *a mensa et thoro*—a Latin phrase meaning separation "from table and bed"—which was a biggie considering the husband's rights to the wife's services.

Usually the legal fees for a separation and a divorce are comparable, and both require as much time and patience.

Divorce and Dissolution—general

Note: An increasing number of states (and/or judges by court rule) demand that the parties undertake mediation before the divorce or dissolution process begins. In this, a mediation professional (often an attorney with additional training) hears each side and attempts to facilitate a reconciliation. If not that, then the mediator may try to minimize the differences for a more amicable custody and property settlement.

Injunctions

An injunction* or restraining order* is imposed by the court, forbidding or prohibiting certain action.

One party to a dispute can go to a judge and, *without* the presence of the other party, obtain a *temporary* restraining order if she or he can convince the court that irreparable harm will be done unless some sort of behavior isn't stopped now and argued about later. This is followed by a full-scale hearing with both parties on whether the temporary restraining order should be made permanent.

Examples of behavior calling for temporary injunctions are a factory emitting poisonous fumes; a neighbor about to cut down a tree you claim is yours; a husband beating up his wife.

Q I am deathly afraid of my husband and what he's going to do to me when the divorce papers are served on him. What can you do to protect me?

A Not much; the law really fails you here. In some states you must wait until you file a divorce petition, in some not. Either way, we can then ask the judge for a restraining order, which would inform your husband that he was not to come around or bother you in any way. It also gives you something to show to the police if you have to call them. Most states no longer have the alternative, which is a "peace bond," by means of which a person could be arrested if he should act up and "break the peace."

The reason I feel the law fails you so badly is that if your husband is crazy enough to come around and start beating you up, he's not going to pay much attention to a piece of legal paper.

We can get the sheriff to cooperate and let us know when that office intends to serve your husband, but if you truly are afraid of your spouse, you'd be safest to stay with friends or family, or at a shelter for abused or threatened women. The latter often has papers already prepared showing what you must allege: prior violence (such as a knife attack), on-going violence so that you fear for your life, or great bodily injury.

Divorce/dissolution basics

Over the years I've found that many clients are unclear about the very mechanics of divorce. For this reason, the nuts and bolts of divorce or dissolution will be discussed before getting into more substantive matters.

Q I told my lawyer I wanted a divorce, and he said I meant a "dissolution." What's the difference?

A "Divorce," a term still used in some states, has a lot of silly fictions. For instance, no matter how agreeable both parties are to splitting up, "divorce" must still be handled like any adversary lawsuit, with a plaintiff and defendant and the placing of blame. The pretense that the matter is adversarial has to be continued to the bitter end, or else the allegation of "collusion" will prevent the divorce from going through.

"Dissolution" is the term being used now in most states, and it removes those legal complications: the words "plaintiff" and "defendant" are replaced by "petitioner" and "respondent," and there's no blame or fault. To dissolve the marriage, the magic words used in the petition are often this mouthful: "an irrevocable difference has led to an irretrievable breakdown of the marriage."

Grounds for divorce include: adultery, bigamy, conviction of a crime involving moral turpitude, cruelty, desertion, habitual drunkenness, insanity, and nonsupport. However, most states have done away with the notion that there is an offending and an innocent party under the "no fault" dissolution laws instead, and those "grounds" are not required.

Usually, with "no fault," the label for the process of legally ending a marriage is "dissolution" instead of "divorce."

Q Where do I get my divorce?

A Usually a divorce is granted in the state where you live, and it is that state's law which governs the divorce proceedings. *Caveat:** If you go off for a "quickie" divorce, that court only has the power to dissolve the marriage—this is what the law calls the "thing," the "res."* That "foreign" court (where you do *not* live) has no jurisdiction to determine custody or property rights.

Q How long does a divorce or dissolution take?

A That depends on two things: the legal processes of your state, and how crowded the "calendar"* of your court is.

The timetable is: you and your attorney prepare and file a divorce petition; next, in most states, your spouse has thirty days to file his or her answer* to that petition, i.e., has an opportunity to deny any allegations. Pretty hard if it's "no fault."

Usually a divorce won't come up for a hearing in less than another thirty days, at which time the judge declares the marriage terminated. In some states this takes effect immediately, but in many others the divorce is not final for another period of time (thirty days minimum again) so that the other spouse can appeal the decision to a higher court.

Time can be shortened if your spouse is willing to sign a "waiver of service and consent," which means that he or she doesn't have to be served with the petition and the divorce can go ahead just as fast as possible because she or he is not going to respond. Then it's a matter of getting it down on the calendar as a "default* divorce," which means there's nobody to fight it. Most judges have days set aside for hearing just these cases, which come up sooner than the other, contested, kind.

If the whereabouts of your spouse is unknown, then the divorce must take place by publication*—a process that increases the amount of time involved. For a certain number of times and for a certain number of weeks, a small notice directed to your spouse is put in the newspaper, announcing your pending divorce. When the time is up from that notice, you can get a default divorce.

By some peculiar logic, the law reasons that if you publish a notice in the newspaper saying that you intend to get a divorce, your spouse will see that newspaper, even though quite often the paper is one that carries only such notices and nobody buys it.

NOTE: The timetable for "dissolution" is usually the about same as for uncontested divorce.

Jurisdiction

A special section here because there are questions on "quickie" divorces and those carry a warning. The courts of some states have said such divorces are no good, that the quickie-state doesn't have the jurisdiction,* the power, to give a divorce to parties who clearly live in another state. Other states hold that the quickies *are good* because of the constitutional guarantee that each state will give "full faith and credit" to the laws of every other state.

Q What's this "quickie divorce" I hear people talking about?

A It usually refers to one obtained in Mexico or Nevada because they traditionally have had a shorter waiting period than the rest of the country. Mexico is usually a one-day wait, while Nevada requires that you establish a residence for a period of weeks. In some states it would be much longer.

Going for a "quickie" would be pointless if you meet the residency requirement and plan to get a divorce where you have been living for some time.

Although some states require none, there is usually a court rule or statute for a thirty-day waiting period after the divorce is filed (assuming you get the waiver from your spouse mentioned previously). This can ordinarily be dispensed with if you can show the judge a good reason why there's a need for speed, such as moving to take another job.

NOTE: The time will, of course, be lengthened if there are all sorts of negotiations as to property settlements or if custody and/or other matters are being fought out, requiring a place on the calendar for a contested* divorce, same as a trial.

Q My wife and I reconciled last night. Does that wipe out the whole divorce process?

A By "reconciled" I assume you mean that you had sexual relations. That used to take the whole case back to square one, but not any more in most states. This is because a set number of days of total separation without sleeping together is no longer required.

Q My wife says she won't give me a divorce. What can I do?

A Tell her to stop watching melodramas; "give" doesn't enter in. First, if you are in a "no fault" state, the divorce or dissolution petition will simply allege "irreconcilable differences." If one party is saying that, I don't see how the other party can successfully "contest" (claim) that there are not these differences. Second, in the states that still demand grounds for a divorce, incompatibility is a common ground and another one where it doesn't seem the party can come in and answer, "But we *are* compatible." Of course, a divorce can be and often is contested, but the soap opera position of "I won't give you a divorce" is simply fiction.

Q What do you think of divorce or dissolution kits?

A They worry me. Divorce is serious business, and the separation of all the rights that were part of the marriage should, I think, be handled by someone who knows what the pitfalls are and who understands the meaning of particular legal words. A number of states have tried to make the divorce/dissolution laws so simple that the parties can handle it themselves, but I can't recall the number of times I've been sitting in the courtroom, waiting for my client's hearing to come up, only to be called forward by the judge asking me to take some do-it-yourselfers through the divorce process. Judges do like things tidy and want to hear the questions phrased as they are accustomed to hear them.

Q I went to Mexico to get a quick divorce from my former husband, and then married my present husband while I was there. Is this legal?

A I think the consensus of attorneys would be that the Mexican divorce was good—if not attacked; i.e., if your (you hope) "ex" fought the Mexican divorce in court as not valid, he would have a good possibility of winning.

One of the earliest cases on this point concerned a southern gentleman who got a "quickie" Nevada divorce and married the "other woman," whom he installed in the house next door. His first wife went after him for bigamy, and the court found that because the man had purchased a round-trip train ticket, he had not intended to make Nevada his residence. Therefore Nevada lacked jurisdiction, there was no legal divorce, and the man was a bigamist. (The moral might be: Don't set up the new wife in a house next door to the old one!)

A Mexican marriage is usually legal under the doctrine that a marriage that is valid where it's entered into is valid elsewhere.

Custody and child support

Custody

The most constant rule reiterated in case after case involving custody of minor children is that the decision will be based on the best interests of the child. That does not mean that people don't often quarrel about whether the court's decision was indeed in the best interests of the child.

Q Is it true that if I go to Reno to get a divorce, I'll lose custody of my children?

A Not necessarily. It's true only in the sense that the Reno court does not acquire jurisdiction over your husband and therefore can't decide custody. All the Nevada court has before it is the marriage, the res, and that's all it can deal with.

The custody of the children must be decided by the court that has jurisdiction over them. If you were getting your divorce where you are living with the children, that court would have jurisdiction over them and be able to decide. The children are considered "wards of the court."

This jurisdiction of the court over the custody, maintenance, and well-being of the children continues until the children are of age.

NOTE: The cases are divided over what courts have jurisdiction re custody when there is jurisdiction over the defendant but the children are living outside that state.

The old rule was that the children were living where the father could be found, and that their residence automatically followed his.

Q If I, the father, have the children when we file the divorce petition, can I keep them until the divorce is heard?

A In many jurisdictions the answer would be "yes," but other factors could enter in so that your wife could challenge your custody immediately. In the ordinary situation, the children would stay with you, since you presently have them, until the hearing that finally determines custody.

NOTE: There are now "men's rights" organizations that can help you with custody problems.

Q My husband and I are getting a dissolution. Can I keep him away from the children?

A Not simply out of general peevishness. Normally he would at least have rights to reasonable visitation. If you can show he's a threat to the well-being of the children or might take off with them, his rights could be reduced, by court order, to supervised visitation or even none at all.

Q The court gave me "reasonable visitation rights" to see my daughter. My ex-wife is living with her parents now, and they won't let me see the child except for about an hour in their house. I don't think this is reasonable. Do you?

A No. Unless there was some restriction on you so that the court was safeguarding the welfare of the child against your having the child alone, you should be able to see her somewhere else and by yourself. The best thing for you to do is ask your attorney to call your wife's attorney and get them to loosen up. The next step would be to take the case back to court and show the judge that your wife is not abiding by the "reasonable visitation" portion of the decree.

Q I got custody of my children, but my husband grabbed them and took off. Can I have him picked up for kidnapping?

A That will vary from state to state. In some states it would be considered the crime of kidnapping; in some, "interference with custodial rights." There are also wide differences among the states about whether or not the police will make any attempt to enforce the law even if, by statute, it is kidnapping.

Q My ex-husband has visitation rights on the weekends, but his girl friend stays over. Can I get the judge to cancel his visitation rights?

A That would depend on a number of factors, including the age of the children and the way your ex-husband and his girl friend behave in front of them.

I don't believe the majority of judges would cut off a husband's right to be with his children on the facts as you've given them to me.

Q I have been given custody of the children on weekends and vaca-tions. When they get out of school, can I leave the state and take them with me on a camping trip?

A Unless there is some restriction on your visitation rights, I see no reason why you shouldn't be able to take the children camping.

Q My parents, our son's grandparents, say that if my wife and I get into a custody battle they're going to join in, too, because they love the boy as much as I do. Can they do this?

A It has happened. In fact, there have been cases decided for the grandparents against either natural parent. A court will always say that the interests of the child come first, so if the judge has to turn to the grandparents, he will. In your case, I would need more facts.

There are several grandparents organizations centered around this issue. A recent case allowed the children to hire an attorney to represent their wishes regarding custody.

Q My husband's parents have so much money, I wonder if I even have a chance at custody.

A Yes, you do. The courts should not decide custody on mere wealth. (His attorney *will* argue the advantages such as fine schools.)

Q I was awarded full custody of the children, but my ex-wife is always telling me how they should be raised. Since I have the custody, don't I get the last word?

A Yes. "Custody" does not simply mean that you have control over those little bodies. The word "custody" is big enough to include everything having to do with the physical, moral, and mental well-being of the children.

Q Do the children have anything to do with who gets custody?

A Yes. The age when the child's wishes are considered and the weight given to the child's testimony vary from state to state by statute.

In some states, the judge talks with the child and attempts to base her decision on that child's preference. This carries the big "if" that the judge must believe that the parent the child selects is a fit parent. In other states volunteers (or employees of the court) are trained to be spokespersons for the child.

As you can imagine, this leads to many bad situations, with the parents going all out to influence the poor child.

Q What chances do I have to show that my wife is an unfit mother for my children?

A More than you used to have. From the common law, the courts have leaned very heavily toward the position that children, especially young children, are better off with their natural mother, no matter how sorry a person she may be. Formerly, even mental instability and child abuse were scarcely considered. This has changed dramatically, but the father still starts out at the short end of the legal stick.

Q Some time ago I read that hundreds of people were not legally married because their prior divorces had never gone through owing to the actions of a divorce attorney. What happened to all the children in all those cases?

A It created a very sticky situation. In some jurisdictions where a man and woman cohabit believing they are validly married, the law treats them as if they were, and this includes providing that children of such a marriage are legitimate.

As I recall, those parties who had thought themselves remarried did quickly marry through another ceremony, once legally divorced, to sensibly tidy things up.

Child support

Historically, the father owes a duty of support to his minor children. This is the basis of the award of child support to the parent being granted custody in a divorce or dissolution proceeding. The law is in a state of flux, as the courts increasingly place the same duty on the wife.

In a case where the husband had been awarded custody, he wanted to stay home with the children. We argued that the husband had been the homemaker and was not trained for other work, while the wife was a skilled professional, and that therefore she should provide child support to the husband. The court agreed.

Q I don't want alimony or child support, but my attorney said I had to ask for a dollar or it would be gone forever. I don't understand what he meant by that.

A He meant that in many jurisdictions, if alimony and child support are not provided for in the divorce decree, the situation can't be changed in the future. However, if just one dollar is asked for, this leaves it open for future modification at a time when you might find that you absolutely had to have some help with the children's living expenses.

Q Since my wife has a terrific job, I don't think I should have to pay so much child support. Can we go back to court?

A You can always go back to court to challenge or modify the support provisions of the decree—the question is whether you are going to win when you do so. If you can show that a change in circumstances has lessened your income, or can convince the court that you made your child support payments as high as they are because at that time your wife was not earning anything, you might be able to get a modification. Remember, though, they are your children, too.

Q My wife won't let me see the children, so I'm not going to pay any child support.

A The court doesn't look kindly on your putting a condition on the payments that were ordered, but at the same time it doesn't look kindly on your wife's disobeying the decree that gave you the right to see the children. One doesn't hinge upon the other, but before you use self-help* (take the law into your own hands), it would be better for you to seek an order that she obey the decree and let you see the children. Otherwise, you are the one who's violating the court order by not making the support payments.

Q My husband skipped out to avoid paying child support. What can I do?

A Make a phone call and appointment. The exact listings differ, so find out who handles child support enforcement in your county. The first step is usually for your prosecutor to go after your husband through the prosecutor of the county where he now lives. If he's moved out-of-state, most states have signed onto Uniform Acts for interstate enforcement. And now we have the federal laws to pursue those deadbeat dads. One way or another he can be forced to pay child support—one being garnishment of his wages.

Caveat: There's a long waiting line!

Q How will the court go about figuring how much I have to pay for support and maintenance?

A Most courts demand a lengthy document showing how much the spouse must spend to care for the children; this would even include a percentage of the utility bills, for instance. The court usually also takes a financial sheet from each. When all of this is considered, the court generally goes by its own rule of thumb—20 percent of the spouse's income is the lowest I've seen. Some courts have what I think is an unrealistic flat fee per child.

Q My living expenses have gone up, and so has my ex-husband's salary. Is there any way I can get the child support payments changed—upward?

A Probably, but you need to show a change in your circumstances since the first decree and any other new facts that have come up since.

Q My ex-husband says he's judgment-proof, so I can just whistle for the child support he owes.

A Tell him the courts don't agree: child support is one of the few debts I know about for which a person can be *jailed*.

Q My ex-husband says he's going to wipe out all the back child support he owes by taking bankruptcy.

A Wrong. Child support is one of the few debts that "ride through" bankruptcy. That means it's still owed and is not affected by bankruptcy.

Q A friend told me that since I'm paying child support, I can declare the children as dependents for income tax purposes.

A The divorce or dissolution decree should state which parent has this right. If it does not, the general rule is that the parent paying over 50 percent of the money necessary to support the child is the one who takes the deduction.

Property

In most divorce or dissolution cases a decision is made as to the division of the property of the parties, alimony or maintenance, and child support. Sometimes the parties themselves reach agreement as to all this and all the court must do is approve it, with the approval being pretty much a matter of form.

However, the court has the right to exercise any reasonable means of attempting to divide the property equally, and so the courts have settled matters in a variety of ways, including: awarding equal parts of the same kinds of property; entering a judgment for money as part of a settlement; ordering that property be sold and the proceeds divided; giving one party the house and balancing this out by requiring that party to pay the other rent.

Remember, division of the property includes division of the couple's debts as well as the assets.

Q My husband and I had a charge account, and when we got a divorce, the judge ordered him to pay all the bills. The store keeps pestering me to pay even though I tell them that it's my ex who has to. I don't, right?

A Sorry. When a debt is in two names, a creditor can go after whomever it wants. In your situation, the court can't make the creditor accept a different debtor. It *can* make your husband reimburse you.

Q Before the dissolution comes through, I'm going to charge a whole new wardrobe to that bastard.

A Please don't. Your idea is not original. The judge is human also, and even though you *can* do this, he won't be looking kindly on your request for support, maintenance, and the division of property when he sees what you have done in a fit of temper. I don't believe you can get enough of a wardrobe to offset the damage you'd be doing to yourself in the future. It's also just too vindictive.

Q When my wife and I break up, do I have to sell the house and give her half the money?

A Not necessarily. Anything can be worked out in the property agreement about who gets the house. The only time you would have to sell the house and split the money is if you can reach no agreement and the court sees no other way around the situation.

Q Since I'm working, does my husband have to pay me temporary alimony?

A Assuming you mean alimony or "spousal support" pending the final decree, it's going to depend on where you live. The old view was that since alimony was based on the husband's duty of support during marriage, the wife was thereby entitled without regard to her ability to provide for herself. Now, the more prevalent view is that spousal support, if any, depends on fairness and the spouse's earning capacity. That includes the award of any temporary monies.

Q I won't pay a dime.

A Fine. I'll bring you cigarettes. If you fail to pay child support and maintenance as ordered by the court, you can be jailed. Pay it.

Q Can I make my wife give back the credit cards, and, if not, am I responsible for what she charges?

A Whether the credit cards should be returned to you would depend on either your property settlement agreement or the judge. If they are not returned, you would still be equally responsible for what she charges until the creditors are given notice. They have no way of knowing the two of you are splitting up.

After the decree, I suggest you write the companies involved and explain that you are no longer responsible, from that date, for anything charged on those cards.

Dealing with the charge accounts has been like meeting on the border to exchange prisoners. I've had a number of couples arrange to come to my office for a ceremony of cutting up the credit cards in each other's presence.

Q So my wife doesn't charge up a bunch of stuff before the dissolution, I'm going to put an ad in the newspaper saying I'm not responsible for her debts.

A I wouldn't advise it. First of all, it's questionable whether that would serve notice on any creditor and let you off the hook. Second, a few people have gotten the bright idea that this forms the basis for a libel suit, the grounds being that you are casting aspersions on her credit.

Q I'm afraid that as soon as my husband is served with the divorce papers he'll take all of the money out of the bank. Should I do it first?

A I'd say no, but I'm more conservative on these matters than some other attorneys. In the states where I have practiced, it wouldn't be illegal for you to draw the money out of a joint account, but I would be concerned about the long-range effect on the judge of hearing that you had stripped the account, as well as the psychology of making your husband feel you've declared all-out war.

I don't see anything wrong in your removing half the money and opening an account in your name only.

Q When I got home last night—kind of late—my wife had thrown all my clothes out on the front lawn and changed the locks on the doors. Can she do that to me?

A She just did. Don't go kicking the door in and getting yourself involved in a crime. If the house is in both your names, owned jointly, you have as much right to the house as she does—but let's have a judge say so. A hearing will determine who has the right to remain in the house pending divorce.

The ultimate outcome can go several ways: the court may decide the house should be sold and the proceeds divided; it might be shown to be economically unfeasible to sell the house, but you would be awarded what would amount to your share by means of rent if your wife remains there; and if there are children, the court may well decide that whoever has custody of the children should remain in the house.

Q What all goes into a divorce/dissolution decree?

A Every divorce decree will have in it words to the effect that the marriage is ended, terminated, dissolved.

If there are children, the decree will also state who has custody, and the rights of the other spouse as to visitation. Custody might be joint.

Besides the above essentials, the provisions in a decree vary from state to state and depend on the complexity of the particular divorce. In some states, if there's a property settlement, the decree itself will simply make reference to that agreement. In other states, the decree will set out all the details of the property settlement agreement. When the parties have been unable to reach an agreement, the decree will then apportion the property. The same will occur with child support payments and support or maintenance for the ex-spouse, if any. Beyond that, you never know how far a decree will go. I had to draw up one decree for the judge wherein the parties promised not to practice witchcraft against each other—I don't know if they abided by it or not.

Interspousal torts* (wrongs actionable in court)

Long past the time when the wife ceased to be considered property owned by the husband, she was still not allowed to sue her husband. In fact, neither spouse could sue the other. To support this ban, law-makers had to follow two lines of reasoning which were not logically connected: 1) preserve the sanctity of marriage; and 2) prevent collusion between the spouses.

Landmark cases in the seventies did away with interspousal immunity and these cases have withstood attacks that this would destroy conjugal harmony, promote collusion and fraud, and that the injured spouse could recover sufficiently under the divorce laws.

Some divorced spouses are now recovering damages for beatings and other harm inflicted during marriage. Some are bringing suit while married. *Interspousal torts* have led to suits for: assault and battery; transmission of herpes or AIDS; battered spouse syndrome; breach of fiduciary duty; intentional infliction of emotional distress; and those brought as Federal Civil Rights claims.

Since I try to stick to contract law in this book I won't go into details on the above list. But, particularly if you're a woman, be aware that you can now sue the abuser and new laws allow those suits even though normally the time would have run.

The law I'm talking about here is different than that discussed under auto insurance. That pertained to one spouse being allowed to sue the other for damages caused by negligence in the operation of a motor vehicle. Those were "arms-length" because of the insurance policy; these are very personal!

CHAPTER IV

Things:
Buying, Selling, and Leasing
Warranties & Guarantees

INTRODUCTION/HISTORY

Looking up what was known as the "law merchant," Black's Law Dictionary (Rev. 4th Ed.) refers to "mercantile law" and says:

"It designates the system of rules, customs, and usages generally recognized and adopted by merchants and traders, and which, either in its simplicity or as modified by common law or statute, constitutes the law for the regulation of their transactions and the solution of their controversies."

Be glad you don't have to read law dictionaries. The last part is the point: ". . . the solution of their controversies." That was the intent of the growing body of law among the traders of Crete, Macedonia, Phoenicia and the rest of the known ancient world. As merchants went from the barter system to a sale for something of value—such as gold—they wanted better rules. These merchants were not interested in any morality in the law; they simply wanted to know what the law was. Clarity.

One rule of the marketplace was *"caveat emptor"**—"let the buyer beware." If you were ripped off, well bully for the clever merchant and too bad for you. And even up to recent times, if you bought from somebody who bought from somebody else, your rights, if any, stopped with that first somebody.

We've undergone a massive change—in large part by putting morality into the market place. With it comes the notion of fairness. Warranties and guarantees (express and implied), suits allowed against manufacturers, recourse for defective products, and strict liability all stem from that idea of fairness.

Buying and selling *things* should be distinguished from buying and selling real estate. At law, things are referred to as "personal property" or "tangibles," and are governed by particular rules of law differing from those for real estate or "real property."

Even though you probably buy or sell most goods with no contract involved, it's the idea of an underlying contract that supplies the basis for the rights and duties developed both by court decisions and by statutes. For the consumer, implied* warranties and strict liability* are among the most important modern outgrowths of this contract idea. (See Section 2 of this chapter.)

"Sale" is defined as the passing of title from the seller to the buyer for consideration. "Consideration" in this context is no different from that discussed previously and can be anything which would support a contract.

It's important that serving food or drink at a restaurant or cafeteria is considered a sale because consumer protection laws are based on that theory.

This chapter does not include questions and answers arising from credit relationships; these are dealt with in Chapter VI, "Credit."

An outline of what's discussed here is as follows:
1. Buying and selling things
    a. Uniform Commercial Code
       1) Bulk sales
    b. Statute of Frauds
    c. Buying and selling things generally
2. Warranties and guarantees
    a. "Guarantee" and "warranty" defined
    b. UCC and express or implied warranties
       1) Express (stated)

      a) General
      b) Automobiles
    2) Implied (unstated)
    3) "As is"
  c. Injury-causing defects
    1) Privity* of contract
    2) Food, drink, and other cases of strict liability
3. Leasing

Buying and Selling Things

Uniform Commercial Code

In a variety of legal areas, national committees of attorneys or legislators or both have drawn up "uniform"* laws, which mean that the law applied to a set of facts will be the same in all the states adopting those uniform laws. (Of course, as different courts interpret the same law, there are different results.) One body of these uniform laws, with which you're involved more often than you realize, is the Uniform Commercial Code. This regulates all sorts of commercial transactions and comprises the statutory basis for your recourse, for example, against an automobile or washing machine manufacturer. (The latter is discussed in more detail under "Warranties and Guarantees," page 148.)

The Uniform Commercial Code was developed in 1957 by the National Conference of Commissioners on Uniform State Laws and adopted by the states thereafter.

Sensibly, the Uniform Commercial Code deals differently, and more strictly, with merchants—people whose business is selling—than with casual sellers. "Merchant" is defined as one who deals in goods of the kind involved, or holds himself out as having knowledge or a skill peculiar to the practices or goods involved in the transaction.

There are, of course, far more regulations of commercial transactions than covered by the Uniform Commercial Code. One of the most pervasive federal invasions into business transactions is through the instrument of the Interstate Commerce Commission. Any item that gets into interstate commerce becomes subject to the ICC. For example, because salt is shipped interstate, restaurants can be regulated under federal laws. The federal government's right to do all this comes from one phrase that is part of one sentence in the Constitution. It is: "The Congress shall have power . . . to regulate commerce with foreign nations, and among the several States, and with the Indian tribes . . ."

Bulk sales

One set of statutes is called the Bulk Sales Act. This comes into play when a person or organization sells out the entire stock of a business. These laws were needed because of fly-by-night operators who came into town and then virtually decamped at night, having sold out the entire inventory in fraud of creditors. If you sell the inventory of your business, you are involved with a bulk sale.

If you are in any other way making bulk sales, either as seller or buyer, it is important to consult an attorney to learn about the many specific papers that must be drawn up in exact form.

Statute of Frauds

The Statute of Frauds is our old friend from the English common law, now codified. It applies here in that a contract for a sale of goods over a specific amount of money must be in writing to be enforced by a court. For the present, simply be aware of the exception that "partial performance" takes it out of the Statute of Frauds.

Buying and selling things generally

NOTE: The transactions covered here are *cash sales* and purchases *only*. Purchases involving credit are dealt with in Chapter VI, "Credit."

The issue of a defective product is covered in Section 2 of this chapter, "Warranties and Guarantees."

Q I tried to return a part to the store because I picked the wrong size, but the salesman said he wouldn't take it back, so I said I'd sue for breach of contract. Is it?

A Usually the general law is that a store must post notice that it will not accept returns. As to your breach of contract suit, it wouldn't be called that. Breach of warranty comes from an "implied contract"* that what you buy is fit for its intended purpose and not defective. However, that "fit" is different from a mistake about size.

Another argument is that there's an implied contract through the custom of the store in accepting returned merchandise in the past. Most stores will accept a return for store credit at the least.

If you're going to stand on principle, is it worth the cost of a lawsuit?

NOTE: The same rules apply to the situations where a store demands a sales receipt before it will accept a return.

Q I sent for a diamond pendant advertised on television, which seemed really inexpensive for one carat. When it finally arrived it was a little chip of a diamond I could hardly see, not one carat at all. I kept watching for that commercial again, and it turned out they were advertising "one point." Isn't that deceptive advertising?

A It's close. You were taken in by verbal "fine print." A "point" is a jeweler's term for both the cut and also the measurement of .01 carat. In other words, you purchased a diamond weighing one hundredth of a carat. In this and other commercials, where the sales pitch is meant to lead you into believing something other than is actually advertised, the sellers are very close to being guilty of misleading advertising or deceptive practices.

When this type of advertising (by television, radio, or the mails) becomes excessively tricky, you have recourse to the FCC (TV, radio) or Postal Service or the state attorney general.

Q I bought a color television from this particular dealer because he advertised a "free gift" of a small black-and-white TV with the purchase of the 25-inch color. My problem is that the black-and-white doesn't work and the dealer says he doesn't have to do anything about it because it was a gift, not a sale.

A Wrong. When you supposedly get one article "free" with the purchase of another article, the so-called free one is part of the sale and its inducement, and therefore the same rules apply to it as to any purchase.

Q I bought some blue jeans on sale and didn't try them on because that size always fits me. Well, the jeans didn't fit. When I tried to return them to the store, the clerk said she couldn't take them back because they were advertised as "All Sales Final." What can I do?

A Not much. You were put on notice by the "All Sales Final" signs and, without fraud or defect, don't have any recourse against the store. This was a special circumstance.

Q I sent in a mail order from a magazine ad that said "Amazing invention! Kills bugs every time!" What I got was two plain little blocks of wood with a printed note that said: "Place bug here and press firmly." Can they get away with that?

A Well, the advertiser didn't promise anything that you didn't get. I suppose it would kill any bug—so long as you caught it first. However, I believe these people are being too clever and that the postal authorities would frown upon this obvious intent to deceive, cute though it may be.

Q We received a catalog from a mail order outfit with a printed notice on the front that said, "Offer expires October 31." I ordered some things October 1, and when they didn't arrive in two weeks I wrote again. The company finally answered my letter with a printed form saying the offer had been canceled. Is this fair?

A No. The company had to leave the offer open for the time stated.
   This comes under the UCC "Firm offer" section, which says that a merchant's written offer to buy or sell goods "which by its terms gives assurance that it will be held open" is irrevocable for the time stated.

Warranties and Guarantees

"Guarantee"*and "warranty"* defined
   Although the words are legally distinct, for our purposes here we'll treat "guarantee" and "warranty" as being virtually synonymous. Basically, the two words relate to promises that can be enforced.

A warranty is a statement or representation by a seller of goods that the condition or quality of goods is as he has represented them to be.

When the expression "express warranty" is used, it means that the seller has explicitly promised that certain qualities of the goods being sold are as stated; if not, the seller will make good on this promise. An example of an express warranty in the sale of a pillow would be that the pillow filling is 100 percent goose down. The "contract" is based upon this being true.

An "implied warranty" is quite different from an express warranty. An implied warranty does *not* come about by any specific statements of the seller, but, instead, is an invention of the courts and, in some instances, the Uniform Commercial Code. An implied warranty is not stated or spelled out. The notion is that certain attributes of the goods must be present as implicit in their sale.

An implied warranty is at the opposite end of the scale from that old rule of the marketplace, *caveat emptor*, "let the buyer beware." The idea of implied warranty is that it's only fair that certain unstated promises are part of the bargain.

Q What is the difference between an express and an implied warranty?
A An express warranty is what you think of as a guarantee. What is meant by "express" is that the seller specifically details verbally or in writing what he guarantees or promises about the goods purchased. An implied warranty, on the other hand, is not stated but is legally "implied" as part of the sale, for example, that the article will be fit for its intended use, free of defects, and safe.

UCC and express or implied warranties

Express (stated)
General
The Uniform Commercial Code (UCC 55-2-313) provides: "Express warranties by the seller are created as follows: Any affirmation of fact . . . made by the seller to the buyer which relates to the goods and becomes part of the basis of the bargain creates an express warranty that the goods shall conform to the affirmation." This means that

although I told you *express warranties* are *explicit,* if the seller asserts or claims that some essential fact is true, the courts are going to create a little fiction and hold that assertion becomes an "express warranty." (Naturally, this is with the qualifications below.)

The question in any sale is whether or not the seller has made an "affirmation of fact" to which he can be held.

No express warranty is created if the seller's words only express an *opinion* about the goods or if his words are only part of a sales pitch or "puffing."

Is the seller making a statement about the quality or characteristics of the goods in an area where he is the expert and the buyer is ignorant? If the answer is yes, then the courts say that the seller's words are an express warranty. If the answer is no, then the courts say that the seller's words are only an opinion and that the buyer could just as well form his own opinion.

Q We bought some asphalt tile that was guaranteed to last ten years, but it started turning a funny color the first time I washed the floor. When we complained, the salesman said, "Show me any place it says the stuff won't turn yellow." It doesn't say so, but my argument is that if it is supposed to last that long, that includes not turning yellow. Who is right?

A You are. First check to see if there's an express guarantee or warranty against discoloration. If so, you're home free. Next, the argument is perhaps some discoloration could be expected within that guaranteed time of "lasting," but discoloration within the time you stated would be a breach of the implied warranty of merchantability.

Q I purchased a sort of game thing that was supposed to help my golf. Right on the front of the instructions it said: "COMPLETELY SAFE— BALL WILL NOT HIT PLAYER." Well, this here player was hit and I had to see a doctor. Can I get the manufacturer to pay my doctor's bill?

A Yes. That statement on the instructions is an express warranty of safety.

Q I answered an ad for a motorcycle that claimed the bike was in excellent condition. The fellow also told me in person that the cycle was in really fine shape and did not need any major repairs. Well, the thing fell apart on me, but the seller says that he didn't give me any kind of warranty. It's true I don't have anything in writing that says "warranty" on it, but I don't think it's fair.

A You're right, it's not fair, and you do have a warranty. The newspaper ad might not be enough by itself to create a warranty, but when you add to it the assurances given you by the seller, I believe a court would find that there was an express warranty. Next time, get it in writing!

Q I ordered some linoleum from a catalog where it was described as being able to flex without cracking. After six months it did start cracking. Is there anything I can do?

A Yes. In a similar case the court held that even though a comparable statement was only in a catalog and was basically advertising, it still was a warranty as to those representations. The test was whether or not the seller made an "affirmation of fact" on which it intended the buyer to rely.

Automobiles

Today's automobile manufacturers usually advertise the warranties on their new cars. Normally these warranties are limited as to time and/or mileage and are also limited to repair or replacement of certain defective parts.

The question is: Can a manufacturer limit the extent of express or implied warranties? The UCC says yes, and the courts have agreed.

Q My new car has been in the dealer's service department so many times I might as well be without a car. Do I have to keep taking it back to the shop, or can I get some other relief?

A Some other relief. A court would look at the reasonableness of the situation and say that at some point the manufacturer must admit it's unable to repair your car under the warranty, with its limitations, and make good your losses.

NOTE: The seller must be given the opportunity to repair and replace, but it only has a reasonable time in which to do so; after a reasonable time has elapsed without the trouble being corrected, the courts find that the warranty is breached. This is the "lemon law."*

Q I bought a used car from a dealer who made a big deal out of the fact that his used cars carried express warranties that they were free from defects in materials and workmanship. The trouble is that when the engine started leaking a lot of oil, the dealer said the problem had nothing to do with materials and workmanship. Can I make him do something about that leak?

A Yes. Courts have held that the problem you describe is a breach of that express warranty.

Q What if I take my newly purchased car back in for repairs under the warranty and the dealer won't fix it?

A You get damages. (They would be based on your expenses incurred by taking it elsewhere.)

The courts have held that the fact repairs must be made isn't a breach of the manufacturer's warranty, but refusing to do the guaranteed repair or replacement is a breach.

Implied (unstated)

An implied warranty comes along with the sale whether the merchant likes it or not. An implied warranty is the opposite of an express warranty in that an implied warranty is not stated.

The Uniform Commercial Code demands that if goods are to be sold, they must be "merchantable."* One of the requirements of this merchantability is that the goods must be "fit" for the ordinary purposes for which such goods are used. (UCC Section 2—314 [2] [c]). This demand for fitness includes the idea that goods must be free from injury-causing defects. (Discussed on page 156 under "Food, Drink, and Other Cases of Strict Liability.")

The concept of fitness and merchantability is hauled in by a legal fiction in which the law calls a philosophy of consumer protection an "implied warranty" when it's not actually implied at all by the parties and the seller made no such promise.

Two of my favorite cases, which have an embarrassment of riches as far as illustrating a breach of implied warranty, are:

(1) The plaintiff bought a used car from the defendant; this car developed engine difficulties before two weeks had passed; was repaired numerous times, with the plaintiff having to pay for half of the repairs; and finally developed new problems, which resulted in a totally destroyed engine—this in a little over a month from the date of purchase.

(2) The plaintiff bought a mobile home, discovering, after purchase, that it was incorrectly placed on the foundation, had ceilings sagging and about to fall, a slashed carpet, a front door that wouldn't shut, broken counter tops, faulty wiring, and other defects.

In both of these cases the court held that the defendants had breached the implied warranty of merchantability.

Q The accident wasn't my fault! The brakes failed [or the steering, etc.].

A Sue the manufacturer. If the cause of the accident for which you are being sued was a defective part or design, you have a right to go against the company that built the car. This includes bringing the company into a suit as the one responsible even though you are the one being sued.

Caveat:* There must have been no alteration in the original part or design since it left the manufacturer.

Q We purchased an air conditioner from a man who promised to install it himself. His unit didn't cool the house, so he told us we had to buy a fan. (He meant for the air conditioner.) That didn't help, but he wants money for the fan and labor besides what we've paid him already for the air conditioner. What can we do?

A Hang on to your money until the air conditioner works—unless there's a contract I don't know about. On the facts given, you probably have what's called an "implied warranty." That means, though nothing was said, the courts find that the man promised the thing would work, i.e., cool the house.

Q I know it sounds like a joke, but when I was driving my just-purchased used car home from the lot, the transmission fell out. My brother-in-law says, "Tough luck. That's what you get for buying a used car." Is he right, and I'm out of luck?

A No. The courts make allowances for used or secondhand cars and other items, but they still must be "merchantable." In your case, that required fitness for ordinary purpose would be fitness for the purpose of driving. Your car obviously was not, and therefore the dealer has breached this implied warranty.

Q What if a lawn mower chews up my foot?

A, The manufacturer is probably liable* on a "warranty" theory; i.e., when the manufacturer sold the equipment, the courts say he, in effect, promised the ultimate buyer the thing wouldn't harm him. You can go through the retailer on to the original manufacturer.

Caveat: You must not have been using or misusing the equipment in a way that no reasonable man could have anticipated.

Q I was picking up a carton of sodas in the grocery store when the bottom fell out and a piece of flying glass gashed my leg. Is the grocery store responsible for that?

A Yes. You could sue the grocery store, the distributor, and the manufacturer. The grounds are that someone is at fault as to the packaging, on the basis of breach* of implied warranty.* You would only have to show that you were not treating the carton of sodas in any rough or unusual way.

"As is"

That old idea of *caveat emptor* still hangs around the marketplace, but now, if the buyer is to beware, the merchant must flag the item offered for sale with a notice of "as is" or other words calling the buyer's attention to the fact that there are no warranties, either express or implied. The Uniform Commercial Code allows "as is" sales—with exceptions. (There are always exceptions.)

The seller may even be aware of defects, but an "as is" notice acts as a warning that the buyer must do his own inspection. If the buyer doesn't inspect or there are even circumstances where he couldn't inspect, the seller is still off the hook unless he has somehow tricked the buyer.

NOTE: The courts lean away from finding that there is no implied warranty, so any notice to the effect that used cars, machinery, and other articles are sold "as is" must clearly call the buyer's attention to that fact or the court will rule in favor of the buyer.

Injury-causing defects

Privity of contract

Privity of contract,"* sounds like the worst of lawyer jargon, but the fact that courts no longer require privity of contract in particular cases is of the greatest importance to you should you be injured by a wheel flying off a passing car, or by a severed thumb in your soft drink (actual case).

The concept of privity of contract is comparable to tracing blood lines in a family tree. The idea was that a manufacturer or producer could not be sued for a defect in goods unless the person damaged by the defect had a contractual relationship with him. In other words, in a suit against a manufacturer, the plaintiff would be thrown out of court unless she could show a line of sales from the defendant/producer to herself.

This demand for privity was prevalent for generations until a Mr. McPherson came along and sued Buick. He objected to having been injured by a wheel that flew off a passing automobile as he walked alongside a road. The result was the landmark decision of *McPherson vs. Buick*, punching a big hole in the concept of privity of contract. The court held that the manufacturer of a product causing personal injury could not escape the consequences by claiming there was no privity of contract.

Now the door is open for suits by any person injured by a defective product and the manufacturer is held responsible.

Food, drink, and other cases of strict liability

To impose "strict liability"* on the manufacturer (in the case of personal injury), it is not necessary for the plaintiff to establish that an express warranty was given. Strict liability is applied to a defect which creates an unreasonable risk of injury. *A manufacturer is strictly liable when an article he places on the market proves to have a defect that causes injury to a human being.* If you can show you have a case of strict liability, then you only need to prove the purchase and the resulting injury. One does not need to prove the actual acts of negligence.

This was first recognized in the case of unwholesome food products and is now extended to a variety of other products, including prescription drugs and medical devices. The courts are divided over whether the strict liability is based on tort (a wrong, such as negligence) or contract. The growing opinion is not to bother with these "terms of art."* However, for our purposes, it is enough to know that if you are injured by something you eat or drink or because of some defect in a product, you probably have a good case against the manufacturer.

The idea of this strict liability is that the public should be able to depend on not being injured by products in the stream of commerce, and, if a person is injured, it is the manufacturer who should bear the expense of that injury.

For example, if you were poisoned by a product purchased at a grocery store, the law is that you or your heirs can proceed directly against the manufacturer. Manufacturers of food are held more accountable than anyone and you will not be forced to prove what they did wrong, but simply the end result, i.e., poisoning.

In one case, a woman became violently ill after snacking on potato chips. She was rushed to the hospital and the potato chips were analyzed. It turned out that, along with the potatoes, the manufacturer had fried the skin of a rat that had perished from strychnine poisoning. The woman recovered—both from the poisoning and from the company.

Q Would anyone believe me if I said I found a roach in my soft drink?

A Yes. Classic cases of foreign objects found in a popular soft drink have included: a mouse, a plug of chewing tobacco, and someone's thumb. Bugs are most common.

Q When I was eating clam chowder at a restaurant, I swallowed a bone and almost choked to death. Can I sue the restaurant?

A You can, but under one court ruling you would lose. In a case with the same set of facts, a court found that a New Englander eating clam chowder should be aware of the possibility of bones and that there was no breach of warranty.

See an attorney. Maybe the court in your state would make a distinction if you're from Arizona instead of New England. But wherever you're from, I believe this was a bad decision.

Q I opened a can of mixed nuts I'd just purchased at the grocery store and popped a handful into my mouth. I bit down on something hard, which turned out to be a piece of shell. It broke off a part of one tooth; I told the store I thought they should at least pay my dental bill, but they wouldn't pay anything at all. Can they get away with this?

A In one case, which was appealed, all the defendants involved—retailer and manufacturer did get away with it. The court held that anyone eating canned nuts should be aware of the possibility of a nutshell, and that the presence of the shell in the can of nuts was not a breach of warranty.

See an attorney! I don't think this case is good law either.

Leasing

Leasing is included in this chapter on buying and selling because a lease is a kind of purchase. It has many, if not all, the rights and duties of ownership for a set period of time and is dealt with in the UCC.

Leasing a home or apartment is discussed in the Real Property chapter—here we'll talk about personal property in the form of an automobile or truck.

Not only advertising, but also straight-forward articles have touted the benefits of leasing your vehicle. They often stress the tax savings. There are pitfalls, however.

If you intend to lease, begin with a check list: tax, capital, costs, acquisition. What *taxes* will you owe for acquiring the leased vehicle? What *capital* must you invest? (Many leases demand a large down payment which is in such fine print and goes by so fast you can scarcely see it on a television commercial.) What *costs* will you have? What *rights* do you acquire—and what *unexpected* duties?

You will often pay higher insurance and have higher maintenance bills.

If you're going to lease for 48 months, don't. You might as well buy the vehicle. Make the lease short term and *find out* if this is truly a lease or if you are indeed purchasing. Check the termination clause carefully; there may be an expensive penalty if you wish to get out of the lease early.

Along with the above, the salesman will probably recite great terms and price if you wish to buy at the end of the lease period. But . . . will your payments all have counted toward the sale? Will you be paying a total that would be a good bargain if you were buying this vehicle now? What will you be credited for residual value?

Close to that termination clause, or part of it, will be one on "normal wear and tear." Look out. "Normal" often is not.

Q I got in way over my head in leasing an expensive car. I didn't understand what all I'm responsible for. They're charging a bundle for repairs and saying I have to pay because the repairs aren't included in "normal wear and tear." I thought I had all sorts of warranties. Now I'm afraid to take the thing out of the garage!

A Many people are finding out that this popular trend of leasing rather than buying carries hidden dangers. You need the help of an attorney to go over that lease contract to see if she can find a way to make a fair settlement for you. You may lose—the old older-and-wiser bit. Note: Vehicle leases are covered by the Uniform Commercial Code also.

In some leases you're in for a bundle for scratches, dents, upholstery and especially tires (no wear) in an agreement in which you've promised *not to detract from the value.*

Q When I signed my lease, I didn't follow all those suggestions you're making now. Is there anything I can do *before* the lease expires?

A Take pictures of every angle of the car and of the tires *before* you turn it in. In ample time before the lease expires, ask the lessor for a written list of what must be repaired and a firm estimate of the cost of those repairs. You could then shop around instead of being stuck with *their* bill. Have your own inspection report made up.

Read the fine print in re how far you can drive each year *without penalty.* Many people don't realize this isn't just an estimate like you make on insurance. This clause usually *penalizes* you for each mile over the number of miles in the lease agreement.

CHAPTER V

Real Estate:
Buying and Selling, Leasing, Optioning, Mortgaging

INTRODUCTION/HISTORY AND REAL PROPERTY DEFINED

Real property is defined as land and anything attached to, or part of, the land, such as houses or barns, crops and minerals. Formerly, ownership of real property meant ownership to the depths of the earth and the heights of the heavens. However, modern conditions, such as highrises, the use of solar energy, airplanes, and dwindling ground water, are whittling away at how far up and how far down a person owns.

The fact that you can own real property represents a revolutionary amount of freedom. The two most important rights flowing from your ownership are (1) that you are able to sell your property, and (2) that you can leave your property to whomever you wish by will. Historically in England, all property was owned by the crown. The few who were allowed control of property did so at the pleasure of the king and with set duties owed to the king, such as providing a specified number of men for battle. A holdover from those days is that should a person leave no heirs, his property returns, "escheats,"* to the state. Although this is surrounded by new rules, such as the demands of due process, the government can still take one's property by eminent domain.

The rights of property ownership, which we take for granted today, had their start in 1290 with the Statute of Quia Emptores. Because of the push for land reform, the lords of the land drew up this statute, which allowed free men the right to transfer a freehold estate so long as the one to whom it was transferred swore on his oath to carry out the other's duties to the king. That Statute of Quia Emptores did not go so far as to let a person dispose of his property upon his death. The situation continued this way until 1540, when the Statute of Wills was enacted.

Real property carries its own rules, such as: it can be conveyed only by a written instrument, and only the courts where the real property is located have jurisdiction over it. A person owning real property has "seisin,"* which means title and possession and something more. This ownership carries with it the right to possession; to exclude others; to dispose of the property by sale, gift, and will; to the use and enjoyment of the property; and to take from the property, such as by cutting trees or mining.

This chapter will cover the most common questions about real estate as far as buying and selling, leasing, optioning, and mortgaging. Other major areas involving real property, such as the duties owed to the public by the owner or lessor, or water and mineral rights, won't be discussed in this book.

The subtopics covered are as follows:

1. Buying and selling real estate: an overview
   a. What is sold?
   b. How much is sold?
      1) Fee simple
      2) Life estate
      3) Lease
   c. How is it owned?
      1) Joint tenancy
      2) Tenancy by the Entirety/Community Property
      3) Tenancy in common
   d. How is it sold?
      1) Contract of sale
      2) Warranty deed
      3) Quitclaim deed

Buying and Selling Real Estate: An Overview

What is sold?

Since land cannot be physically handed over, in the old days the owner walked the land with the buyer and then delivered a symbolic stick. Today, delivery of the deed is the symbolic transfer of the land. The deed is recorded in the courthouse of the county where the land lies in order to keep a record of ownership. It is also to give notice.* This same record includes any encumbrance* on the property, again for purposes of notice.

Normally the sale of land is the sale of all rights that the owner possesses, the whole bundle of rights that are included in title and possession. Most commonly, too, this is done without condition or reservation.

However, in transferring title, the owner of land may retain certain rights, such as the right to mine the minerals under the land or the right to pass over the land with, for instance, a road. The latter right is called an easement,* or, if you want to stop all party conversation call it an "incorporeal hereditament."* (Another conversation stopper is to say that you have willed your land in "fee tail male special," which means that you have willed your land to the eldest son born of a particular woman.)

Besides reserving an interest in the land to himself, a seller can also place strings on the conveyance, or gift or will, so that if a certain event either happens or fails to happen, the land will revert to him. Examples would be: ". . . so long as the property is used as a church," or "but if liquor is sold there it shall revert . . ."

Also, how much one promises to convey depends on whether the deed is "warranty"* or "quitclaim,"* which is discussed later.

Q I say I can use my property any way I want to! Right?

A Wrong. In our society, the use and enjoyment of your property are looked at in conjunction with your neighbors' use of their property. This balancing of interests includes everything from your disturbing your neighbors' enjoyment to the government's enacting zoning laws.

Q The neighborhood has built up around me, so that now I'm told I can't keep my pigs. That's unconstitutional, isn't it?

A Originally, it was found to be unconstitutional. In most situations, an ordinance must allow for nonconforming uses that existed before the law was passed; this is called a "grandfather clause." However, there is sometimes a conflict between the public interest and the rights of an individual: that's you. Unfortunately, even without an unconstitutional retroactive application of an ordinance, the town could probably force out your pigs by calling them a "nuisance," which has a particular legal meaning comparable to the English meaning you're accustomed to.

Q If I own the air rights above me, can't I stop the airport from ruining my peace and quiet by having planes fly overhead?

A Some courts have allowed an injunction and some haven't. Some courts find that you own only a reasonable amount of airspace, which would not be as high as the planes are flying; other courts have said that the planes are a legal nuisance, just as you claim.

All the circumstances would have to be considered, but you are most likely on the short end of the legal stick, particularly if you purchased your home with knowledge of the flight patterns.

Q We bought a condo on the beach with a marvelous view of the ocean, but now somebody is putting up a high-rise right in front of us that will cut off our view. My brother-in-law says that when I bought the condo I bought the view. Is that right?

A Possibly. See an attorney. Traditionally, you did *not* buy rights to a view, but there is a body of thought moving away from this concept, and in your favor.

Q A factory nearby has started using a different kind of fuel, and the fumes are killing my rose bushes. Isn't this some sort of interference with my property rights?

A Yes. The idea of a legal "nuisance,"* such as the fumes you describe, is based upon your rights as a property owner, which include "enjoyment" of your land. You can try various legal means to stop the emissions, such as injunction and probably a class action. The health of you and your neighbors may well be affected.

Q We purchased several acres from a woman who had a large tract and kept some acreage for herself. The deed had in it some kind of a clause about a road for her to cross our land, but now she's decided to develop her acreage and there's all sorts of traffic on that private road. That wasn't part of the deal as far as we were concerned. Can we stop the traffic?

A I'd need more facts to be able to advise you. This is an involved area of law when an easement like your roadway is changed by way of more traffic than was expected when you accepted that reservation in the deed.

The way the easement is described in your deed is critical. Was it limited to ingress and egress (travel in and out) by the grantor, or was it more comprehensive, such as just stating that a roadway was reserved? If it was the former, then you win. A court will consider how much more burdensome the present use is than that originally contemplated.

Q I bought land to build a solar home. Now the neighbors are putting up a house that will block the sun. Can they do this to me?

A It may be worth a fight in court because right now there's no way of knowing how the case will be decided in your jurisdiction. All sorts of regulations are cropping up alongside the growth of solar homes.

Legislatures have declared that the right to use the natural resource of solar energy is a property right, which has been defined as a right to an unobstructed line-of-sight path from a solar collector to the sun.

A number of states now have statutes guaranteeing your rights to unobstructed sunlight for solar uses so long as you meet the standards or conditions set out for solar users.

*Caveat:** The strength of your position will depend, in large part, on whether or not the land was sold for solar building.

Q Some oil company representatives came by my farm and said they'd been drilling in the area and would be willing to try my land if I gave them some sort of deed or lease. I don't understand. Does this mean if I want to get money from the oil I have to give up my property?

A No. See a lawyer to ensure that you can continue to live and farm there and either sell or lease the mineral rights *under* the land. One common arrangement is that you will receive a percentage on the oil produced, usually called a royalty, while you retain the full rights to the surface.

Caveat: Be sure the lease defines how much land the oil company will dig or tear up in its search for oil and that it will be returned as close as possible to its original condition.

Q Our property is one parcel out of several acres owned by the woman who sold our land to us. Until we got ready to build a house, we didn't realize there's no way to get to our lot without going over the acreage that woman owns. She says we can buy some more land from her to put a road on—otherwise we're out of luck. Can she do this to us?

A No. In your situation, the courts say you have what's called "easement of necessity."* This means an owner of landlocked property has a right of access to that property, a right to pass over the property of the original owner, to get to a road.

How much is sold?

Real property is unique in that more than one person can have a variety of interests or estates* in the same piece of property. For instance, let's call an acre of land "Sunnyville." Among the variety of ways a number of people can own estates in Sunnyville is this: A, B, and C are "joint tenants"* with a "fee simple"* estate; D leases the house on the Sunnyville land; and E has been granted the mineral rights. A person could also have a life estate* in certain property which would pass to another upon her death.

Fee simple

This is the most complete interest a person can have in land and carries with it full rights to sell or devise* (leave by will). If there is no will, this property will pass to the heirs of the deceased.

A fee simple is still not quite *total* ownership. That idea of the state is still in there.

Life estate*

The second largest estate in land is a life estate, which means just what it sounds like: the possessor of a life estate can basically treat the property as if it is his, but only for his lifetime. Therefore he cannot, of course, devise it, but he can sell or lease his interests during his life. At the death of the owner of the life estate, the property passes to whomever was named in the original conveyance or back to the original owner who gave the life estate.

Lease

A leasehold estate is quite different from a fee simple and a life estate in that it is considered personal property by some courts, although, at common law, a lease was considered the equivalent of a sale of the premises for a term. Today, a number of courts follow contract law rather than real property law when dealing with leases.

More important, the rights of the tenant have gone from being virtually nonexistent, under the *caveat emptor* of early sales law, to comprising an entire body of law. Among them is the Uniform Landlord Tenant Relations Law.

Q I'm selling some commercial property I own to a church at considerably below market price, and I want the church to use the property instead of selling it at a profit. Is there anything I can do to make the church stick by the bargain and use the property for church purposes?

A Yes. You deed the property to the church as you would normally do, but add the words: "for so long as the property is used for church purposes" (detailing exactly what you mean by church purposes) and then add a "but if" clause so that if the church ceases to use the property for its purposes, it will "revert," return, to you.

Q I noticed that my deed conveys the property to me "and my heirs." Why mention anything about heirs?

A A deed "to so-and-so and his heirs" doesn't mean anything other than that you are getting the maximum interest in property, a fee simple.* Traditionally, to do this, the words "and his heirs" had to be included. That is the only meaning those words have in this context.

Q I want to deed my farm to my son, but not to his wife. How can I accomplish this?

A If you phrase the wording in the deed "to my son and his heirs," the "and his heirs" part comes carrying historical baggage that will lead the courts to interpret it as deeding your son a fee simple, with which he can do whatever he wishes. That would include turning it over to his wife if he liked. To keep your son's wife from taking any interest in the property, a number of "words of art"* are available, such as: "To my son for life and then to his issue [children] but should he die without issue then the property shall pass to . . ." You can also set up a trust.

Q Before she died, my mother said she was going to will me the house for life, so that I'd have a place to live. The will says: "to Martha Ann for life and then to her children . . ." Do I have to stay here, or can I rent the house to someone else?

A You can rent it for any length of time up to your death. You sell no more than your "life estate."

Q We just bought a home and found that the sellers had actually taken the hot water heater with them! They say there wasn't a word in the deed about the hot water heater. Can they do that to us?

A No. The hot water heater, along with things such as the furnace, built-in ovens, a dishwasher, and wall-to-wall carpeting, all come under the heading of "fixtures," which automatically pass with the property.

Most contracts list what items shall be considered as fixtures, but if there is no list, the basic rule is that whatever is attached,* whatever would have to be torn loose from the property, is a fixture.

How is it owned?

Besides the above three major ways of owning rights to or in property, explained above, a person can also be a "joint tenant," a "tenant by the entirety," or "tenant in common."

Joint tenancy

The two major points are that (1) each joint tenant has an undivided interest in the entire estate, and (2) upon the death of one joint tenant, his interest automatically—and not by his will—passes to the other joint tenant(s) unless it specifically does not. Also, the joint tenancy is destroyed if one joint tenant attempts to sell his interest. That ringing legal phrase "undivided interest in the entire estate" means that no joint tenant can separate out what he or she owns of the entire parcel; together they own the whole thing.

Historically, joint tenancy had very technical rules that had to be followed or the courts would not recognize it as a joint tenancy. These were called the "four unities": time, title, interest, and possession. In other words, the joint tenants must have had their same interests created by the same deed, commencing at the same time, and with the simultaneous right to possession. Therefore, no one could create a joint tenancy between himself and another person because the second person's interests wouldn't have come at the same time; instead, you would have to deed your land to a "straw man" who would deed it back, *in joint tenancy*, to you and your desired joint tenant. Now more and more states are doing away with these technicalities, and if the parties intend to create a joint tenancy, the courts will say that they have done so.

If the joint tenants want to split up and each one hold a specific part of the property, they must have a judge "partition"* the property. This means that the court would tell each former joint tenant what part of the land he or she will now own.

Tenancy by the Entirety: Community Property

"Tenancy by the entirety"* is created (in non-community property states) when property is deeded to a husband and wife. Like a joint tenancy, they each own an undivided interest in the whole parcel and have "right of survivorship,"* one taking the whole enchilada when the other dies.

"Community property"* is similar to the above in those states that follow the "civil law"* of Spain as opposed to the majority that are based on the English "common law." Property deeded to both husband and wife belongs to the community. This is also true of property deeded to husband *or* wife that is not specifically "separate property."* Some laws are different in community property states; even the federal estate taxes are modified to fit.

Tenancy in common

This is different from joint tenancy in that each of the tenants in common can own a different amount, such as one third or one fifth, and those "unities" of joint tenancy are not present except unity of possession. Also, tenants in common do not have that right of survivorship described above.

Q I am thinking of going into a land-buying deal, and the promoters told me that I would own one eighth of the parcel as a "tenant in common." Does that sound all right to you?

A Yes. In a tenancy in common, as contrasted to a joint tenancy, you can own any fraction of the whole in common with other people. The other major distinguishing point of a tenancy in common is that you can sell or leave your interest by will.

Q In my wife's will she left me everything she possessed, but she owned some property separately with a business partner. Now that character claims he gets all the jointly owned property. I tell him the will says different. Who's right?

A Unfortunately, the business partner. When property is owned jointly, one of the characteristics of the joint ownership is that, upon the death of a joint owner, all of that owner's interest passes to the survivor. Your wife's will does not affect the jointly held property.

Q I owned a farm before I was married, and now I want to deed half of it to my husband and own it jointly with him. Can I just make up some papers naming my husband as a joint tenant with me?

A Probably. It depends on your state law. Traditionally, you could not do this, but would have to go through the process of conveying the property to a "straw man" so that he could turn around and convey it to you and your husband jointly. (A "straw man" is a figurehead, someone used to set up a deal who actually takes no interest.)

Now many states have done away with some of the super-technicalities of joint tenancy, and you would be able to deed the property to yourself and your husband as joint tenants.

Q I inherited some money from my mother and would like to invest it in a piece of property that I want own separate from my husband. Can I do this?

A Yes. It's important that you inherited the money. That's one of the occasions when property doesn't become "community." Now, just be sure the deed is made out to you, a "married woman, as her sole and separate property."

Q We don't live in a community property state but my husband says half of everything is his. I say that's not right. My dad has been reducing his estate by gifts and I think the interests he's been deeding me in commercial real estate are mine!

A You're right—so long as your father deeded those interests to you alone as your sole and separate property. Otherwise the presumption for a married woman in your state is that it's a "tenancy by the entirety"* with your husband.

How is it sold?

Contract of sale

Normally, the sale of real estate begins with a contract of sale. (One is translated at the end of this section on "Real Estate: Buying and Selling.") The contract of sale is an agreement on the terms as to the transfer of title by means of a deed. Like any contract, the contract of sale must be sufficiently definite for a court to enforce. This means that the contract must set out a description of the property being sold, what interest is sold, how the property is to be paid for, and what kind of deed is to be given.

The description of the property is usually the "legal description,"* which is often written in surveyors' language as degrees and minutes, metes and bounds, including phrases such as "thence northwest . . ."; this determines the precise boundaries of the property you are buying. The description should correspond *exactly* to the deed you receive, and even if you think you cannot understand a legal description, you can certainly check to see if those incomprehensible words match on both the contract of sale and the deed.

Don't dismiss this as so much legal jargon, because the legal description is exactly what you are buying and it can be vitally important in any number of disputes, including ones over where your property ends and your neighbor's starts.

In some rural parts of the country, the legal description will be set out in boundaries couched in layman's terms, such as "south from the old oak tree three hundred yards to the boulder at the edge of the river, then east eight hundred yards to the old Jones fence post."

The contract of sale will include the purchase price of the property and method of payment. As a buyer, you can always insert a clause stating that the contract is conditional or contingent upon your obtaining financing and at what interest rate.

The third major provision of a contract of sale is that the "seller will furnish good and merchantable title."* The contract will usually give the seller a choice of furnishing an abstract or title insurance as proof of this. (These are discussed on pages 176-177.)

The contract of sale will stipulate the type of deed to be supplied. It should normally call for a "warranty deed" (discussed in the next subsection), unless there are unusual circumstances of which you are fully aware.

Time of sale, i.e., "closing" will be set out. The sale of property is often negotiated by a real estate agent. This, of course, calls for another contract—*read it.*

You can, naturally, contract with any number of realtors to sell your property, on an open or "multiple" listing. NOTE, however: if you sign a so-called exclusive with any one realty company, its exclusive right to sell the property means you will still owe a real estate commission if you do the selling yourself, unless you reserve the right to do so. Pay attention to this part of the contract, as well as to the period of time stated in the contract for which you are making the company your agent. There will also be a clause stating for what additional period of time and under what conditions the real estate company will get a commission *after* the contract terminates. (If the agents who have the exclusive are truly not trying to sell your house, see an attorney. You may have grounds to break that exclusive contract.)

Under either form, check upon what conditions you would still owe a commission even if you sold the property yourself.

Q What does it mean where the contract for sale says that the seller "will furnish good and merchantable title"*?

A This means the seller will show by an abstract (or title insurance in its place) that he does have the right to sell the property as described, that he can convey good title to it. In other words, the seller must show that there are no defects in the chain of title down to him, which would be a "cloud on the title."*

Q Can I have a verbal agreement for the sale of land?

A No. An agreement for the sale of real property (land) must be in writing. It must describe the land, the parties, and the terms. The basis of this is the old English Statute of Frauds.*

Q We've signed a contract to buy a house, but I don't see where it says we are getting that "fee simple" you said meant everything.

A Most contracts, and the deed, too, of course, do recite a "fee simple estate," but if yours doesn't, check and see that it does provide for a "warranty deed" and says the seller does "grant, bargain, and convey all of his right, title, and interest in and to," whereupon *if* the seller does own a fee simple estate, that is what you'll get.

Caveat: In the latter case, where "fee simple" isn't recited, it's important that you get title insurance or an abstract showing you are buying nothing less than a fee simple.

Warranty deed* defined

The type of deed people deal with most often is called a "warranty deed." This guarantees or warrants certain promises as to the conveyance from the seller to the buyer. The signifying words in the deed are "grant and warrant," which make the seller responsible for what are called "warranties of title."

Warranties of title are normally (1) the covenant (promise) of seisin* and the right to convey, which mean that the seller warrants he has good title and the right to sell; (2) the covenant against encumbrances, which means there are no mortgages or liens* against the property except those expressly set out in the deed; (3) the covenant of quiet enjoyment, which is a kind of catchall basically meaning that the buyer is assured he will not be thrown out by someone with a better title.

One of the most important aspects of buying property with a warranty deed is that it creates a chain of responsibility, so that any purchaser suffering from a broken promise (breach of warranty) down the line can go back to each former seller to enforce his rights. Therefore, a buyer is not limited to a damage suit against the one from whom he purchased his property but can go all the way back to the one who originally breached the warranty.

Quitclaim deed* defined

A quitclaim deed is completely different from a warranty deed in that a quitclaim deed promises nothing. A quitclaim deed is saying, "*If I have any interest, I am conveying it to you.*" A quitclaim deed puts the buyer on notice that the seller is not claiming to have good title, or any title. If you want to sell the Brooklyn Bridge, a quitclaim is the way to do it!

A quitclaim deed is often used to clear up a cloudy title. For instance, when someone dies without a will, all the remote and unlikely but possible heirs might be asked to sign a quitclaim deed. Another example would be in the case of a divorce, one spouse may surrender his share of a jointly owned property to the other, or when a co-tenant wants to buy out the other; that other could give up his claims to the land by way of a quitclaim deed.

Q My sister and I each inherited adjoining pieces of property but the line between wasn't real clear. She says she'll give me a quitclaim to what we believe is my portion. Isn't it supposed to be a warranty deed?

A No. This is a proper use of the quitclaim, saying, in effect, "I convey my interest—*if any*— to this piece of property." Your sister can't really "warrant" it because it may already belong to you.

Q We're buying a parcel of land next to our cabin in the mountains. The neighbor says he'll just quitclaim it to us—that it's simpler that way. Right?

A Wrong. For him maybe. If there turns out to be any trouble with the title, such as his right to sell it, you have no recourse with a quitclaim. Get a warranty deed.

Recording, chain of title, abstract vs. title insurance

Recording

The idea of "recording"* is to give notice* to all the world of the current status of any piece of real property. The county clerk keeps the record books into which are placed the papers representing any transaction involving any piece of real estate in that county. These will include deeds, mortgages, and other liens. The law varies from state to state, but if someone does *not* record a transaction, such as putting a lien on a piece of property, that person loses his rights to assert a lien against subsequent owners because he has failed to give notice of those rights by recording them.

These record books are set up alphabetically in two basic ways, so that you can look up the property under the name of the grantor,* the one selling or otherwise disposing of a piece of property, or, in reverse, under the name of the grantee,* the one acquiring the piece of property.

Recording does not make a deed any more or less valid. The recording is for purposes of notice. It doesn't matter whether or not a purchaser has checked out the title in the record books; the law assumes knowledge of what she might have found if she had checked the record. If there is, for instance, a recorded mortgage on the property, a purchaser cannot claim he didn't know about it.

*Chain of title**

"Chain of title" is a descriptive phrase that means just what it sounds like: Able sells Sunnyvale to Baker, who gives it to Cain, who wills it to Deborah. Able to Baker to Cain to Deborah is the "chain of title" of Sunnyvale—assuming it was recorded. If Cain, for example, sold off a bunch of little pieces of Sunnyvale and did not record those sales, they would be referred to as "out of the chain of title."

If Baker mortgaged the property before giving it to Cain and nothing was ever recorded to show that the mortgage was paid off, that's a "cloud"* on the title.

Abstract versus title insurance

An "abstract" is the history of that "chain of title" we just discussed. Someone preparing an abstract goes back all the way (to the original land grant from the king, for example) to be sure that everything on the record appears to be proper, that the same legally described piece of property goes nicely from A to B to C to D to whomever is now disposing of the property. This is done less frequently these days; instead, the seller supplies "title insurance." The title insurance is designed to reimburse the buyer if anything guaranteed in the warranty deed turns out to be untrue. The primary example of this would be that the seller did not have good title to the property—the right to sell it.

Caveat: A title insurance policy will usually state it does *not* cover whatever the insurance company can think of the insurer might collect on. *Notice particularly*: A title policy normally will *not* cover anything visible on the land, such as phone and power line easements and "squatters."

Q What is an abstract?

A An abstract is the record of sales and purchases of real estate back to the original deed or grant of land from the government or the king. It shows whether or not there's any defect in what's called the "chain of title." An example is: Mr. Black sells an acre of land to Mr. White, who sells it to Mr. Green. The abstract will show all that and whether the acre has been properly described each time and whether there are any liens, mortgages, or other claims against that property. A defect would be, for example, if Mr. Black made out a deed to Mr. White and his wife, but she didn't sign the deed when Mr. White sold it to Mr. Green. That's the "cloud" business again.

Q I've had to furnish title insurance each time I've sold a home, but I still don't understand what I'm paying for.

A Although sometimes the buyer is responsible for it, in most states the seller guarantees "good title" to the property being sold by means of title insurance. This will supposedly reimburse the buyer if there are any defects in the title, such as another party having a claim or the seller having no right to sell what he is purportedly selling. However, most title insurance policies add clauses for anything that could conceivably come up, stating that the policy doesn't cover those instances; not much is left in. It is worthwhile as a title check, however, because you can be sure that the company has gone over the entire chain of title with a fine-tooth comb.

The time to complain about a lack of coverage is *before* you purchase the property and acquire the policy; with your attorney's help, you can get some coverage back in. The insurer will never change it later when you complain that your problem isn't covered.

Squatters and adverse possession

You can lose your land to "squatters" or trespassers. Although the details vary from state to state, the essentials are the same: squatters can take by what's called "adverse possession." This means that, when certain requirements are met, someone who came on the land *illegally* in the first place cannot be thrown off.

Generally, a person acquiring land by this adverse possession must have taken possession without the consent of the owner, have been there openly and notoriously, and have remained there continuously for a certain period of time. I remember these elements of adverse possession as COHAN—continuous, open, hostile, adverse, notorious.

In most states, the length of time for this is five years or more. Some states add the requirement that the adverse possessor must have paid the taxes and acted under what appeared to be a right to be on the land. Other states do not have these requirements, which are called "color of title."*

On the same general theory, the public can acquire rights as trespassers by passing over the land for a certain period of time. For instance, if the neighborhood makes a practice of using the corner of your lot as a shortcut and they have been doing it long enough, you cannot then put up a blockade to stop them. You might even have the obligation to keep this path safe for them!

Translation of Exclusive Listing Contract

with Real Estate Agent

In consideration of the services of the hereinafter named real estate BROKER, OWNER hereby lists with said BROKER,

The owner lists his property with the broker with the consideration for the contract being the services of the broker. (These services have been interpreted as the agent's time in showing the property and obtaining prospects as well as the expenses of advertising the property.)

from _____ ,to _____ , 11:59 P.M., the property described above,

The "from _____ ,to_____ , 11:59 P.M." refers to the length of time this contract lasts, the period during which the owner allows the agent to have an exclusive contract. NOTE: You, as owner, can say how long this period is, e.g., thirty, sixty, or ninety days. The broker will, of course, try to get you to agree to the longest period.

and OWNER hereby employs and grants said BROKER the exclusive and irrevocable right to sell the same within said time at the price, terms and conditions herein stated, or at such other price, terms or conditions which may be accepted by OWNER,

The owner agrees the broker has the exclusive right to sell the property for that stated period of time on the terms set out in the contract or on different terms if they turn out to be acceptable to the owner. (The word "irrevocable" in there is misleading because any agency contract *can* be canceled if you're willing to pay the damages done the agent by the cancellation.) and to accept deposits thereon and retain same in BROKER'S trust account, on behalf of OWNER herein, until the closing of, or defeat of, the transaction.

The grammar is dreadful, but the meaning is that the owner agrees that any deposit made on the property by a buyer may be held by the broker in his trust account on behalf of the owner until the owner is paid off at the closing or the deal falls through.

Price to include all items currently fixed and attached to the premises.

The purchase price the owner sets for the property includes "fixtures," which are those things such as carpeting and furnaces physically connected to the property. *Be careful here.* To avoid future trouble, you need to add to this contract in writing what you and the broker agree are meant by "fixtures"; i.e., are items such as drapes and your security system to be included as fixtures?

OWNER hereby agrees to pay said BROKER _____ % of the selling price, plus applicable gross receipts tax, for BROKER'S services,

Okay.

(1) in case of any sale or exchange of same within said listing period: by the undersigned OWNER; the said BROKER; or by any other person,

If the owner, the broker, or anyone else sells the property, the broker still gets the commission.

(2) upon the said BROKER finding a prospective purchaser who is ready, willing and able to complete the purchase as proposed by the OWNER,

If the broker finds a prospective purchaser ready and willing to complete the purchase at the price and terms the owner has established, but the owner reneges, the broker still gets his fee.

or (3) if at any time within _____ days following the termination of this contract, the said property is sold or exchanged to any person who, prior to the termination of this contract, either inspected or was shown the property during the term of this contract and whose name BROKER submitted to OWNER in writing or who was personally introduced to OWNER as a prospective purchaser, provided, however, that this subparagraph (3) shall not apply if OWNER has again listed said property with another BROKER, following the termination of this contract and prior to the sale or exchange.

The broker still gets his fee if, after the contract ends, the property sells to someone to whom the broker had previously shown the property and whose name he had furnished the owner in writing. The number of days this clause shall be in effect is left open for you to fill in. This provision does not apply if the property was listed with a different broker prior to the sale.

In the event of forfeiture of deposits made by a prospective purchaser, the sums received shall be divided between the BROKER and the OWNER, one-half thereof to said BROKER, but not to exceed the fee agreed upon herein, and the balance to the OWNER.

If a prospective purchaser forfeits his deposit, the deposit is divided equally between the owner and the broker unless the broker's half would be more than his agreed commission. If that is the case, the owner gets any sums over that amount.

Cancellation of this listing can only be made with the consent of the listing BROKER.

The English is clear, but the law is wrong. "Cancellation" is the same as the "irrevocable" discussed above; the contract *can* be canceled at any time if you're willing to pay the broker's out-of-pocket expenses and other damages. Of course, if the cancellation is by mutual agreement, nothing is owed the broker.

The OWNER agrees to refer to the BROKER all inquiries from other brokers, salespersons and prospective purchasers received during the term of this contract. OWNER warrants no other listing contracts are in effect on this property and authorizes BROKER to place a sign on the property.

The first sentence is English. The second sentence means you're in trouble if you've already given a listing to a different broker.

The OWNER agrees that the BROKER shall not be liable for damages of any kind occurring to the premises, unless such damage shall be caused by the negligence of the BROKER.

This recites what the law is anyway. The broker is not liable for any damages to the property unless they're his fault.

Mineral, water, and timber rights, if any, of OWNER on said property will pass coincident with said property, unless specifically excluded in this contract. No representation of any value is made by reason of this paragraph.

The owner is again agreeing to what the law is: that unless he reserves mineral, water, and timber rights, they pass along with the other rights he is selling.

Evidence of merchantable title shall be in the form of 1. _____ new owner's policy of title insurance issued by a responsible title company, furnished and paid for by _____ , or 2. _____ abstract of title certified to date of closing of the transaction; furnished and paid for by_____ .

Good and merchantable title (see pages _____) shall be by means of either title insurance or an abstract (see page ___). Normally, these are paid for by the seller, but here the contract allows you to insert whether it's the seller or the buyer who pays.

The OWNER and BROKER, by their respective signatures hereon, agree that they will not discriminate against any prospective purchaser because of race, creed, religion, color, age, sex or country of national origin.

Okay.

OWNER certifies, that to the best of OWNER'S knowledge, the information herein, regarding said property, is correct and that property will be conveyed in the same condition, reasonable wear and tear excepted, as of the date of this agreement. I/we hereby certify that I/we have read and understand this contract and have received a copy of same. Seller authorizes Lien Holder to reveal loan information to the BROKER.

The owner makes himself responsible for the accuracy of the information in the contract and that he's not going to tear up the house any more than when he signed the contract, He once again agrees to the existing law: that signing the contract means he's read it and has received a copy of it, Finally, he allows the lienholder to give the information about his loan to the broker.

Contract of Sale Translated

THIS AGREEMENT, made this _____ day of _____ 19__ between undersigned SELLER(S) and undersigned PURCHASER(S) WIT-NESSETH: SELLER(S) agree(s) to sell and convey and PURCHASER(S) agree(s) to purchase upon terms and conditions hereinafter set out, the following described real estate in county of _____ state of _____. Type of Property: _____

Address:_____

Legal Description: _____

By this contract, on the stated date, the sellers agree to sell and the purchasers agree to buy the property at the stated address and according to the legal description.

Price to include all items currently fixed and attached to the premises including, but not limited to the following: electrical, plumbing, heating, cooling and ventilation systems and their fixtures; built-in appliances; fire, smoke and security systems and their devices, water conditioning system (if owned by SELLER(S). The SELLER(S) certifies these aforementioned items will be in good working condition at time of closing. SELLER(S) further agree(s) that, at the time of closing, the lawn and landscaping, window and porch shades, venetian blinds, storm windows, storm doors, screens, curtain rods, drapery rods, TV antennas, mirrors, floor coverings, awnings, wall-to-wall carpeting,

_____

_____

will be in the same condition, reasonable wear and tear excepted, as of the date of this agreement; provided, however, that the following fixtures of a permanent nature are to be excluded from the sale:

_____

The price includes the fixtures* listed, leaves a place for other items buyer may be demanding, and gives the seller a place to *exclude* items that would normally be called "fixtures" and pass with the property. Then the seller promises that none of them will be in a different condition than on the date of this contract.

NOTE: Scratch out the phrase "including, but not limited to" because this list is exactly what you do want the sale limited to; you want to prevent any future arguments that something else was to be considered a fixture.

NOTE ALSO: this is another document not writ in stone, and therefore in your bargaining you can certainly cross out any item in that list which you don't want to pass with the property.

1. The purchase price is $_____to be paid as follows:

(a) $_____ earnest deposit to be escrowed with BROKER on behalf of the SELLER(S). Any funds paid by the PURCHASER(S) shall be deposited in BROKER'S trust account.

(b) $_____ total down payment including earnest deposit.

(c) $_____ balance as follows: To be secured by a new mortgage for years. Conventional mortgage will be closed at prevailing rate of interest. FHA and/or VA mortgage to be closed at the maximum rate of interest allowable by FHA and/or VA unless otherwise committed. PURCHASER(S) will make diligent effort to obtain said mortgage and will make application for mortgage within _____ days.

Should PURCHASER(S) be unable to obtain a mortgage financing commitment by _____ , 19___ , all earnest deposit, less cost of credit report, shall be returned to PURCHASER(S) within five (5) days of said date and this agreement shall be terminated.

This almost sounds like English, supplying a blank for the total purchase price, followed by:

(a) a blank to fill in the amount which is offered by buyer (or acceptable to seller) as "earnest" money customary to bind the bargain, and which will be held in the broker's trust account pending a final contract;

(b) a blank to fill in the *total* down payment, including the earnest money; and

(c) a blank to fill in the balance and how long it will take to pay off this balance. *Caveat*: the purchaser is agreeing the financing will be by way of a *new* mortgage.

NOTE: The last paragraph gives the purchaser an out if he can't obtain financing, as we've discussed.

2. Subject to such conditions as may be herein set out, upon full compliance of the agreement to be performed by PURCHASER(S), SELLER(S) to convey title by statutory general warranty deed to PURCHASER(S);
Legal Name(s)_____
Address (for mailing Deed)_____
subject to conservancy district liens, zoning ordinances, patent reservations, easements and restrictive covenants, if any, of record.

When the purchasers have performed their part of the bargain with the exception of some special proviso, the sellers agree to turn over the title by means of a general warranty deed.

NOTE: The sellers are making no guarantee as to any of the conditions affecting the property that are listed in those last lines above. Any of those conditions might have a serious impact on the property, so the buyer *must* be sure to check them out.

"Conservancy district liens"—a debt placed against the property based on special regulations, sometimes governmental, for protection of rivers or area. "Zoning" you know but check it out: you could be prevented from having signs, an excess of cats, a pet pig, giving a hair cut, running a B&B, etc. "Patent reservations"—a variety of possibilities granted by the king or government. "Easements"—a right to pass over your land, such as electric wires, or the neighbor's road. "Restrictive covenants"—look out!—can affect what you do with and to your property, the sale thereof, and how you build your house—to just name a few.

NOTE ALSO: Supposedly the buyer is here warned off only if the conditions are "*of record.* " However, they might not be "of record" for this piece of property, e.g., zoning, and some might not be of record at all, For the safety of both buyer and seller, this ambiguous phrase should be cleaned up. It's not clear if "of record" modifies the entire "Subject to" list or only "restrictive covenants."

3. It is agreed that closing costs in connection with this transaction shall be paid as follows, or as shown on the Closing Costs/Prepaid Items Addendum attached hereto and made a part hereof:_____

4. Rents, taxes, and other items where applicable and payable on the above described property shall be prorated between the parties through (date) _____19___

5. Closing Date: _____ 19___ . SELLER(S) agree(s) to give possession of the premises to PURCHASER(S) on _____19___, Time _____ AM/PM.

Okay.

6. PURCHASER(S) declare(s) that PURCHASER(S) (is/are) purchasing said property upon PURCHASER(S) own examination and judgment and not by reason of any representation made to PURCHASER(S) by SELLER(S) or agent for SELLER(S) as to its condition, size, location, value, future value, income therefrom or as to its production. PURCHASER(S) further accept(s) property in present condition including but not limited to, roof, all plumbing, electrical and all mechanical equipment. BROKER herein is not in any way responsible for the condition of the property and in no way warrants same.

Paragraph 6 protects the sellers (as well as the real estate agent) by stating that the buyers are relying on their own examination of the property and their own judgment and not on any representations, as listed, by the sellers.

The purchasers are also here agreeing that—whatever their condition may be—they accept the roof and plumbing, electrical and mechanical equipment as is.

NOTE: The entire paragraph 6 is for the purpose of eliminating any claim as to breach of warranty in relation to the physical condition of the property. Your warranty deed does not have anything to do with this.

7. Time is of essence. If any payment or any other condition hereof is not made, tendered or performed by either the SELLER(S) or PURCHASER(S) as herein provided, then this contract, at the option of the party who is not in default, may be terminated by such party, in which case the non-defaulting party may recover such damages as may be proper. In the event of such default by the SELLER(S) and the PURCHASER(S) elect(s) to treat the contract as terminated, then all payments made hereon shall be returned to the PUR-

CHASER(S). In the event of such default by the PURCHASER(S) and the SELLER(S) elect(s) to treat the contract as terminated, then all payments made thereunder shall be forfeited and retained on behalf of the SELLER(S). In the event, however, the non-defaulting party elects to treat this contract as being in full force and effect, the non-defaulting party shall have the right to an action for specific performance and damages.

The phrase "time is of the essence" is taken from legal opinions where the court found one party had breached the contract by "acting too slowly when the facts demonstrated that time was of the essence." Here it means nothing at all. If one party was claiming the other defaulted because of the amount of time taken to perform, a court would still have to look at whether or not the amount of time lapsing was unreasonable or whether in this particular sale time was indeed of the essence.

The next part of the above paragraph is using legal jargon to get across the idea that if the seller defaults, the purchaser gets his money back, while if the buyer defaults, then the seller can keep what's paid in, treating it as damages.

Finally, the last lines of that paragraph 7 kindly allow the non-defaulting party to bring a lawsuit for "specific performance* and damages"; he could do so, anyway. Specific performance means you must *perform* what you promised. Here it means that if you're the seller, you must go ahead and sell; if the buyer, you must complete the purchase.

8. This instrument comprises the entire understanding and agreement of the PURCHASER(S) and SELLER(S) on the subject matter herein contained and shall be binding upon and inure to the benefit of the PURCHASER(S) and SELLER(S), their heirs, executors, administrators, successors and assigns.

This written contract is the whole contract and continues in force whether or not one or the other dies.

Leasing: An Overview

Lease Defined

A lease can be any contract that creates the relationship of landlord and tenant. By this contract, the person with title and right to possession gives up possession or use to the "tenant." Since the lease is a contract, there must be consideration; this is usually rent on the tenant's side. The other side's consideration is allowing occupancy of her premises. (See types listed below.)

An interesting point is that since a landlord gives up the right to possession of the property, he then has no more right than any trespasser to come onto the land or into the dwelling during the period of the lease. That's why most formal leases set out specific provisions allowing the landlord entry under certain conditions or for inspection of the premises.

At common law, a lease was considered as virtually a sale of the premises for the term of the lease. Many courts now say that a lease is the sale of a kind of interest in land, that interest being considered personal property, like the sale of any "thing"; other courts find that a lease is not much more than a contract and, therefore, controlled only by contract law. Here I will discuss the basic three types of land possession, because, although law books commonly list four, the distinctions between two of them are so technical that they are of little use to anyone other than an attorney.

1. Naked possession with no lease or contract is called a "tenancy at sufferance." Here the tenant has no rights, including no right to any notice of eviction. This kind of possession usually comes about when a lease has expired and the tenant stays on and "holds over."

2. The next step up is a "tenancy at will," wherein there is no time set as to length of occupation or for regular payments of rent. NOTE, HOWEVER: You might very well be involved in this kind of casual renting where there is no formal lease, yet you must be given the same amount of notice as what has evolved as your customary rent-paying period; in other words, if you are paying rent every thirty days, then the landlord has to give you thirty days' notice of eviction from the date of your last payment.

3. Periodic, or year to year. This is one of our legal cuties in that "year to year" doesn't necessarily mean year to year at all. If you are leasing for a set period of time, whether it's from week to week or month to month, this is called a "periodic tenancy" or an "estate from year to year." This kind of lease continues until you are given proper notice as

set out in the terms of the lease. The notice to quit can't come before the end of a proper period.

Remember that if you lease for a year or a month, it is exactly that and not one day over. For instance, a lease for a year starting January 1 does not go to the next January 1 but to December 31.

NOTE: Statutes and ordinances can change the amount of time required to give the tenant notice of eviction.

Q I moved out of my apartment at the end of the lease, but the landlord says that since I didn't turn over the keys, I owe another month's rent. Do I have to pay?

A Under common law, the keys are symbolic, and if you keep the keys, then you have symbolically kept possession of the premises and, therefore, owe rent. NOTE, HOWEVER: your state statutes may change this technical rule, so be sure to check them.

Q We are renting trailer space by the month. The owner just said we had to get out. Can he do that to us without any reason?

A Yes. If your lease does not state that it will continue for any set period, the landlord has the right to end the lease, no excuse required. In your case this would call for only one month's notice.

Q In his will, my father left me the house for my lifetime. Can I rent it out?

A Yes.

Q My brother-in-law and I have been arguing about ninety-nine-year leases.

A Since I don't know the details of your argument, I'll just say that ninety-nine-year leases have been gaining steadily in popularity— mostly in commercial transactions. If you are contemplating signing such a lease, my suggestion is to see an attorney.

Q I leased a house for a year, and the lease ran out a month ago but I'm still here. Do I keep paying rent?

A At common law, when the lease period ends, the landlord has no duty to give the tenant notice prior to eviction and the tenant has no duty to pay rent. In most states, that is changed by statute, and the landlord would probably have to give notice and also bring a court action to evict you. Some states have three days notice and then the sheriff is notified.

If you want to remain in the house, I suggest you make arrangements with your landlord either on the old terms or by negotiating what you might want for new terms. Whatever the statutes may be in your jurisdiction, you don't want to risk an eviction, which would be inconvenient at the least. Also, if you want to stay on, I suggest you continue paying rent so that the landlord would not be able to bring an action on the basis of nonpayment.

Lease purchase or lease option

NOTE: You will find a separate section on options generally later in this chapter.

There are all sorts of creative new ways to deal with property outside of the traditional buying or renting; these include the lease purchase and lease option.

In the *lease purchase* you have contracted to buy the property—price, terms, and all. The agreement can be drawn up so that you rent the property for a certain length of time, with all or part of the rent payments going toward the down payment or purchase price. Then, at the end of the predetermined length of time, title shall be transferred.

There are no limits to the variations that can be arranged between landlord and tenant/buyer and seller. It is simply a matter of making up your own contract rather than following a form. For instance, you could arrange for the lease payments to count toward the purchase price with a balloon payment at closing.

In the *lease option*, the lessee (recipient of a lease) has a right to purchase the property for a set price at some time in the future. Her mind isn't yet made up.

One thing to be careful about here is that the courts have been firm in holding that either the price to be paid for the property must be set or there must be a specific formula for determining what the price will be. Another point is that although there must be consideration for the seller to keep a naked option* open, this is no problem in the lease option because the lease itself is sufficient consideration.

Sometimes the lessee, the prospective buyer, can exercise the option any time he wishes. However, the contract is more clearly enforceable if a time is set within which the prospective buyer must make up his mind.

A lease option can be of benefit to both the seller and the buyer. The buyer is not forced to come up with the purchase price at once and is able to plan for a fixed amount in the future. The seller has the benefit of being able to depreciate the rented property, which can be very important financially.

The main thing to remember in any sort of creative property transactions (where you are tailor-making your own provisions) is to go back to the basic contract stipulation: your contract must be sufficiently specific for a court to enforce. This means that what you are acquiring, when you are acquiring it, and the terms under which you are acquiring it must be clearly set out.

Your lease option should contain:

1. *The financial arrangements*: the term of the lease and amount of rent, as well as the future purchase price (or formula therefor) and provisions as to payment and interest.

2. A requirement for *recording* both the lease and the option.

3. A requirement for *merchantable title** by means of an abstract or title insurance.

Another arrangement would be a lease with a right of first refusal. This is not an option but gives the tenant a right to buy the property before anyone else, should the landlord decide to sell. (The price cannot exceed a bona fide third-party offer.)

Landlord and tenant—rights and duties

General

At common law, leases were treated in the same way as goods in the marketplace, carrying with them that warning *caveat emptor*. Many modern courts, whether using the lease-as-personal-property idea or holding that a lease is basically just another contract, have decided that a lease carries an implied warranty of fitness for intended use. (Implied warranties are discussed fully in Chapter IV.)

If a court is going to imply that a lessor has made a promise that leased premises are fit for intended use, what is that use? Habitation. Therefore, the courts taking this position are saying that the premises must be fit to live in or else the landlord has breached the warranty.

Once you get to this point, you are faced with the biggest question of all: how bad must the condition of the premises be for a court to say they aren't habitable? The answer varies from one jurisdiction to another. Rat and bug infestations will usually qualify the place as uninhabitable, while minor problems will not. It's all that space between the two extremes where there's no set answer unless the situation has already been considered by the courts in your jurisdiction.

A similar result is reached by courts taking a more traditional view, saying, instead of breach of implied warranty, that unlivable conditions can create a "constructive eviction."* "Constructive eviction" is one more legal fiction because there has been no real eviction; instead, the courts are saying that conditions are such that the results are the same as if the tenant has actually been dispossessed.

Q Yesterday a rat jumped up on my baby's crib in our apartment. I called the landlord, and he said that he was just in the business of renting apartments, not guaranteeing what went on inside. I'm frightened but don't have the money to move. What should I do?

A Since you're without the money to move, you're probably without funds to pay an attorney. Check the phone book to see if your town has a legal aid service and, if not, then call the local bar association to find out who represents the indigent.

In many states you don't have to pay the rent until the landlord has corrected the situation. Also, a number of courts say that you can sue the landlord for damages once you have given him notice of these conditions and a reasonable time to alter them.

Not only states but cities have so many laws on the books dealing with "tenants' rights" that you should certainly check out legal assistance, as above, or at least call your local housing authority. The landlord may very well be breaking the law by not dealing with the rat situation. However, the traditional view has been that the tenant's duty to pay rent does not depend on the condition of the premises, so *find out before you refuse payment.*

Q We rented a furnished cottage at the beach, but were driven out the first night by bedbugs. I've told the owner I want back the deposit we had to pay, but he refuses, saying that the deposit was to hold the space and doesn't have anything to do with whether or not we could stay there. Who's right?

A It's a fine line when you're talking about an advance deposit. The conservative view would side with the landlord, but in a similar case dealing with a suit to recover advance rent, the court found the situation to be an "outrage" that should not be sanctioned by the law.

Q I was just flabbergasted when the landlord sent his property tax notice on to me. He said since I have the house, I have the taxes. Is this true?

A Usually not. Unless you agreed to pay taxes in the lease, the landlord gets to keep the privilege of paying the property taxes.

Q After the house I was renting burned, the landlord's attorney called me and said it was up to me to repair the fire loss. I said that couldn't be, that it was the landlord's house, not mine. The attorney said that the terms in the lease called for me to make all necessary repairs and return the premises in the same condition. Does this add up to my having to rebuild?

A Yes. When the lease has both provisions—repair and delivering the premises in the same condition as when you leased—the rule is that the tenant must restore the premises in case of destruction by fire.

See an attorney! This is a harsh rule, and if a court finds any way around it in the language of the lease, *and* if the fire was not your fault, you will not be forced to rebuild. Who benefits from the insurance?

Pay rent

In the old English common law, rent had to be paid before sunset on the day due. The tenant owed that rent even if the landlord had failed to keep up his end of the bargain, such as making repairs. On the other side, the landlord could not easily cut off the tenant's rights for simple nonpayment of rent.

In the case of nonpayment, the landlord either had to go through a lengthy technical process aptly named "distress" or to "attach" the tenant's personal property (hold it pending payment of the debt due). A close relative of this today is the old innkeeper's lien, which gives her a right to hold the luggage and belongings of a hotel guest who skips out without paying.

Much of the old law has been changed by innumerable statutes and ordinances. However, even today a tenant wades in murky waters when he arbitrarily decides to refuse to pay the rent because of some action (or lack of action) of the landlord, while, at the same time, the landlord must be careful about how and why he goes about evicting the tenant.

Q Our rented home burned, and besides the terrible loss of our personal things, now the landlord says we must keep on paying rent until the end of the lease. I say this is fantastically ridiculous. Who is right?

A Historically, the landlord is. This rule is applied to leased houses, but not to apartments. See an attorney! There may be something to the contrary in your lease or in the laws or decisions in your state. Harsh common-law rules such as this one have usually been changed.

Q I was just a little late in paying my rent. Now I receive a notice of eviction! Help!

A I need to see your lease.

1) If there's a grace period or even provisions for a "late fee," I'd say the latter implies you can be a few days late. (Of course, I don't know what you mean by "a little late.")

2) Under common law,* the landlord had to give you as much notice as the length of the rent period.

3) Under statutes, you're often allowed some time to "cure the defect" such as nonpayment.

4) Bad news. Many states have statutes whereby you can be physically ejected after, say, a 3-day notice to pay.

Q We've found a place we like better than where we are. We have 9 months left on a year's lease. If we just move out and let the landlord keep the damage deposit, she doesn't have anything to squawk about, does she? And anyway we don't owe those future payments!

A She can "squawk about" non-payment! In a clear-cut case like yours, the contract is breached and the landlord can take you to court for the payments you'll owe and any damages. And, yes, you do owe those future payments now by law, probably statute, and a doctrine called "anticipatory breach of contract." This latter means that one's actions now show the contract will be broken in the future.

Upkeep or repairs

One practical note not mentioned in the preceding discussion is that, whether you are the landlord or tenant, you should walk through the premises to be leased before the lease is signed. Together, make a list of every spot, scratch, or other defect, and then you both sign it. This is of primary importance to avoid trouble later when the tenant moves out.

Along the same lines as above, it is important to note that there have been rapidly increasing numbers of suits by tenants against landlords for return of the "damage deposit." Also some state statutes now carry a substantial penalty against the landlord if she wrongfully withholds return of that deposit. In the old days, a tenant never saw his damage deposit again.

Specifically as to repair, historically the landlord has no duty to keep up the premises after the tenant takes possession. In those cases, the landlord was liable for injuries on the leased premises only if he did the repairs negligently or concealed defects.

NOTE: The landlord is liable for injuries caused by an unsafe condition on those parts of the premises over which he retains control, such as hallways, stairways, and sidewalks.

In case of injury caused by defects in or around leased premises, see an attorney. An increasing burden is being placed on the landlord, so you need to know where the law stands in your state.

Q I've been trying to organize the other tenants in the building to join me in a suit against our landlord because the whole place is in such a bad condition not any single one of us could fix it. What luck do you think we would have?

A There have been many suits comparable to yours in the last few years. In one, where the landlord sued for nonpayment, the court found that the tenants had shown that the landlord was in violation of several provisions of the housing code and found that that code was part of the contract. It concluded that the tenants' obligation to pay the rent was dependent upon the landlord's performance of this obligation, so the landlord lost.

Q When I was cooking dinner last night in my apartment, the stove exploded and I had to be treated for burns. Is it the landlord's fault?

A Usually your action would be against the manufacturer if the stove was defective, but there was an exploding-stove case where the court gave judgment in favor of the plaintiff tenant and against the defendant landlord. Your answer might depend upon whether the landlord had been notified there was a problem, and then failed to fix it or fixed it improperly.

Q Our lease doesn't say anything about repairs one way or another, but our landlord has always been good about keeping the place up. The trouble is, he undertook to replace some linoleum in the kitchen and the way it was put in caused me to trip and fall. Is the landlord responsible for my doctor bills?

A Yes. Even though the landlord had not contracted to make the repairs, once he did so *negligently*, he would be liable.

Q I fell down the apartment stairs because my heel caught in a tear in the carpeting. Can I collect damages from the landlord?

A Probably. The hallway and stairs are normally under the landlord's control, and he's responsible for injuries caused by his failure to make repairs. Remember, though, the landlord must have had a chance to find out about the defect in time to repair it. The same goes for conditions such as ice on the sidewalk or too dim a light in a corridor.

Q When I leaned against the railing around the balcony on my apartment, it gave way and I fell. I broke my ankle. Will I win if I sue my landlord for damages?

A Whether or not the law will be in your favor depends on the answer to additional questions: (1) What does your lease say about repairs? (2) If the landlord was obligated to make these repairs under the terms of the lease, did he have notice and sufficient time to repair the railing? (3) If the landlord did not have this obligation in the lease, was the balcony under the landlord's control or yours? (4) Most basic of all, what was the nature of the defect that caused the railing to break?

Lease Translated

The following lease is standard "boiler plate" (repeatedly turned out for everyone, not tailored to a specific situation) and is used for both residential and commercial leases. If you're offered one of these leases and told, "Sign here," remember you have a right to negotiate and strike out.

This standard lease uses the words "Lessor"* and "Lessee"* throughout. "Lessor" is the one renting out, turning over possession and control of the premises; "Lessee" is the one receiving them, the tenant.

LEASE

This Indenture, made this ____ day of _____ ,19___ ,by and between_____ hereinafter, whether singular or plural, masculine, feminine, or neuter, designated as "Lessor," which expression shall include Lessor's heirs, executors, administrators, assigns, and successors in interest, and_____ hereinafter, whether singular or plural, masculine, feminine, or neuter, designated as "Lessee," which expression shall "include all Lessees, jointly and severally, and shall include Lessee's heirs, executors, administrators, assigns, and successors in interest, WITNESSETH:

The agreement, made on the ___ day of _____, 19___ is between the lessor and the lessee, under the following terms: . . .

The word "Indenture" is used to mean "contract" or "agreement," but is actually misused because the original meaning was "deed."

You can ignore all those singulars and plurals and assigns and successors in interests because they are used to attempt to make the lease binding upon the transfer of rights on the death of one party, and to make lawyers feel more secure. You're not agreeing to anything not already the law.

I. DEMISE OF PREMISES. Lessor, for and in consideration of the covenants and agreements herein contained to be kept and performed by Lessee, Lessee's heirs, executors, administrators, assigns, and successors in interest, and upon the terms and conditions herein contained, does hereby let, lease, and demise to Lessee the following-described premises situated at _____in the County of _____ State of _____ to-wit: _____

Don't take the heading "Demise of Premises" to mean "death" of the premises. Actually, "demise" is a legal word, here meaning "lease"—and I don't know why it didn't simply say "lease."

The translation of the above is simply that the lessor, for the consideration of lessee's promises, leases the premises described to the lessee.

"Let, lease, and demise" is another illustration of lawyers always speaking in triplicate.

II. TERM OF LEASE. The term of this Lease shall be for a period of _____ (___) (months) years, beginning on the _____ day of _____ 19 ___ , and ending on the _____ day of _____, 19___.

Okay.

III. RENT, Lessee, for and in consideration of this Lease and the demise of the said premises by Lessor to Lessee, hereby agrees and covenants with Lessor to pay as rent for the said premises, without notice or demand, the sum_____Dollars ($_____) in the following manner, to-wit:

Lessee agrees to pay the amount of rent stated and for that period of time.

IV. USE OF PREMISES. Lessee, for and in consideration of this lease and the demise of the said premises by Lessor to Lessee, hereby agrees and covenants with Lessor to use and occupy the said premises for the purpose of _____ and for no other purpose without first obtaining the written consent of Lessor therefor; to conform and comply with all applicable municipal, state, and federal ordinances, laws, rules, and regulations in using the said premises; and not to use or suffer to be used the said premises in any manner in contravention of any applicable municipal, state, or federal ordinances, laws, rule, or regulation, or so as to create any nuisance, or so as to tend to increase the existing rate of fire insurance for the said demised premises.

Lessee agrees to use the premises for the stated purpose or get the lessor's consent in writing should there be a change in purpose.

Also, the lessee agrees not to use the premises for an illegal purpose, or create a nuisance, or increase the fire hazard.

V. CONDITION OF PREMISES AND REPAIRS. Lessee, for and in consideration of this Lease and the demise of the said premises, hereby agrees and covenants with Lessor that Lessee has examined the said premises prior to the execution hereof, knows the condition thereof, and acknowledges that Lessee has received the said demised premises in good order and condition, and that no representation or warranty as to the condition or repair of the said premises has been made by Lessor, and, at the expiration of the term of this Lease, or any renewal or extension thereof, Lessee will yield up peaceably the said premises to Lessor in as good order and condition as when the same were entered upon by Lessee, loss by fire or inevitable accident, damage by the elements, and reasonable use and wear excepted; that Lessee will keep the said premises in good order and repair during the term of this Lease, or any extension or renewal thereof, at Lessee's own expense and will repair and replace promptly any and all damage, including damage to glass, that may occur from time to time; that Lessee hereby waives any and all right to have such repairs or replacements made by Lessor or at Lessor's expense; and that, if Lessee fails to make such repairs and replacements promptly, or, if such repairs and replacements have not been made within fifteen (15) days after the occurrence of damage, Lessor may, at Lessor's option, make such repairs and replacements, and Lessee hereby agrees and covenants to repay the cost thereof to Lessor on demand.

Watch out for this one. If you are the lessee, you are here agreeing to accept the premises in the condition they're in, as well as affirming that lessor hasn't made any promises or warranties as to the condition. Moreover, you are promising to return the premises in good order when the lease expires, but are not responsible for damages by fire, inevitable accident, or storm.

NOTE: You are also here, as lessee, promising to take care of any damages or needed repairs at your own expense and specifically give up any right to demand that repairs or replacements be made by the lessor. Furthermore, if you fail to make the repairs promptly, then the lessor may do it himself and you are responsible for his costs. Negotiate this, too.

VI. LIABILITY OF LESSOR. Lessee, for and in consideration of this Lease and the demise of the said premises, hereby agrees and covenants with Lessor that Lessor shall not be liable for any damage to persons or property arising from any cause whatsoever, which shall occur in any manner in or about the said premises, and Lessee hereby agrees to indemnify and save harmless Lessor from any and all claims and liability for damage to persons or property arising from any cause whatsoever, which shall occur in any manner in or about the said premises. Further, Lessee hereby agrees and covenants with Lessor that Lessor shall not be liable for any damage to the said demised premises, or to any part thereof, or to any property or effects therein or thereon, caused by leakage from the roof of said premises or by bursting, leakage, or overflowing of any waste pipes, water pipes, tanks, drains, or stationary washstands or by reason of any damage whatsoever caused by water from any source whatsoever, and Lessee hereby agrees and covenants to indemnify and save harmless Lessor from any and all claims and liability for any damage to the said demised premises, or to any part thereof, or to any property or effects therein or thereon.

Be careful here, too. If you are the lessee, you are agreeing that if any person or thing is damaged because of the condition of the property, *you are the only one responsible,* not the lessor; and *if the lessor should be sued, you will reimburse him for any costs.*

NOTE: In the last half of that paragraph, you, the lessee, are agreeing that the lessor is not responsible for any damage to the premises or contents because of a leaking roof, bursting pipes, or any plumbing problems, etc. You also agree to reimburse the lessor if he has to pay out for any claims for damage.

VII. ALTERATIONS, ADDITIONS, AND IMPROVEMENTS. Lessee, for and in consideration of this Lease and the demise of the said premises, hereby agrees and covenants with Lessor that Lessee shall not make, or suffer or permit to be made, any alterations, additions, or improvements whatsoever in or about the said demised premises without first obtaining the written consent of Lessor therefor; provided, however, that such consent, if given, shall be subject to the express condition that any and all alterations, additions, and improvements shall be done at Lessee's own expense and in accordance and compliance with all applicable municipal, state and federal ordinances, laws, rules, and regulations, and that Lessee hereby covenants and agrees with Lessor that in doing and performing such work Lessee shall do and perform the same at Lessee's own expense, in conformity and compliance with all applicable municipal, state, and federal ordinances, laws, rules, and regulations and that no liens of mechanics, materialmen, laborers, architects, artisans, contractors, sub-contractors, or any other lien of any kind whatsoever shall be created against or imposed upon the said demised premises, or any part thereof, and that Lessee shall indemnify and save harmless Lessor from any and all liability and claims for damages of every kind and nature which might be made or judgments rendered against Lessor or against said demised premises on account of or arising out of such alterations, additions, or improvements.

This says that any alterations, etc., can be made only if the lessor gives his written consent and then everything shall be at lessee's expense. It is also the lessee's duty to comply with any applicable laws.

If *anything* causes expense to the lessor, the lessee will pay it and the lessee shall not do anything that lets someone put a lien on the property.

NOTE: A lessee might want to strike out most of this so that there could be bargaining over who would pay what and how much for any charges on the property.

VIII. OWNERSHIP OF ALTERATIONS, ADDITIONS, AND IMPROVE-MENTS. Lessee, for and in consideration of this Lease and the demise of the said premises, hereby agrees and covenants with Lessor that any and all alterations, additions, and improvements, except shelving and movable furniture, made at Lessee's own expense after having first obtained the written consent of Lessor therefor, in accordance with the provisions contained in Paragraph VII, hereof, whether attached to the walls, floors, premises, or not, shall immediately merge and become a permanent part of the realty, and any and all interest of the Lessee therein shall immediately vest in Lessor, and all such alterations, additions, and improvements shall remain on the said premises and shall not be removed by Lessee at the termination of this Lease. The shelving and/or movable furniture, which Lessee is privileged to remove, must be removed by Lessee at Lessee's expense on or before the termination of the Lease.

Here the lessee agrees that anything changed, added to, or improved becomes the *property* of the *lessor* with the generous exception of shelving and movable furniture. If the latter is to be moved, it must be done before the lease ends.

I'd like to watch when any of those additions "shall immediately merge and become a permanent part of the realty. . . ."

IX. ASSIGNMENT AND SUBLETTING. Lessee, for and in consideration of this Lease and the demise of the said premises, hereby agrees and covenants with Lessor that neither Lessee nor Lessee's heirs, executors, administrators, assigns, or successors in interest shall assign this Lease or sublet the said demised premises, in whole or in part, without first obtaining the written consent of Lessor therefor; that no assignment of this Lease or any subletting of the said demised premises, in whole or in part, shall be valid, except by and with the written consent of Lessor first obtained; that the consent of Lessor to any such assignment or subletting shall not operate to discharge Lessee, or any one of them, or Lessee's heirs, executors, administrators, assigns, or successors in interest from their liability upon the agreements and covenants of this Lease, and Lessee, Lessee's heirs, executors, administrators, assigns, and successors in interest shall remain liable for the full and complete performance of all of the terms, conditions, covenants, and agreements herein contained; that any consent of Lessor to any such assignment or subletting shall not operate as a consent to further assignment or subletting or as a waiver of this covenant and agreement against assignment and subletting; and that following any such assignment or subletting, the assignee and/or sublettee shall be bound by all of the terms, conditions, covenants, and agreements herein contained including the covenant against assignment and subletting.

The lessee can*not* sublet the premises unless the lessor agrees in writing.

In this paragraph, the lessee also agrees to remain responsible for everything recited in the lease even though the premises are sublet.

Finally, just because the lessor lets you sublet it once doesn't mean that you can do it anymore.

X. UTILITY AND OTHER CHARGES, Lessee, for and in consideration of this Lease and the demise of the said premises, hereby agrees and covenants with Lessor to pay promptly all utility and other charges of whatsoever kind and nature, including charges for electrical, gas, garbage, sewage, telephone, and other services, which may be incurred in connection with Lessee's use of the said premises, and to save harmless Lessor therefrom.

Pay them.

XI. LESSOR'S RIGHT OF ENTRY AND TO MAKE ALTERATIONS, ADDITIONS, AND IMPROVEMENTS, Lessee, for and in consideration of this Lease and the demise of the said premises, hereby agrees and covenants with Lessor that Lessor, Lessor's heirs, executors, administrators, assigns, agents, attorneys, and successors in interest shall have the right at any time to enter upon the said premises to inspect the same and to make any and all improvements, alterations, and additions of any kind whatsoever upon the said premises, providing such improvements, alterations, and additions are reasonably necessary or convenient to the use to which the said premises are being put at the time, but at no time shall Lessor be compelled or required to make any improvements, alterations, or additions.

Everybody and his brother has the right to inspect the premises at any time. If you're the lessee, I suggest that you change this unlimited right of entry to particular times, such as business hours.

This paragraph also gives the lessor the *right* to make any improvements or repairs, etc., but calls your attention to the fact that he doesn't have to.

XII, TAXES, OTHER ASSESSMENTS, AND INSURANCE. Lessee and Lessor hereby covenant and agree that all taxes and other assessments of whatsoever kind and nature which have been or may be levied upon the said demised premises and upon any alterations, additions, and improvements thereon shall be paid by_____ at the time when the same shall become due and payable, and that all taxes and other assessments of whatsoever kind and nature which have been or may be levied upon the personal property located upon the said demised premises shall be paid by_____ at the time when the same shall become due and payable. Lessee, for and in consideration of this Lease and the demise of the said premises, hereby agrees and covenants with Lessor to carry and maintain in full force and effect during the term of this Lease and any extension or renewal thereof at Lessee's expense public liability insurance covering bodily injury and property damage liability, in a form and with an insurance company acceptable to Lessor, with limits of coverage of not less than $_____ for each person and $_____ in the aggregate for bodily injury or death liability for each accident and $_____for each accident for property damage liability, for the benefit of both Lessor and Lessee as protection against all liability claims arising from the premises, causing Lessor to be named as an additional-named insured on such policy of insurance, and delivering a copy thereof to Lessor. Fire and extended coverage insurance upon all buildings, residences, alterations, additions, and improvements upon the said premises shall be provided for as follows:_____ and fire and extended coverage insurance upon all of the contents and other personal property situated upon the said premises shall be provided for as follows:

Watch out for those first two blanks! It's open as to whether the lessor (as expected) or lessee will pay the property taxes and all assessments.

NOTE: It is the *lessee* who in this lease agrees to carry public liability coverage for bodily injury and property damages—the amounts need to be inserted.

NOTE ALSO: This leaves blank whose responsibility it is to pay for fire and other damage to the premises and personal property.

XIII. HOLDING OVER. Lessee, for and in consideration of this Lease and the demise of the said premises, agrees and covenants with Lessor that no holding over by Lessee after the expiration of this Lease, or any renewal or extension thereof, whether with or without the consent of Lessor, shall operate to extend or renew this Lease, and that any such holding over shall be construed as a tenancy from month to month at the monthly rental which shall have been payable at the time immediately prior to when such holding over shall have commenced and such tenancy shall be subject to all the terms, conditions, covenants, and agreements of this Lease.

This is just a recitation of what the law is as to staying over when the lease ends.

XIV. BANKRUPTCY AND CONDEMNATION.

I'll not translate this one, but just remind you that if you're seeing an attorney about bankruptcy or if the property is being condemned, you'll need legal advice on how it affects your lease.

XV. DESTRUCTION. Lessee, for and in consideration of this Lease and the demise of the said premises, agrees and covenants with Lessor that if at any time during the term of this Lease, or any extension or renewal thereof, the said demised premises shall be totally or partially destroyed by fire, earthquake, or other calamity, then Lessor shall have the option to rebuild or repair the same, provided such rebuilding or repairing shall be commenced within the period of thirty days after notice in writing to Lessor of such destruction or damage, and to rebuild or repair the same in as good condition as they were immediately prior to such calamity. In such case, a just and proportionate part of the rental herein specified shall be abated until such demised premises shall have been rebuilt and repaired. In case, however, Lessor shall within thirty days following notice in writing to him of such damage elect not to rebuild or repair said premises, Lessor shall so notify Lessee and, thereupon, this Lease shall terminate and become null and void.

If the premises are destroyed, the lessor has the option of whether to rebuild or not. If he doesn't rebuild, he must notify the lessee within thirty days and the lessee actually does then get off the hook, with the lease becoming null and void. Be aware that, if this is a business property, the landlord's decision not to rebuild can put you out of business overnight!

XVI. SIGNS.

If you're worried about putting up signs, you're into commercial real estate and shouldn't be using a form. See an attorney.

XVII. TERMINATION. It is expressly understood and agreed between the parties aforesaid, that if the rent above reserved, or any part thereof, shall be behind or unpaid on the day of payment whereon the same ought to be paid as aforesaid, or if default shall be made in any of the covenants or agreements herein contained to be kept by Lessee, Lessee's executors, administrators, assigns, and successors in interest, it shall and may be lawful for the Lessor, Lessor's heirs, executors, administrators, agents, attorneys, assigns, or successors in interest, at Lessor's election to declare said term ended and to re-enter the said premises, or any part thereof, either with or without process of law, to expel, remove, and put out, the Lessee, or any other person or persons occupying the same, using such force as may be necessary in so doing, and to repossess and enjoy the same premises again as in its first and former state, and distrain for any rent that may be due thereon any property belonging to Lessee, whether the same be exempt from execution and distress by law or not, and Lessee in that case hereby waives any and all legal rights which Lessee now has or may have, to hold or retain any such property under any exemption laws now in force in the State, or in any other way; meaning and intending hereby to recognize in Lessor, Lessor's heirs, executors, administrators, assigns, or successors in interest, a valid first lien as provided in the laws of _____upon any and all goods, chattels, and other property belonging to Lessee and located in said premises as security for the payment of said rent and fulfillment of the faithful performance of conditions in the manner aforesaid, anything herein-before mentioned to the contrary notwithstanding. And if at any time said term shall be ended at such election of Lessor, Lessor's heirs, executors, administrators, assigns, or successors in interest, as aforesaid, or in any other way, Lessee, Lessee's heirs, executors, administrators, assigns, or successors in interest, do hereby covenant and agree to surrender and deliver up the above-described premises and property peaceably to Lessor, Lessor's heirs, executors, administrators, assigns, or successors in interest, immediately upon the termination of said term as aforesaid, and if Lessee shall remain in possession of the same ten (10) days after notice of such default, or after the termination of the Lease in any of the ways above named, Lessee shall be deemed guilty of a forcible detainer of said premises under the statute and shall be subject to all the conditions and provisions above named, and the eviction and removal forcible or otherwise, with or without process of law as above stated. And it is further covenanted and agreed by and between the parties hereto that the Lessee shall pay and discharge all costs, attorney's fees, and expenses that shall arise from enforcing the covenants of this indenture by Lessor, Lessor's heirs, executors, administrators, assigns, or successors in interest.

This language makes me ashamed to be an attorney. The first sentence takes an inordinate number of lines to phrase in every conceivable—and some inconceivable—way that any possible legal rights of the lessee shall be done away with if he should be behind in his rent or any part of it. It gives all rights to the lessor, including not having to abide by the law, and even allowing him to attach the lessee's furniture and other property. Lessee may be removed by force!

This paragraph adds, of course, that the lessee agrees to pay any attorney's fees of the lessor, no matter who wins in court.

If you're the lessee, this is a bad paragraph; you should read it closely, go over it with the lessor, and then mutually initial those parts which, I hope, you are going to scratch out. If you're the lessor, the paragraph is just fine.

XVIII. FAILURE TO TERMINATE. Lessee, for and in consideration of this Lease and the demise of the said premises, agrees and covenants, with Lessor that the failure, neglect, or omission of Lessor to terminate this Lease for any one or more breaches of any of the covenants hereof, shall not be deemed a consent by Lessor of such breach and shall not stop, bar, or prevent Lessor from thereafter terminating this Lease, either for such violation, or for prior or subsequent violation of any covenant hereof.

If the lessor doesn't assert his rights at the time of any default, he can do so later if he wants to. Watch out!

The lease ends with the repeated recitation of its being binding on all heirs, executors, etc., and the statement that it is the entire agreement between the parties. I should hope so! NOTE: Most of the issues discussed in this section are part of the Uniform Landlord-Tenant Relations Law, which more and more states are adopting. It is important that you find out if your state has adopted this law and what your rights would be under it.

Options*

An option is an agreement giving one party the right to buy a specific piece of property in the future. Like any contract, an option must have consideration of some kind in order to bind the parties. When the option is part of a lease, as discussed previously, the lease is considered sufficient consideration.

Since an option deals with the sale of land, it must be recorded.

Most courts require that an option either include the specific price for which the property is to be sold or a definite formula for arriving at that price.

An option must sufficiently identify the property to be purchased.

Q Can you hold property for a dollar?

A Yours is one of those "dollar questions" that come up fairly regularly. Usually, when I hear this one, the person asking about "holding property" means an option, and yes, you could buy an option on property for a dollar. As in other contracts, the dollar is not magic; it is simply one kind of consideration that will support a contract.

Mortgages

A mortgage is often the largest credit transaction a person enters into. The reason it's under property law here, and not in the credit chapter of this book, is that a mortgage attaches to realty and is usually considered separately from other credit agreements. A mortgage has special rules, such as those relating to foreclosure, because it is, actually, a conditional conveyance; i.e., title is transferred to the mortgage holder upon the happening of the "condition," which is nonpayment.

A mortgage is one of the most formal of credit agreements because it must be "filed of record."* (When a mortgage or deed of trust is handed to the clerk keeping the "deed book" for her to put in the record of that property, this is called "filing of record.")

The procedure of filing a mortgage is both sensible and important. The record makes it possible for anyone to go to a specific place and find out the status of any parcel of property, including whether there is a mortgage or lien outstanding against that property. The buyer and the mortgage holder are thereby both protected.

A mortgage is a credit agreement wherein the borrower puts up his property as collateral for the money loaned by the mortgage holder. The mortgage is an "encumbrance" on the property, meaning it is a "burden." (A "lien" is also an encumbrance.) If not paid off, the mortgage, lien, or other encumbrance passes along with the title upon sale of the property. The most important difference between a mortgage and a deed of trust is that when the borrower defaults, the mortgage holder must go through a foreclosure with rules to insure fairness set by statutes, while a deed of trust allows the lender to snatch back the property without the protective regulations that control foreclosure. In most states, a defaulting borrower has a year in which he can redeem or, in effect, buy back the property foreclosed against; a person who gives a deed of trust can't do this. The deed of trust is outlawed in a number of states. Some jurisdictions call a "deed of trust" a "contract of sale."

Usually, upon default in making the specified payment on a certain date, the mortgage holder can "accelerate the debt," which makes the entire amount of the loan due immediately instead of as deferred; and if the loan is not paid off then, the mortgage holder can bring a foreclosure action. All of this is governed by state statute. But see also 15 USC § 1635, discussed on page 212 of Chapter VI, "Credit."

Q The savings and loan that has my mortgage has been sending me letters and notices and is now talking about a foreclosure sale. Why can't I just let them have their foreclosure and walk away from the whole deal?

A You can, but you'll be followed by debt if the property sells for less than the amount you owe the creditors. In other words, if you owe $70,000 on the property and it sells for $50,000 at the foreclosure sale, the lender will get a judgment against you for the $20,000 difference.

Q The bank wouldn't accept my mortgage payment. They said this was because it was late, but they were mistaken. My barber says the rule is that now it's the same as if the whole mortgage was paid off and my property is free and clear. Is this true?

A No! I don't know where this notion began, but every now and then, it crops up and somebody tells me that when the lender refuses a payment the entire debt is wiped out. Wrong.

Send a registered letter "return receipt requested," stating that the payment was offered on time and is now re-offered, as protection should the bank attempt to foreclose.

Q When you read about a foreclosure sale taking place on the "courthouse steps," is that really the way it's done?

A Usually, yes.

Q I'm frequently a little late with my mortgage payment and have never had any trouble. Now, this month, I get something in the mail that says across the top "Notice of Acceleration."* What does this mean?

A It means that the mortgage holder is calling the entire amount due, i.e., moving up or accelerating the payment. First, double check to see if you have a grace period for late payment.

The next question would be whether, by accepting your previous late payments, the mortgage holder had set up a pattern whereby you had a "right," so to speak, to make those payments late. Normally *not*. The usual mortgage provisions will have in them words to the effect that allowing one or more defaults does not waive the lender's rights to acceleration.

Acceleration is usually the first step in the process of foreclosing on a mortgage, but see an attorney. There are a number of things you can do, including simply talking to the lender or attempting refinancing.

CHAPTER VI

Credit

INTRODUCTION/HISTORY

Moneylenders have always been with us, and our contempt for usurers was immortalized by Shakespeare's Shylock in *Merchant of Venice*.

The word "usurer" comes from a medieval Latin word meaning payment for the use of money. The states have historically set upper limits on interest rates, and any rates illegally charged in excess of these were called usury. The term is also applied to high, though legal, interest rates.

Credit transactions predated the notion of interest. However, it is in recent times that a society has become so credit-based that it needed legislative protection. People's jobs have been lost and their lives ruined because of erroneous credit reports. Single women have been discriminated against. The pervasive use of abusive collection practices has necessitated the enaction of protective federal and state laws.

Because so many of our daily transactions involve credit, you need to know about this legislation. I have, therefore, begun this chapter with some important aspects of the federal Consumer Credit Protection Act, followed by the Uniform Consumer Credit Code adopted by the states.

i. Federal Consumer Credit Protection (with Truth in Lending Provisions) Title 15 USC section 1601 et seq.*

ii. Uniform Consumer Credit Code

1. Borrowing money
    a. Installment loans with and without collateral or security

       1) Finance charges and disclosures (federal)

       2) "Calling it due" or "acceleration"

   b. Promissory notes

   c. Credit agencies and reports

2. Buying on credit

   a. Credit agreements and disclosure (open-end, revolving, and non-open-end)

   b. Billing and disputes

       1) Your rights as to quality and payment

       2) Billing errors and "paid in full"

   c. "My card is lost!"—unauthorized purchases

3. Collecting

   a. Liens: mechanic's; garageman's; innkeeper's

   b. Repossession and self-help

   c. Collection agencies

   d. If they "turn it over to an attorney"

       1) General

       2) Compromise

       3) Courts and judgments

       4) Execution, attachment, liens, garnishment

4. Bankruptcy: a glimpse in passing

i. Federal Consumer Credit Protection (with Truth in Lending Provisions) Title 15 USC Section 1601 et seq."

The federal Consumer Credit Protection Act, together with its truth in lending provisions, was passed by Congress in 1977 and is an attempt to codify fairness. In credit and lending transactions, at least, it is the ultimate move away from the *caveat emptor* rule of the marketplace.

The law library in your local courthouse is the place to look for a large set of books labeled "United States Code Annotated (USCA)"; the one with "Title 15" on the spine, commencing with Section 1601 (§ 1601), will provide you with the full text of the provisions highlighted here.

Billing and credit card practices

In this section dealing with disclosures, the act defines the word to include the annual percentage rate, the method of determining the finance charge and the balance upon which the finance charge will be imposed. It then goes into the same detail as to the finance charge itself so that you must be provided with all the information necessary to figure out how much of an extra load you'll be carrying on the amount you charge.

You must be informed of interest and service or carrying charges as well as loan fees, fees for investigation of credit reports, and the premiums for any sort of insurance that might be demanded as part of the extension of credit. We are told:

(u) The term "material disclosures" means the disclosure, as required by this subchapter, of the annual percentage rate, the method of determining the finance charge and the balance upon which a finance charge will be imposed, the amount of the finance charge, the amount to be financed, the total of payments, the number and amount of payments, and the due dates or periods of payments scheduled to repay the indebtedness.

The act includes "model disclosure forms," which are supposed to "utilize readily understandable language" so that the debtor will know exactly the cost of any credit. It carries criminal liability for willful and knowing violation.

Right of rescission as to certain transactions 15 USC § 1635

The first part of this section deals with any consumer credit transaction in which the creditor will acquire a *security interest in the borrower's home*. The simplest example of this would be when a person gives a mortgage on his home as collateral for a loan. In this situation, the borrower has a "right to rescind," or call off the deal, until midnight of the third business day following either: the finalization of the transaction; or delivery of the rescission (negating, canceling out the deal) form together with the disclosure forms. The latter proviso means that time doesn't start until the lender has supplied the borrower these forms.

The second part of this same section is something you need to be aware of in order to know your rights. When a debtor calls off the deal, as per above, he is not liable for any finance or other charges:

Within twenty days after receipt of a notice of rescission, the creditor shall return to the obliger [debtor] any money or property given as earnest money, down payment, or otherwise. . . .

The creditor also has to do whatever is necessary to void that mortgage or any other security. There are other rights under the same section.

Open-end consumer credit plans 15 USC § 1637

An open-end credit plan might be a revolving charge account with a department store or the credit furnished by one of the bank card companies. The creditor plans repeated transactions, defines the terms of these transactions, and provides for a finance charge on the unpaid balance. Such a plan is governed by the provisions of this section of the disclosure act. It sets out:

1. the conditions under which a finance charge may be imposed and the time within which credit may be repaid *without a finance charge*;

2. the method of determining the balance upon which a finance charge will be imposed;

3. the method of determining the amount of the finance charge;

4. an explanation, when there is more than one way of computing a finance charge;

5. a notice of any other charges that may be imposed;

6. the debtor must be informed whether the property purchased will be security or collateral, so that, if payments are not made, the property can be taken back, or if some other type of property will be used as security;

7. a statement setting out the debtor's and creditor's responsibilities.

The act details all the points that the creditor must cover in the statement required with each billing cycle.

Transactions other than open-end consumer credit plans 15 USC § 1638

This section is an important grab bag providing you with rights as to kinds of credit other than that charge card.

It's important for you to know that you have rights to specifically defined information about every part of a transaction that includes any sort of financing. You even have the right to have phrases explained to you, as, for example, the meaning of "amount financed," "annual percentage rate," or "total sale price."

This particular section is also quite important in that it regulates an area where consumers experience much trouble: unsolicited mail or telephone purchase orders.

Civil liability 15 USC § 1640

Lookee here! You get *damages* if your creditor is breaking these credit laws. And they can be substantial. For instance, you get whatever damages the creditor caused you *and* twice the amount of any finance charge if your creditor violated your rights.

Truth in Lending: Liability for unauthorized purchases 15 USC § 1643

Pay attention. Here's a biggie that a surprising number of people don't know about—to their detriment. Under Section 1643, a credit card holder can*not* be liable for more than *$50* of unauthorized purchases on his or her card. This is exactly what the act says about your obligation— *and that of the credit card company.*

c) the card issuer gives adequate notice to the cardholder of the potential liability;

d) The card issuer has provided the cardholder with a description of a means by which the card issuer may be notified of loss or theft of the card, which description may be provided on the face or reverse side of the statement required by section 1637(b) of this title or on a separate notice accompanying such statement;

e) the unauthorized use occurs before the card issuer has been notified that an unauthorized use of the credit card has occurred or may occur as the result of loss, theft, or otherwise; and

f) the card issuer has provided a method whereby the user of such card can be identified as the person authorized to use it.

For purposes of this section, a card issuer has been notified when such steps as may be reasonably required in the ordinary course of business to provide the card issuer with the pertinent information have been taken, whether or not any particular officer, employee, or agent of the card issuer does in fact receive such information.

NOTE: You're *not liable* at all if you've given notice *before* unauthorized use occurs.

The next part of this federal disclosure chapter deals with credit advertising. (If you wish to pursue that topic, see the provisions of §1661 through 1665a. of the act.)

Correction of billing errors 15 USC § 1666

This is designed to end the frustration of wondering if there is anyone at the receiving end. If you write within sixty days of the bill and:

1. give your name and account number;

2. inform the creditor there's a mistake in your bill and for how much; and

3. explain why you think so,

then the creditor *must reply* within thirty days and proceed to try to work it out with you.

Garnishment restrictions 15 USC §§ 1671 et seq.

This chapter includes details about garnishment and its mechanics and regulations. Here I'll only comment on the federal restrictions that are the most important for you to know, whether you are an employee or an employer.

First, there is no such verb as "garnishee"—as in "I'll garnishee you!"—nor can garnishment happen without the creditor first getting a judgment against the debtor. The verb is "garnish"; after you get a judgment, you can "garnish" the debtor's wages.

The federal act defines "garnishment" as any legal procedure through which the earnings of any individual are required to be withheld for payment of any debt.

There are exceptions and formulas pertaining to the amount that can be withheld from a paycheck. The *important part* is that no more than 25 percent of the paycheck after deductions can be garnished. This goes up to 50 percent to enforce any support order for spouse or dependent child. Of course, one exception is for any taxes due.

NOTE: It's against the law to fire any employee because of garnishment for any one indebtedness; if the employer violates this, he's liable for a fine up to $1,000 or one year in jail, or both (15 USC §1674).

Credit reporting agencies 15 USC §§ 1681 et seq.

The preface to this section shows that Congress recognizes that "consumer reporting agencies" have "grave responsibilities" and must exercise them "with fairness, impartiality, and a respect for the consumer's rights to privacy."

People have felt, sometimes with good reason, that they were secretly being blackballed, and could not find out by whom; tragedies have occurred. The provisions of this subchapter are meant to remove that threat of serious harm which can be done by an erroneous, or even malicious, credit report on a person.

This subchapter sets out to whom a credit report may be furnished and forbids "reporting of obsolete information," which means anything adverse beyond seven years.

You must be informed if anyone requests an investigative consumer report about you. NOTE ALSO: Every reporting agency must provide you with the nature and substance of *all information* in its files relating to you at your request. Be careful not to overlook the fine print. This may serve as your notice.

Damages again! You have the right to bring a law suit against any credit reporting agency if it breaks those rules on purpose or even if it just doesn't take the care it should. You get any *actual* damages its noncompliance caused you and this time you get to go after *punitive damages,* too! Punitive damages are punishment. The amount is based on how much you need to take away from a credit reporting agency to make it hurt. You can also recover any attorney's fees and costs that you had to incur to enforce this.

Equal credit opportunity 15 USC § 1691

The purpose of this chapter is to make it unlawful for any creditor to discriminate against any applicant:

1. on the basis of race, color, religion, national origin, sex, marital status, or age;

2. because all or part of the applicant's income derives from any public assistance program; or

3. because the applicant is exercising his or her rights.

Debt collection practices 15 USC § 1692

I've reprinted this section of the Act so that you can understand why Congress thought you needed protection:

§ 1692. Congressional findings and declaration of purpose

(a) There is abundant evidence of the use of abusive, deceptive, and unfair debt collection practices by many debt collectors. Abusive debt collection practices contribute to the number of personal bankruptcies, to marital instability, to the loss of jobs, and to invasions of individual privacy.

(b) Existing laws and procedures for redressing these injuries are inadequate to protect consumers.

(c) Means other than misrepresentation or other abusive debt collection practices are available for the effective collection of debts.

If a debt collector is attempting to locate someone, these federal acts set forth in detail how this may be done. The restrictions include that the collector: shall *not* state to others that the consumer owes any debt; shall *not* attempt collection by postcard; shall *not* use anything on any envelope indicating it's in the debt collection business or that the communication relates to a debt; and will hold off if the debt collector knows that the consumer has an attorney.

NOTICE: If you are or may be harassed by a bill collector, you should be aware of the federal law, which attempts to remove as much pain as possible from the process. A debt collector may not communicate with the consumer in connection with the collection of any debt:

1. at any unusual time or place that would be inconvenient to the debtor (this includes no telephone calls or appearances before 8 a.m. or after 9 p.m.); and

2. at all (with exceptions, of course) if the debtor has an attorney; and

3. by calling the debtor at work if there's reason to believe the employer prohibits this kind of call.

It is now forbidden for a collector to harass a debtor's family and associates.

If you notify a debt collector in writing that you do not want any more communications, then that bill collector must cease and desist. It can have no further communication with you except to tell you it's ending its efforts or to notify you that it intends to invoke a specified remedy. An example of the latter would be telling you that the debt is being turned over to an attorney or that you will be sued—not as a threat but as an actuality (§ 1692c.).

Harassment or abuse 15 USC § 1692d.

This is so prevalent, I'll give you the federal list of prohibited conduct:

§ 1692d. Harassment or abuse

A debt collector may not engage in any conduct the natural consequence of which is to harass, oppress, or abuse any person in connection with the collection of a debt. Without limiting the general application of the foregoing, the following conduct is a violation of this section:

(1) The use or threat of use of violence or other criminal means to harm the physical person, reputation, or property of any person.

(2) The use of obscene or profane language or language the natural consequence of which is to abuse the hearer or reader.

(3) The publication of a list of consumers who allegedly refuse to pay debts, except to a consumer reporting agency or to persons meeting the requirements of section 1681a(f) or 1681b(3) of this title.

(4) The advertisement for sale of any debt to coerce payment of the debt.

(5) Causing a telephone to ring or engaging any person in telephone conversation repeatedly or continuously with intent to annoy, abuse, or harass any person at the called number.

(6) Except as provided in section 1692b of this title, the placement of telephone calls without meaningful disclosure of the caller's identity.

The debt collector is breaking federal law if it makes false or misleading statements to the debtor, The following section includes a list of what some of these forbidden misrepresentations might be.

§ 1692e. False or misleading representations

A debt collector may not use any false, deceptive, or misleading representation or means in connection with the collection of any debt. Without limiting the general application of the foregoing, the following conduct is a violation of this section:

(1) The false representation or implication that the debt collector is vouched for, bonded by, or affiliated with the United States or any State, including the use of any badge, uniform, or facsimile thereof.

(2) The false representation of—

(A) the character, amount, or legal status of any debt; or

(B) any services rendered or compensation which may be lawfully received by any debt collector for the collection of a debt.

(3) The false representation or implication that any individual is an attorney or that any communication is from an attorney.

(4) The representation or implication that nonpayment of any debt will result in the arrest or imprisonment of any person or the seizure, garnishment, attachment, or sale of any property or wages of any person unless such action is lawful and the debt collector or creditor intends to take such action.

(5) The threat to take any action that cannot legally be taken or that is not intended to be taken.

(6) The false representation or implication that a sale, referral, or other transfer of any interest in a debt shall cause the consumer to—

(A) lose any claim or defense to payment of the debt; or

(B) become subject to any practice prohibited by this subchapter.

(7) The false representation or implication that the consumer committed any crime or other conduct in order to disgrace the consumer.

(8) Communicating or threatening to communicate to any person credit information which is known or which should be known to be false, including the failure to communicate that a disputed debt is disputed.

(9) The use or distribution of any written communication which simulates or is falsely represented to be a document authorized, issued, or approved by any court, official, or agency of the United States or any State, or which creates a false impression as to its source, authorization, or approval.

(10) The use of any false representation or deceptive means to collect or attempt to collect any debt or to obtain information concerning a consumer.

(11) Except as otherwise provided for communications to acquire location information under section 1692b of this title, the failure to disclose clearly in all communications made to collect a debt or to obtain information about a

consumer, that the debt collector is attempting to collect a debt and that any information obtained will be used for that purpose.

(12) The false representation or implication that accounts have been turned over to innocent purchasers for value.

(13) The false representation or implication that documents are legal process.

(14) The use of any business, company, or organization name other than the true name of the debt collector's business, company, or organization.

(15) The false representation or implication that documents are not legal process forms or do not require action by the consumer.

(16) The false representation or implication that a debt collector operates or is employed by a consumer reporting agency as defined by section 1681a(f) of this title.

This section is becoming similar to one of those television commercials advertising pans or knives that keep telling you there's more to come. Here Congress is still not through with those bill collectors but now defines what falls under the label of "unfair practices":

§ 1692f. Unfair practices

A debt collector may not use unfair or unconscionable means to collect or attempt to collect any debt. Without limiting the general application of the foregoing, the following conduct is a violation of this section:

(1) The collection of any amount (including any interest, fee, charge, or expense incidental to the principal obligation) unless such amount is expressly authorized by the agreement creating the debt or permitted by law.

(2) The acceptance by a debt collector from any person of a check or other payment instrument postdated by more than five days unless such person is notified in writing of the debt collector's intent to deposit such check or instrument not more than ten nor less than three business days prior to such deposit.

(3) The solicitation by a debt collector of any postdated check or other postdated payment instrument for the purpose of threatening or instituting criminal prosecution.

(4) Depositing or threatening to deposit any postdated check or other postdated payment instrument prior to the date on such check or instrument.

(5) Causing charges to be made to any person for communications by concealment of the true purpose of the communication. Such charges include, but are not limited to, collect telephone calls and telegram fees.

(6) Taking or threatening to take any nonjudicial action to effect dispossession or disablement of property if—

(A) there is no present right to possession of the property claimed as collateral through an enforceable security interest;

(B) there is no present intention to take possession of the property; or

(C) the property is exempt by law from such dispossession or disablement.

(7) Communicating with a consumer regarding a debt by post card.

(8) Using any language or symbol, other than the debt collector's address, on any envelope when communicating with a consumer by use of the mails or by telegram, except that a debt collector may use his business name if such name does not indicate that he is in the debt collection business.

The debtor has further rights, which he can investigate, but they will not be dealt with here. This subchapter, like the others under this Title 15, provides for damages if the debt collector violates those preceding sections.

ii. Uniform Consumer Credit Code

In addition to the federal act, discussed above, states can adopt the Uniform Consumer Credit Code, the second version of which was drawn up in 1974. A state would adopt the UCCC to provide its citizens with its laws and therefore would not have to look to the federal government for protection.

The UCCC is not detailed here because it is quite similar to the federal in its attempts to protect credit consumers by such means as limiting the amount on finance charges, requiring disclosure, and providing for rescission of a sale.

NOTE: The UCCC applies only to transactions of $25,000 or less and is intended for individuals or families. Organizations are not protected.

The UCCC takes us beyond that concept of protecting the little old lady in tennis shoes by providing that if a court finds *any* agreement "unconscionable," it may refuse to enforce the contract. The court can also find *parts* of an agreement unconscionable and refuse to enforce those parts.

One important provision of the UCCC requires that if a buyer defaults in her payments, the seller must elect either to take a money judgment or to repossess the security, not both.

Borrowing Money

Installment loans with and without collateral or security

Probably the most popular arrangements for borrowing money are installment loans and promissory notes.

An installment loan divides the debt into portions payable at successive periods as set forth in the loan agreement. This contract should state the amount of each payment, the interest or finance charge, the number of payments, and the duration of the payments. It will normally also include the creditor's rights should the debtor default. Read this part carefully. Before you sign you may be able to insert *debtor's rights* if you do *not* default.

Interest is usually the consideration for the loan agreement. For example, a bank is saying, in effect, "We will charge you 16 percent interest for the use of our money for six months."

An installment loan may be with or without collateral or security. One case defines "collateral"* as some security in addition to the personal obligation of the borrower. Collateral is something of value put up to ensure the debtor's performance so that, if the debtor does not keep his promise to repay, the creditor may fall back upon the collateral as security.

When you hear a reference (as in bankruptcy proceedings) to a "secured" or "unsecured" debt, it means a debt with or without collateral security. "Unsecured" debt rests on nothing but your promise to pay.

Finance charges and disclosures (federal)

Remember that the federal laws also provide protection against lenders and others giving loans.

Since this federal act (Title 15) requires any lender to make clear exactly how much a loan is costing a borrower, it supersedes any state laws to the contrary. This means that unless the federal law itself makes exceptions, it applies everywhere in the country.

The idea behind the federal disclosure act is to prevent a lender or creditor from, for instance, telling you an interest charge and then slipping in more costs under another heading, such as "loan fee" or "service and/or carrying charge."

If the installment payments you are making on a loan are higher than you understood them to be, check to see if your lender has violated 16 USC 1601 (discussed above). If you still have questions, see an attorney.

Q I bought a used car that was advertised at a 9.5 percent interest rate and the installment sales contract didn't have the annual percentage rate in it. Now that I figure out my installment payments, it seems I'm paying 12.5 percent. Can they do that to me?

A No. Failure to enter the annual percentage rate (APR) in the installment sales contract is a violation of both the Uniform Consumer Credit Code and the federal act. You can go after the dealer for damages.

Q We had to hire an attorney because the lender wouldn't release the mortgage even though we rescinded our home improvement loan application within the proper time. Can we get attorney's fees?

A Attorney's fees have been recovered in similar cases.

"Calling it due" or "acceleration"

If your loan agreement has in it any phrase to the effect that "upon default of borrower, creditor shall have the right to accelerate the total amount due," this means that if you miss a payment, your creditor can demand the entire amount be paid immediately. If you are then unable to pay off the entire amount, the creditor can proceed with its legal remedies, which will include forfeiture of your collateral, if any. This same clause of the credit agreement usually contains a reference to "waiver of default," which means that just because you were allowed to make a late payment once, the creditor has *not* given up the right to call it all due at another time.

If you are in default, remember your rights under the federal act as to restrictions on garnishment and debt collection practices (see pages 215 and 216). These are also discussed in more detail later in this chapter. However, there is so much confusion about garnishment, note for right now that any creditor must *first* have a judgment before it can garnish your wages—and then the amount that can be taken is restricted by the federal act and probably by your state laws, too.

Q I got an installment loan to pay for my new car. I missed one payment, and the bank sent me a "Notice of Acceleration." I tried to pay some on it and the bank wouldn't take it. That's not fair! Will they still take my car?

A Probably. It's most likely that when you signed the installment loan papers you agreed that "in case of default," missing that payment, the creditor had the right to call the entire amount due, which is what's meant by the "Notice of Acceleration." Harsh though it is, the bank does not have to accept partial payment.

Go talk to the bank and see if you can work out some arrangement; if you can't, then see an attorney.

Promissory notes

A promissory note is about the same as a formalized IOU. It's a written promise to pay a certain sum of money at a certain time. In legalese, a promissory note is an "unconditional provision in writing made by one person to another, signed by the maker, engaging to pay on demand, or at a fixed or determinable time in the future, a sum certain of money to order or to the bearer."

Credit agencies and reports

These are covered in detail in this chapter, starting on page 216. The main thing to remember is that you do have rights concerning what is reported about your credit standing and to whom it is reported.

If you are turned down on a loan or on an application for credit purchasing, you do have a right to know the reason, to dispute the credit report (and have the dispute recorded), and even to go to court if the agency has either: (1) refused to comply with the federal or state laws; or (2) done so only in such a way as to show it was unreasonably careless. Don't be afraid to make them straighten out your credit report.

That includes noting where a bill was not paid because *the amount was disputed.*

If any of the above has occurred, see a lawyer to invoke your rights.

Q I was fired from my job, can't find a new one, and get an instant "no" anytime I try to borrow money to tide me over. I think it's probably because of some kind of credit report. Is there anything I can do to find out?

A Yes! The federal act (set out in Section i. at the beginning of the chapter) recognizes the actual tragedy caused some people by misleading and/or erroneous credit reports.

Write a letter to each person or organization where you have sought credit, and also to prospective employers who have turned you down for a job, demanding the reason for your rejection. You are entitled to this disclosure under Title 15 USC Sections 1681 et seq. If you are refused, you can bring suit under this act.

NOTE ALSO: If anyone has requested an investigative report on you, the act is violated if you are not informed.

Q I found out I'm getting a bad credit report over a bill I didn't pay because I was disputing it. I can't get the agency to change the report. Is there anything I can do?

A Yes. Write a letter telling the agency that it will owe you damages under the federal act, Title 15 USC Section 1681. Remind them also that, besides damages, you can collect "punitive damages," which are meant as a financial punishment. They often grumble but the reporting agency *must* show you your report.

Buying on Credit

Credit agreement and disclosure (open-end, revolving, and non-open-end)

Be careful here! When you sign an application for credit with a store or credit card company you may not realize what you are agreeing to, and what rights you are waiving. In fact, you probably don't realize that you're most likely signing a contract.

Remember, you have rights to full disclosure as to how much you are paying for the privilege of credit in the form of various charges with a variety of names; and the right not to be discriminated against in the way of credit. But do you know what you have promised? Look out! You may be making a prior agreement that the outfit involved can come into your home and repossess what you have purchased; or that you will pay for attorneys, costs of collection, and court costs if the creditor decides you have failed to make a proper payment, even if it turns out that you, the buyer, were in the right.

Q If you pay your creditors one dollar, they can't touch you, right?

A Wrong! In my thirty years of practice, one thing has remained constant: clients—on their own, or with the assurances of brother-in-law and barber—have frequently informed me of that rule of law. Trouble is, there is no such rule.

Many (not all!) creditors will accept a good-faith attempt to pay off a bill, but seldom without interest and finance charges. That "dollar" doesn't enter into it.

Q My husband charged some expensive boots while we were married. Now the store says it can collect from me even though we're getting a divorce. I say those boots are his debt and the store can go whistle. Right?

A Wrong. Debts incurred during marriage are joint or community debts—even for his boots.

Q I'm really scared. We didn't pay on our big sectional in the living room because we discovered it was all stained when we bought it. Now the furniture place says that if we don't pay up they're coming to get it! That's bad enough but they say we'll also owe for the cost of the repo and any attorney fees! We'll be ruined!

A Get a lawyer! The contract you signed to buy that sectional on the installment plan probably purports to give the store the right to do all that. But it broke the contract by selling you furniture in damaged condition. If you want to keep it, you can no doubt work out a compromise where the price is reduced to your satisfaction—and the store won't do all those bad things it's threatening.

Billing and disputes

Your rights as to quality and payment

A store, and even a car dealer, must make good on defective merchandise; you obviously didn't contract for goods that later showed a hidden defect in workmanship or material. Therefore, you have a right either to withhold payment or to have an adjustment made on your bill.

NOTE: If the purchase is by means of a credit card, under the federal act cited in this chapter the credit card issuer has a duty to withhold payment on your behalf upon your request and recitation of all the pertinent facts: your card number, date of transaction, amount, merchant, complaint, and offer to return or return of the defective merchandise. The withholding is, of course, pending resolution of the issue.

Q Can I deduct the cost of a defective iron from my bill?

A Yes, assuming you return it. The same holds true if you're talking about a credit card purchase; the company must allow you the same defenses or reasons for nonpayment as you would have against a retail merchant for an in-store charge.

Billing errors and "paid in full"

If for any reason you have a valid dispute over your bill, write to the creditor involved, give your account number, and point out the mistake. (See page 212 for more details.)

The creditor has a duty to answer your objection within a certain amount of time. NOTE: during this period, the creditor cannot charge you interest or other finance charges on the amount in dispute.

Q I have been writing letters and telephoning a local department store over an error made in my bill. They don't answer and instead are sending meaner and meaner collection letters. Can I sue?

A Yes, but first write the store a letter and keep a copy of it instead of leaping into court. The federal law now demands that the store must answer you in thirty days. (You are not to be charged finance charges while the matter is in dispute.)

Head up your letter with your account number. In the body of the letter, recite how much the bill is, and how much of it you are disputing, and give your reasons.

Mention that you are proceeding under state statutes and Title 15 USC Section 1666 of the consumer code.

Then, if you are still not answered, see an attorney.

Q I'm going to write "paid in full" across my checks to Macy's and Sears—then I won't have to pay any more on my account if they cash them, right?

A Wrong. The only time the "paid in full" routine works is if there is a true dispute over the amount owed. NOTE: If you have a good-faith dispute over the amount due and you thereafter write "paid in full" on your check, preferably on the back where it will be endorsed, it truly is paid off *if* the creditor cashes that check.

"My card is lost!" —unauthorized purchases

Many people don't realize that they are responsible for only up to $50 for the unauthorized use of a lost or stolen card. In part, this is because of scare tactics used in offers of insurance to protect you against enormous unauthorized purchases on your credit card. Besides that, if the company is going to be allowed to charge you $50 for unauthorized purchases, it must comply with the federal laws (see pages 211-212), including a prominent statement in its credit agreement with you that you may be liable for up to $50 and what to do in case of loss or theft. (You must comply with the latter.)

Collecting

Liens: mechanic's, garageman's, innkeeper's

A "lien" is a hold, an attachment, on property. A lien makes property into collateral for a debt.

Statutory liens vary from state to state, but under the common law there are three: a mechanic's lien, a garageman's, and an innkeeper's.

MECHANIC'S. This one is *not* what it sounds like; instead, a person who has done work on a structure, such as a house, has a right to file a lien against that property until paid for work done. An example would be brick layers whom the contractor was obliged to pay but did not. The way to do this, and the amount of time a contractor or subcontractor has to do it in, are set out in the statutes in each state and are often highly technical.

GARAGEMAN'S. This is a common-law lien that is often complicated by statutes. A garageman's lien entitles someone making repairs (or doing other work) on a vehicle to hold that vehicle until paid.

NOTE: if the garageman allows the vehicle to be taken away, the lien is lost.

INNKEEPER'S. This is an old common-law lien allowing an innkeeper to keep the luggage and any other belongings of a guest until his bill is paid. It still applies today, even if the inn involved is a "Holiday" one. If, of course, the guest skips, taking his luggage, without paying the bill, the lien is lost.

Q I work for a contractor and haven't been paid for painting a new house. The house hasn't been sold yet. The other guys say I can put a lien on it. Can I?

A As a subcontractor, you do have a right to a lien for work and materials. Your state statutes will set out when and in what form you must file this lien. The filing is crucial because it's only fair to put the buyer on notice that there is a lien on the property.

Repossession and self-help

In the bad old days, the most notorious use of "self-help" was in the form of repossessing automobiles. There were, and still are, people who do nothing but "repo" work. Only quiet trickery was needed because the laws merely demanded that the repossessor didn't cause a breach of the peace.

Finally, a Mr. Fuentes objected to this on constitutional grounds, claiming that he had a valid reason for nonpayment and was entitled to his day in court. Fuentes said that since the state statute allowed his automobile to be repossessed without a hearing, he was denied his right to due process. The U.S. Supreme Court agreed. It said that state statutes must provide for notice or an opportunity to be heard before seizure.

Courts have also questioned the violation of the Fourth Amendment search and seizure rights, which the Fuentes case did not decide.

Q The garage manager and I got in a yelling match over the price I supposedly owed for the repairs on my car—way over the estimate. Well, I just jumped in my car and burned rubber. Now the character says I can't even drive around town because the garage has a lien on it. Is that right?

A Nope. Unless common law has been changed by statute in your state, the garage lost the lien when it lost the car. It did have a right to keep it 'til paid however, and you do owe. How much is a whole other ball game.

By the way, in some states, if garage personnel can slip into your car and drive it away, the lien re-attaches. (It's also legal.)

Q I was kinda slippin' down the back stairs of the hotel when the manager caught me and grabbed my suitcase. He said he could hang on to it 'til I paid. Can he do that to me?

A Yes.

Q I was behind in my car payment and someone just jumped in the car and drove off, repossessing it, I guess. Can they do that to me?

A No—but you might have to go to your state supreme court to get a ruling to that effect. You have a right to your day in court in which to raise any defenses to your default. By taking your car, the creditor has violated that right of yours.

Collection agencies

Collection agencies are now set about with sanctions against violations of the laws governing their actions in:

1. skip tracing or acquisition of location information;
2. phone calls and letters;

3. harassment or abuse;

4. lies and tricks or false and misleading representations.

Q I heard an attorney say, "That's a 'page two' collection letter." What does that mean?

A It refers to a classic case that continues to delight me. The company decided to be clever and sent out letters that started in mid-sentence on "page two" as if someone had accidentally failed to include page one. This "page two" pretended to refer back to "page one" with such phrases as "we will be forced to take the foregoing action against you" and other implied threats. When one debtor receiving this "page two" letter took the company to court, the court held that the creditor was liable, legally responsible, for any threats the debtor could reasonably believe were implied. *That* was the "Gotcha!"

Q We haven't been able to get the loan paid back to a creditor, and because of this, he's been not only writing but phoning and even coming out to our house. He's been saying that he'll have our house seized and sold. I don't understand how he could just take it for this debt.

A He can*not*. This threat is untrue because the creditor would first have to have a judgment and attachment before any foreclosure. He is, therefore, in violation of a section of the Federal Consumer Credit Protection Act. (See Section 1692e. on pages 219-220.) You can sue *him*!

Q I've been suffering from headaches and loss of sleep because of a creditor's phone calls calling me a "deadbeat," criticizing my morals, and saying he's going to take me to court. Do I have to take this?

A No. You could take *him* to court. In a comparable case, the court found there was substantial emotional harm and the plaintiff/debtor was awarded damages.

Q We've been getting many letters from a collection agency threatening us with suit, garnishment, and attachment. They literally made my husband sick. When I called the agency, they told me not to make a federal case out of it.

A You *can* make a federal case out of it. A case like yours, which went to the federal court, allowed a suit for damages for physical injury resulting from what the court found to be intentionally inflicted mental stress.

Q I am so angry! I live in an apartment and the mail is sorted by the manager. A collection agency had right on the envelope in red letters after my name the word "debtor." Can I get them for libel or something?

A Yes. You can "get them" on the "or something" part of your question. Courts have found that using the word "debtor" on the envelope is intended to embarrass and makes a jury case for damages under the state statutes.

Q A collection agency has been calling me at work and late at night. Can they harass me like this?

A Not without repercussions. See an attorney. There are statutes protecting you from harassment or threats over the telephone, as well as from having your job endangered.

If they "turn it over to an attorney"

General

If your account is turned over to an attorney, as that bill collector threatened it would be, you may be better off. This is because the odds are that the attorney will work out a more reasonable solution and compromise than the debt collector would have.

True, the collector is right when he says that it will cost you more to go to court, but you don't have to let it go that far.

Compromise

If you can make any sort of small monthly payment, tell the creditor's attorney. She is very likely to be willing to work out such a compromise with you.

Another possible compromise is to figure out if you can pay a substantial portion of the debt. Remember, the creditor's attorney is probably working for a percentage of the amount collected and would rather not spend her time going to court. Therefore, if you are able to offer about two thirds of the amount due, or at least something over 50 percent, the attorney will probably be willing to take it as paid in full. Write and ask.

Q I just got a letter from a collection agency which said that if they had to go to court, I'd have to pay attorney's fees and court costs. Can they do that to me?

A That depends on the original credit agreement and the statutes in your state. Most standard credit agreements do contain a clause making you liable for costs of collection, but don't take this for granted: read your agreement.

If that clause isn't there, most states do *not* give the creditor attorney's fees; consult your lawyer.

NOTE: that letter threatening suit probably told you how much more expensive it would be for you if they had to resort to a lawsuit; it will be more expensive for them, too. If you can come up with a substantial portion of the amount owed, the creditor will most likely be willing to settle for that lesser sum.

Q I'll garnishee him!

A Not yet you won't. And besides that, you're using the word wrong. The "garnishee" is the person who owes a debt to your debtor, such as your debtor's employer.

Garnishment can take place only after you've gotten a valid judgment against someone. Then it's one way of collecting that judgment. The garnishee pays you instead of paying the debtor the money.

The garnishment process requires a good deal of paper work, and I'd advise you to hire a lawyer.

Courts and judgments

If you are a creditor and are not owed too large an amount, most of the states have a "small claims court" you can go to without an attorney. In some states, lawyers are not even allowed in small claims; and in all the states, you don't have to worry about any sort of complicated "pleading"; you merely fill out a form (provided by that court) in which you simply outline the facts involved.

Normally, the "filing fee" is quite small in small claims.

If, instead, you are the one being sued as the debtor, the attorney for the creditor will probably have a number of collections he's running through at the same time. Because of the ease and low filing fee, the attorney for the creditor is likely to proceed in a lower court, such as small claims (if attorneys are allowed) or magistrate's court. These are courts of "limited jurisdiction," which means they can hear only certain cases with a ceiling on the amount of money in dispute or damages claimed.

For any court other than small claims, I'd say that you need to get your own attorney—if you have a defense for nonpayment. (If you have no defense, of course, don't go to court; pay the debt.)

If you lose, you usually don't owe the creditor's attorney fees unless you've agreed to that in a credit contract, but you do owe what are called "court costs," which normally are not very large.

If you lose, the creditor has a judgment against you and can act upon the judgment in a number of ways.

Compromise is still available—even after judgment.

NOTE, HOWEVER: If the creditor goes to court and gets a judgment in a different state from the one in which you live, he has to go through another process to make the judgment good against you in your state.

Execution, attachment, liens, garnishment

The terms "execution," "attachment," "liens," and "garnishment" all relate to what happens after a judgment. Usually, anyone who threatens to garnish your wages without first getting a judgment in court is making an empty threat.

Once the creditor has the judgment, she can "execute on a judg-ment" by attaching property, a process of seizure.

One criticism of small claims and other lower courts is that a person may get a judgment, but then the legal process shuts down and there's never any follow-through on execution and attachment by the sheriff.

Whether you're the creditor or the debtor, it's important to know that execution and attachment have to follow set legal procedures. For instance, to execute on a judgment by attaching the debtor's car, most states require a complete identification of the car as being the one owned by the debtor—you even need to have the engine number. This often isn't easy to obtain.

After judgment, a "lien" can be put on a piece of property, which means that property cannot be sold without paying off the debt repre-sented by the lien. Basically, a lien is a sort of hold on property.

Garnishment is based on a proposition that the Supreme Court of the United States approved many years ago: if money is owed to your debtor, you can collect in his place. In modern practice, this has come to mean that a judgment creditor—a person to whom a sum of money awarded by a court is owed—can demand that the employer who owes wages to the debtor can be forced to pay a part of them to the creditor.

Remember: the federal laws on garnishment (see page 216) limit the amount of wages or salary that can be garnished.

Bankruptcy: A Glimpse in Passing

From the Middle Ages through the founding of our own country, a person could be imprisoned for debt. There was even a "debtor's gaol." A debtor could also end up virtually having to sell himself for the debts owed and become a "bond servant," a servitude little better than slavery.

In the United States you can't be jailed for debt except for failure to pay child support and taxes. You also get a chance to wipe out all debts—except those—and start over by taking bankruptcy. Support payments and taxes "ride through" bankruptcy, i.e., are still owed.

Historically, if someone took bankruptcy, all his assets were ap-plied to all his debts, with priority given to some. The debtor was allowed to keep only such things as one pig, one milk cow, six chickens, an ax, and the tools of his trade.

Now bankrupts are allowed to keep assets up to a certain amount, their home (if valued under a certain amount), and a good deal else. Usually, as a matter of form, the assets are marked as "none." The disadvantage is, of course, bankruptcy's effect on one's credit. Bankruptcy is a serious step because it severely limits who is willing to give you credit. It takes many years of care to rebuild your credit reputation. Bankruptcy can be taken only once every seven years. That's why used car salespeople so generously advertise that they will sell to bankrupts; they know the person can't take bankruptcy to get out of paying!

If you are contemplating the need for a bankruptcy, see an attorney specializing in it. There is an enormous amount of paper work involved. Most attorneys won't touch bankruptcies for under $1500 (low), and the ironic thing is that the bankruptcy judge will usually ask first if the attorney has been paid. There's also a "filing fee" of $60 or more.

There are different types of bankruptcy. You don't necessarily have to go for a total wipe out.

CHAPTER VII

Contracts with Doctors and Hospitals

INTRODUCTION/HISTORY

Wise women, healers, are found as far back as we can trace humanity. And we know that those men referred to as doctors have been with us since some time before Hippocrates, who was born in Greece around 460 BC. The Hippocratic Collection probably belonged to his medical school and deals with anatomy, the clinical approach, diseases he found particular to women and children, and treatments ahead of some today in that they espoused diet along with drugs and surgery. He also believed good and bad "humours" in the body influenced the mind.

His Hippocratic Oath has been administered to would-be doctors through the ages up to now where it's often used at med school graduations. One line of it is: "First, do no harm." In this chapter we'll look at that in its breach.

The topics covered in this contract approach to the patient-physician and patient-hospital relationship are as follows.

1. What is the contract between patient and HMO? Physician?
   a. General
   b. Malpractice: breach of contract or negligence?
2. "Patient's Bill of Rights" and Contracts with Hospitals
3. "Informed consent"
   a. General
   b. Physician's test
   c. Patient's test
4. Malpractice: doctor and/or hospital

a. Defined

b. Proof

c. Damages

5. The more frequent areas of malpractice: physicians

   a. General

   b. Duty to refer patient to another physician or specialist and HMOs

   c. Surgery and postoperative care

     1) General

     2) Damage to other organ or removal of healthy organ

     3) Plastic or cosmetic surgery

     4) Post-op

6. The more frequent areas of malpractice: hospitals

   a. General

   b. Fall from bed

   c. Drugs and injections

   d. Failure to supervise the physicians

7. Dying

   a. Contract to terminate: Living Will

What Is the Contract Between Patient and HMO? Physician?

General

Offhand, it would seem that a contract with a physician would be the same as any other contract for services. Indeed, it is true that the patient-physician relationship has the basic elements of any contract: offer, acceptance, and consideration. However, although it's clear that the patient is promising to pay, what is the physician promising to do as his part of the bargain? Seldom is a doctor caught with his warranty or guarantee hanging out, such as having contracted to put the patient "in good health"; even the less positive promise, that of curing a disease, is unlikely. She offers her skills for your money.

In almost all cases a doctor promises to "treat a condition"—not to cure it. The courts demand no more of him than that his treatment of the patient's disease or disorder drops no lower than the standard of care provided by physicians in the same or a similar community.

HMOs, health management organizations, bring a new equation into the traditional picture of your contract with the doctor. This is because now they contract with the physician to treat you and contract with you to accept that treatment for a set price. They often own or manage the hospital your doctor will send you to, if that's necessary.

Q I went to a new doctor for a simple checkup. Then I got a bill for $372.50. That's not right and I don't think I should have to pay!

A Sorry. This is one of those times where the law implies a contract: when you went to the doctor and sought his services, the law says you knew and, in effect, accepted that the doctor would charge his fee. Therefore, you have offer, acceptance, and contract.

If you refuse to pay and this physician brings suit to collect, your only defense would be that those charges were so unconscionable, so out of reason and out of step with those of other doctors in your area, that the court should refuse to enforce collection of that amount. A comparable approach would be to claim there was a verbal understanding as to the amount the doctor was going to charge for the checkup, and he has violated that understanding.

A note to the doctor wouldn't be out of line; politely state that you don't understand why the bill is so high and ask him to explain.

Always avoid a lawsuit when possible. "I'll see you in court!" sounds good but is often expensive.

Malpractice: breach of contract or negligence?

Most of the civil law can be divided into two areas: tort and contract. "Tort" means a wrong, while contract law has to do with agreements and their breach.

Most malpractice cases are dealt with—by attorneys and courts—as coming under the tort law of negligence, i.e., a physician's actions have fallen below the duty of care owed to a patient. In a smaller number of cases, malpractice suits have been based upon the idea of a breach of contract; i.e., the damage done a patient is the result of the physician's failure to provide the service as promised or—that legal fiction—as "implied" by a court.

In fact, no sort of fancy legal theorizing is necessary to see that a malpractice suit could be treated as a breach of contract simply on the grounds of faulty workmanship like a plumber or carpenter might do.

Q I have an HMO as my medical provider. Their doctor diagnosed me with diabetes but said I didn't have to worry about how high my sugars went, that he was only concerned about the lows. Now I have all sorts of complications and think he should have sent me to a specialist, an endocrinologist. Can I sue?

A Sure you can. Will you win? is the question. I think the HMOs who instruct their doctors not to refer out to a specialist (or not to order expensive tests) are asking for trouble. Let a lawyer go over your contract with the HMO to see what they promise to do for you. If it's not breach of contract, then, as we discussed earlier, it could be negligence, a tort: the HMO and its doctor fell below a reasonable standard of care in failing to refer you to a specialist. And don't forget the other malpractice: that particular doctor failed to provide correct diabetic treatment.

"Patient's Bill of Rights" (as Pertaining to Hospitals, Not Individual Doctors) and Contracts with Hospitals

Naturally, the same problems come up when attempting to analyze the patient's contract with either the hospital or physicians. The patient promises to pay for services rendered, but what services and in what manner? In 1972 the American Hospital Association attempted to address this complex issue by adopting the "Patient's Bill of Rights." One version of it reads as follows:

Provide considerate and respectful care.

Provide complete, understandable, current information regarding your diagnosis, treatment, and prospects for recovery.

Provide names of anyone directly responsible for your care and let you know their role in your care.

Provide as much information as you feel is needed from your physician before consenting to any procedure during your hospitalization. Any questions concerning your illness, the treatment to be given, and the probable medical outcome should be asked during this time.

Provide you with every consideration of privacy concerning your medical care. Your hospital records will be kept confidential and will be released only to those agencies or persons having your permission for access to this information.

Allow you to refuse treatment to the extent permitted by law and to be informed of the medical consequence of your refusal.

Respond with a caring attitude to your requests for service, aid, and comfort as promptly and effectively as possible.

Allow you to leave the hospital, even if your physician advises against it, unless statutes prohibit dismissal.

Inform you _____ Hospital is a teaching hospital. A variety of health care personnel are here as part of their education and are an integral part of our health care team. Their presence helps bring the most current knowledge in the health care field to your bedside.

Offer you the opportunity to participate in available research studies or procedures. You are not obliged to participate in these research projects.

Provide you with the reason for any delay in your treatment.

Provide you the opportunity to examine and receive an explanation of your bill.

Offer appropriate consideration to someone who can act in your behalf if you are unable to request or comprehend the above listed hospital responsibilities.

Q The patient's rights refer to having someone who can act in my behalf. How do I set that up?

A With a Durable Power of Attorney.* You make someone (with a successor named if that person can't or refuses to serve) your "Attorney in Fact." That person isn't really an attorney; it's just a term. If you are in a coma or cannot conduct your affairs for some reason, this person will have the right to act for you, such as to sign checks, pay bills, or collect insurance. It's commonplace to also give that person (or someone different, or in addition to) the power to decide for or against medical options available to you. This includes your "right to die." (Sample at the end of this chapter.)

NOTE: You should discuss the "right to die" or "living will" with your spiritual advisor and your doctor. Many doctors and hospitals are bad about following that request—even though the hospital may demand you have a living will and a power of attorney.

NOTE ALSO: Remember to indicate organ donation if that is your wish. Don't leave this difficult decision to your loved ones.

Q When I check into a hospital, is that hospital making a kind of contract with me?

A You betcha! No contract is valid unless it can be enforced on both sides. You know the hospital would certainly claim you contracted to pay if you tried to leave without doing so. If that's so, the hospital owes contractual duties to you. They're not usually set out in the forms you sign, but are included in the "Patient's Bill of Rights."

Some attorneys might disagree, but I think a malpractice suit can be based on your contract with the hospital as well as on negligence.

"Informed Consent"

General

"Informed consent" is not some shibboleth of attorneys; it fits right in with basic contract law. There can't be an agreement if one party (the patient) doesn't understand to what he is agreeing. This parallels a minor's lack of competency to contract, for instance (see pages 20-22).

The general rule is that the patient, or the person who can legally give consent for the patient, must consent prior to treatment or surgery. From this it logically follows that the consent must be meaningful, i.e., "informed." You must know what you're agreeing to have done and at what risk.

The traditional view, as to finding whether or not there has been informed consent, is the "reasonable physician's test," or a determination of what the medical custom is in the locale involved.

The more modern view looks not to the practices of the medical profession but rather to the patient's need to be informed, so that he can accept or reject the proposed treatment based on facts of which he has been made aware.

This patient's viewpoint has been taken as far as being made a matter of law in some states. Under this rule the patient must be properly informed if the treatment involves a material risk, if other methods of treatment are available, and if the information will not be detrimental to the patient's health. (How's that last for "ignorance is bliss"?)

The states placing this mandatory burden of disclosure on the physicians argue that the question of whether there is sufficient information cannot be left to the medical establishment because doctors won't necessarily demand a sufficiently high standard to enable the patient to make his own decisions as to what is to be done to his body.

Physician's test

A minority of the states follow the position that informed consent is to be measured by community medical standards. Even with this medical test, the courts have still stepped in in some cases to say the physician or surgeon has failed to disclose or disclose sufficiently, material risks to the patient.

The amount of information disclosed increases in some instances, such as with elective surgery. An illustration of the reasonable physician's rule is a case in which a surgeon removed a thyroid and the patient was left in a condition of numbness and pain, and with muscle spasms. The patient had not been informed of these possible effects, but the court let the doctor off the hook because, although these problems were known to result, the number of them was small.

As to hospitals, the "Patient's Bill of Rights" says that a patient has a right to be informed of "medically significant risks" of a proposed procedure. The "Patient's Bill of Rights" does not use the reasonable physician's test.

Patient's test

A majority of states have moved to the side of making the Patient's test the rule as to when, and to what degree, informed consent is required.

The most potent argument in support of the position that disclosure should be measured from the patient's viewpoint is that the patient is the one who must personally and emotionally deal with pain, suffering, possible disfigurement, and, of course, the cost of the procedure.

A plaintiff must do more than simply show lack of informed consent. An example of this is a case wherein the doctor performed an amniotomy to induce labor. The result was a healthy baby but a mother who hemorrhaged to the extent that a hysterectomy was necessary. In this case, the mother said she had not been informed that this was a risk involved in the procedure to which she had consented.

The plaintiff-mother lost. The court said that she had not shown that with knowledge of the risk she would have refused the procedure.

Q What's "informed consent"?

A Well, you're familiar with the release you're asked to sign before surgery. That release says that you're consenting to the surgery and—the biggie—that you (or your heirs) won't hold anybody liable for the results of that surgery.

Now that brings us to "informed consent." It applies to more than surgery, but sticking to our example, the law is that if the surgeon didn't sufficiently explain the operation and its hazards, you didn't really consent at all. You can't consent to what you don't understand.

Q I keep hearing about "informed consent" between doctors and patients. Just what does this mean?

A Courts have been allowing more and more lawsuits by patients, based on the theory that the doctor or hospital did not give the patient sufficient information about a procedure or medication for the patient to give his "informed consent" to it.

An example would be if a doctor prescribed medication which was the only drug available to cure the patient's condition, but which had a possible side effect of causing pernicious anemia. These facts should be set out before the patient and his agreement given or else the patient would lack "informed consent."

Today the courts are increasingly strict that all the facts be laid before the patient. If they are not, and the patient suffers adverse effects, she can successfully sue (or her survivors can), other conditions being met.

Q You keep talking about informed consent, but it doesn't work that way. I've been having a bunch of tests and someone's always shoving a paper at me, saying, "Sign here." What am I supposed to do? Cancel the test? I don't even get time to read the thing!

A I know. It seems like that's often the way it goes. Only the really tricky procedures are discussed with a patient. You can ask for time to read that paper and then think about to what you're consenting. You might want to actually say, "No, thank you."

Always find out if you have other options and be sure you understand the actual risks involved.

Malpractice: Doctor and/or Hospital

Defined

As I mentioned earlier in this chapter, malpractice is usually considered to be the tort of negligence rather than a breach of contract. A good argument can be made for each, however. Clearly, the implied contract between the patient and the M.D. creates a duty owed by the doctor to the patient. At a minimum, this duty should be to give the patient the standard of care furnished by other physicians in the community and at the level of expertise claimed by the particular doctor.

The majority of courts say that malpractice is only proved sufficiently to go to a jury (as opposed to being thrown out of court) if a plaintiff proves: (1) the defendant-doctor had a duty to conform to a specific standard of conduct in her treatment of the plaintiff; (2) the defendant-doctor's treatment fell below that standard; (3) the plaintiff was damaged; and (4) it was the conduct of the defendant-doctor that brought about this damage.

Proof

It is difficult for a plaintiff-patient to prove malpractice on the part of a physician because expert testimony is usually required and doctors are reluctant to testify against one another. It is infrequent for a judge to find that the facts of the malpractice suit are such that a layman can say whether or not there has been malpractice. However, the case may be allowed to go to a jury without expert testimony when the alleged malpractice is that the surgeon left instruments and sponges inside a patient's body.

Many states have medical/legal boards that will provide an expert if the board decides there has been malpractice. They usually don't.

Q How can I prove malpractice?

A With difficulty. In most cases of malpractice, it is necessary to have testimony from a doctor—and most doctors don't like to testify against another doctor.

With a very powerful lobbying group, medical associations have influenced an increasing number of state legislators to pass statutes forcing plaintiffs to submit to a medical-legal review board before they can go to court. In a number of states, although a plaintiff does not have to submit to such a review panel, it is only by doing so—and being approved—that the plaintiff-patient is furnished a testifying doctor.

Supposedly, these panels are the result of increasingly high medical malpractice insurance brought about by frivolous suits. However, unless the physicians were losing these suits, it's difficult to see why the insurance rates would go up.

These review panels have been attacked as a denial of equal protection because malpractice victims are treated differently from other plaintiffs, and also because it is the most seriously injured who are affected. In some cases, the statutes creating the panels have also been held an unconstitutional delegation of judicial power and denial of due process by limiting the patient's rights to go to court.

Usually this review is required before the plaintiff can file suit. However, suit *is* allowed, though no expert is furnished, even if the committee finds in favor of the physician and against the plaintiff, which is the norm.

Q A friend of mine had an appendectomy and the surgeon did something so that afterward her right leg was completely crippled. It seems like anybody would know this shouldn't happen when you have an appendectomy, so I wonder if she could make a case without having a doctor testify against her surgeon.

A It seems so to me, too, but you never know.

The patient did recover damages in a similar case where it was proven that the surgeon had severed the nerves and muscles involved, so that the crippling was caused by the inability to use those muscles.

Q Why is a doctor's malpractice insurance so expensive?

A I've heard insurance companies say it's because of suit-happy money-hungry attorneys. I don't agree.

The More Frequent Areas of Malpractice: Physicians

General

There are so many malpractice cases against physicians that they are classified by topics and subtopics, such as: infections by contaminated needles; injury to or removal of healthy organs; paralysis; disfigurement; and drugs and dosages.

A particularly large area of malpractice occurs with prescribed drugs; just one of its subtopics has been negligence in the physician's administration of weight control drugs, such as amphetamines. These have resulted in drug dependence, a variety of contraindications, and the unpleasant experience of withdrawal. Those were dropped in favor of the newer varieties, which are now showing dangerous side effects.

Q I questioned the number of tests my o.b. was ordering for me and she said it was a condition of her treating me. Have I contracted to spend that much extra money?

A I can't say what's "extra" without knowing more about your condition and the tests. I can tell you that many doctors (and maybe especially o.b.s) are practicing "defensive medicine." They say the number of malpractice suits has forced them to cover every base, no matter how remote.

As to any contract, you probably agreed to pay her bill in some form of installments and may have agreed to something like "all reasonable and necessary tests."

Q When my doctor put me on those diet drugs, he had me check off separate lines in a list warning of the dangers and then sign. Now I hear that it's considerably more dangerous than first thought and my odds are greater for being a victim of pulmonary hypertension and a heart condition. Have I contracted away my right to sue?

A If you were fully warned, I think so. You knew what you were getting into, assumed the risk. The only question is, Is this affected by the new findings? You knew the risk existed but didn't know the likelihood. Was it to be reasonably expected? Should your doctor have known? It would be up to a jury. Let's hope you're not planning a wrongful death suit!

Duty to refer patient to another physician or specialist

Is it malpractice if a physician fails to send a patient to another doctor who is qualified in whatever treatment is called for where the original physician is not? Most courts have found there is such a duty in theory, but it is difficult to prove in specific cases. Supposedly, this duty begins when the original doctor knows—or should know—that the disorder is beyond his capabilities or facilities or, more simply, that the patient is not improving under his treatment.

This question becomes critical as more and more people are cared for by HMOs who sometimes instruct their physicians not to refer patients out to expensive specialists.

There have been many shocking cases based on this type of malpractice—and some shocking results also. In an example of the latter, the patient not only lost her eyesight, but also lost her suit against the physician who, despite the plaintiff's requests, failed to call in an eye specialist to treat the patient's inflamed eye in a case of typhoid fever.

The court held that the physician had no duty to bring in the specialist. This was despite the fact that when an ophthalmologist did examine the plaintiff, he said it was too late to do anything, but had he been called in earlier, he might have saved the eye.

On the other hand, in one case the patient had cancer of the lip and jaw. The doctor treated this with nothing but injections, failing to use radiation therapy or surgery.

The court held that the physician was liable because he should have told the patient either that the treatment was not stopping the cancer, which was progressively growing worse, or that other treatments were available.

For our contract purposes, the interesting question is whether you, as a patient, are put at risk by the HMO's contract with its physicians. To what have you agreed when signing on with an HMO? These questions are legally distinct from the question of the duty of care owed you by your independent doctor.

Surgery and postoperative care

General

There are so many cases alleging malpractice in this area that they, too, are divided into subtopics.

Some of the cases involving surgery and post-op care appear so gross that one would think it's simply a matter of common sense that the result shouldn't have occurred. Most of them, nevertheless, require expert testimony. To find a surgeon who will testify that another surgeon has committed malpractice is difficult; to go the next step and prove that there was negligence or breach of contract is even more difficult.

Damage to other organs or removal of healthy organ

Numerous cases are brought because of damage done by surgeons to veins, muscles, and organs of patients. That's cases *brought.* The numbers dwindle when one looks at how many plaintiffs have been successful in showing, to the satisfaction of a judge, that he or she should be compensated for the damage done. Horrendous fact situations are frequently labeled as a risk of the surgery. Plaintiff-patients have been more successful when there has been the outright removal of a healthy organ.

In one instance, surgery was scheduled for the removal of a diseased kidney; the healthy kidney was the one removed. (Here the plaintiff did win the case.) This case was so publicized that subsequently when a surgeon took off the drape from an anesthetized patient who also had to have a kidney removed, he was met by a diagram drawn in Mercurochrome on the patient's abdomen. It read "Not this one, Doc," and an arrow pointed to the words "This one."

Plastic or cosmetic surgery

Cosmetic surgery is elective surgery for the purpose of improving one's appearance, as opposed, for example, to ensuring or maintaining the necessary functions of organs.

Since this surgery is directed toward a specific result, it would seem that surgery which does not achieve that result is a breach of contract or express warranty. Wrong. Plastic surgeons are taught *not* to make any promises as to the outcome of the surgery, so it's difficult to prove breach of contract. In fact, most medical malpractice insurance specifically does *not* cover any actions against a physician or surgeon that are based on a promise to accomplish a specified end or cure.

The courts have held that disfigurement alone does not prove the surgeon was at fault.

Even if the case is not thrown out before it gets to a jury, that jury often has a disapproving attitude toward the plaintiff-patient who has elected to have cosmetic surgery.

Case: A woman with breathing problems went in for surgery purely to have this difficulty corrected. Instead, the surgeon decided she needed more fixing up and removed a hump from her nose and a scar from her forehead. Besides an altered appearance, which probably would not have been a sufficient allegation, the woman suffered a debilitating infection. She won her suit against the surgeon.

Case: A patient had elected surgery to remove thickened skin at the end of his nose. The surgeon didn't stop there but refashioned the nose to his pleasure. The patient felt that his appearance was altered for the worse and his breathing was also impaired. Although the patient claimed the physician had warranted that the surgery would improve his appearance, and went beyond permission, the patient lost.

Case: A patient went in for dermabrasion to have wrinkles removed but came out with her skin in a variety of colors. She won without expert testimony because the judge believed that clearly she should have been told her chances of a good result were only fifty-fifty.

Case: A woman won a malpractice suit based on breach of contract and was awarded damages resulting from the surgeon's broken promise to use only specified procedures in plastic surgery on her nose. Her case was better than most because the surgeon had expressly promised not to make any incision on the woman's face and instead had made two.

Case: A facelift resulted in an area of dead tissue on one woman's face, a "gristle-like" scar on one cheek, pleated skin on her neck, and a part of the face sewn to her earlobe, leaving a small "tit" or "scallop" that required further surgery. The woman not only lost, but her case was thrown out of court before it could get to the jury.

Post-op

Another area in which claims of malpractice flourish is post-op care. The cases range from situations where instruments and sponges and various types of swabs are left in the patients to matters of medical judgment.

Between those two extremes, it appears that a larger number of cases are brought because of infections alleged to have resulted from the surgery. Most of these, in turn, have been decided on the basis that a resulting infection does not, by itself, show breach of contract or negligence. The plaintiff-patient is not likely to win.

In one case where the patient actually did win his lawsuit, the facts were extreme. The elderly patient, recuperating after hip surgery, fell while being given a whirlpool bath. The fall broke open the wound, which was then exposed to unsterile water, draped with an unsterilized towel to stop the bleeding, and then closed by surgical tape placed on the wound without any cleansing. Nothing was communicated to the treating physician that day and the patient suffered a serious staph infection.

The More Frequent Areas of Malpractice: Hospitals

General

Historically, all hospitals have enjoyed "charitable immunity,"* which means they cannot be sued. This has changed. The first cracks appeared when courts allowed hospitals to be sued if the plaintiff could collect on the hospital's liability insurance. In one of these cases, a woman went in to have surgery on a leg that was one inch shorter than the other; three operations later she emerged with that leg two more inches shorter, but her damages were limited to the amount of insurance carried by the hospital.

Of the innumerable cases alleging malpractice on the part of hospitals, probably the most common relate to infection. These usually don't get very far.

Nevertheless, a patient does have an implied contract with the hospital and the hospital owes the patient a duty of care. What the standard of care is varies immensely.

Fall from bed

There are so many cases of patients being injured because of falls from their beds that these cases are put in the categories of: patient medicated; patient not medicated; supervision; restraint.

A helpless patient falling from the bed is not, in itself, enough to make a case. The patient would first have to show that the hospital either knew, or had reason to know, that the patient was likely to fall from the bed.

At times the courts have considered such factors as sedation or other mind-affecting medication, but their presence won't necessarily prove that the patient should have had special attention.

One light in the darkness is that some courts have held that it's actually a matter of common sense whether the patient should have been supervised or put under restraint and, therefore, the case has been able to go to the jury without expert testimony.

Drugs and injections

Again there are many, many cases where patients have been damaged by drugs and injections. Sometimes the harm is caused by defective drugs, sometimes by the administration of the improper drug or dosage.

In a number of these cases, attorneys for the patients (or their survivors) have tried to use the breach of warranty argument. However, the courts have often said that the hospital provides a service rather than the sale of a drug.

Hospital's failure to supervise the physicians

Cases show the increasingly active part the hospital is taking in supplying medical care. The hospital has a duty to supervise the personnel with whom the patient has made no direct contractual relationship.

Dying

Because of advanced medical technology that can artificially keep a person's heart and breathing going, the courts have had to determine when a person actually does die. This determination is changing all the time, but right now most states define the time of death—"legal death"—as when the brain stops functioning. Brain dead.

With this continuing controversy over the definition of "death" and "when to pull the plug," hospitals are demanding and individuals are requesting what are called "Living Wills" or "Right to Die" documents. They are frequently part of a "Durable Power of Attorney" (see p. 241) which takes effect when the person giving the power is no longer able to take care of his or her affairs. Most hospitals now have a form that's offered to patients who don't already have a Living Will.

There has been criticism that many people do not know what it means when they stipulate to such things as "no hydration," so some states are now legislating that the document clearly show the individual understands each part of it.

The "Right to Die" that I include in the Durable Power of Attorney, when desired by the client, accompanied by an Affidavit acknowledging the meaning of each clause is as follows:

Health Care: in accordance with the "Right to Die" Act of the (State) statute cited infra, I demand that my wishes to comply therewith be carried out through the authority given to my primary and successor attorney acting together or any combination of them surviving me by this document despite any feeling to the contrary held by any relative or friend. In exercise of my attorney's authority as granted herein, my attorney should try to discuss with me the specifics of any proposed decision regarding my medical care and treatment if I am able to communicate with my attorney, even if only by blinking my eyes. If such is impossible, then my wishes in my "Right to Die" document shall be followed. Accordingly, if the physician in charge of my care and one other licensed physician have certified in writing that I am suffering from a terminal illness or being in an irreversible coma (both as defined in statutory citation of the Right to Die Act), then my attorney is authorized as follows:

a) To execute for me any documents necessary to carry out the authorizations described herein below, including releases of liability required by any health care provider; and

b) To give or withhold consent for any medical care or treatment, to revoke or change any consent previously given or implied by law for any medical care or treatment, and to arrange for my placement in or removal from any hospital, convalescent home, hospice, or other facility; and

c) To require that medical treatment which will only serve to prolong the inevitable moment of my death or irreversible coma not be instituted or, if previously instituted, to require that it be discontinued; and

d) To require that procedures used to provide me with nourishment and hydration not be instituted or, if previously instituted, to require that they be discontinued but only if my attending physician shall also have determined that I will not experience pain as a result of the withdrawal of nourishment or hydration; and

e) To execute for me any documents necessary to carry out my wish that any usable organs be donated upon my anatomical death, including releases of liability required by any health care provider or other person or entity.

CERTIFICATION
I HEREBY CERTIFY THAT I HAVE READ AND UNDERSTAND THE PROVISIONS OF THIS ARTICLE AUTHORIZING MY ATTORNEY TO RE-FUSE MEDICAL TREATMENT FOR ME UNDER THE CIRCUMSTANCES SPECIFIED IN THE ARTICLE AND THAT SUCH PROVISIONS HAVE BEEN EXPLAINED TO ME IN DETAIL TO MY SATISFACTION AND THAT SUCH PROVISIONS ABSOLUTELY AND CORRECTLY STATE MY WISHES AND DEMANDS UNDER THE CIRCUMSTANCES DESCRIBED.

The document is signed by the person giving the power and witnessed.

NOTE: By statute some states demand you fill in a more detailed "Living Will." It may be a form as, e.g., "I ___do ___do not choose to exercise my option . . . I ___do ___do not wish hydration . . ." etc.

CHAPTER VIII

Contracts with Attorneys and Going to Court

INTRODUCTION/HISTORY

"The first thing we do, let's kill all the lawyers" (Shakespeare, Henry VI) in centuries before and after the bard.

Lawyers have always been with us if you take the word to mean "one who argues the case for another."

Early on in English common law, you could only be heard in a court of law if your case fit within the four corners of the King's Writ. Therefore, Courts of Equity came into being to hear all the other cases. These decisions, based on fairness, were thus "equitable."

Two kinds of lawyers developed: "barristers" argued in court (and were usually independently wealthy); "solicitors" prepared the briefs for the barristers and did the other legal work.

Historically, in the United States, we also had cases heard in equity but had no formal division of duties among lawyers. (I'm often asked the difference between lawyer, attorney-at-law and counselor. None, in practice. It's mostly what the individual thinks sounds best.)

Up through the Depression years, many people became attorneys without ever going to law school. They interned with a lawyer, "read for the law"—and often looked down on those who did it the "easy way" by going to law school.

Lawyers are neither as bad (usually) as they're made out to be, nor as good (too often) as we'd like to think we are.

Besides representing you, arguing your claims and rights with all the skill and vigor we can muster, attorneys are also officers of the court, sworn to uphold the Constitution. Therefore, when you see a television show depicting the slick lawyer getting the criminal off on a "legal technicality," remember that "legal technicality" is usually a large constitutional principle. It protects you from a midnight knock on the door by the secret police or a conviction under some retroactive law making it a crime that you were once a Boy Scout or that you voted Republican ten years ago.

As I've recommended for all contract situations, when hiring an attorney, *get it in writing.* This includes your arrangement for the payment of any fees. (For details, see page 258.)

As to going to court, discussed subsequently, for now let me paraphrase:

"The truth emerges when two men argue opposite sides as unfairly as possible."

1. Attorneys
    a. General
    b. What is an attorney?
    c. How to find an attorney
    d. Advertising versus "solicitation"
2. Attorney-client relationship
    a. General
    b. Fees, retainers, and liens
    c. The client is boss
    d. Privilege and confidential communication
        1) General—defined
        2) Crimes
    e. Malpractice
        1) General
        2) Allowing time to run out
        3) Settlement instead of suit
        4) Withdrawal
3. Going to court
    a. Mechanics of suit

b. The trial
c. After judgment
d. The appeal

Q I got a contract from my attorney, but it really doesn't say what I can expect him to do for me.

A It depends on the attorney. When he was sworn in, he took an oath to the effect that he would "well and faithfully prosecute" your suit—but interpretations vary.

Surprisingly, the single biggest complaint from clients is *not* about the results obtained from their attorney, but, rather, about the lack of communication. Many clients feel that their case has become buried in the files, and are too shy to call to check, are afraid to set that meter running, or can neither catch the lawyer in nor receive a call back.

In defense of the lawyer, I'll say that usually he is working on your case, but doesn't believe there's anything to report and is himself dealing with other lawyers, which is often time-consuming and without results.

If an inordinate amount of time has passed with no word from your lawyer, call. Even if he doesn't call back, he will have gotten the message and that may move him to act.

To avoid this situation, I have my secretary photocopy all correspondence in and out and mail it to the client stamped FOR YOUR INFORMATION ONLY. NO ACTION NEEDED.

Back to your basic question: What can you expect from your attorney? Overall, your attorney owes you a duty to advance your cause with diligence and all the skill he can muster.

Q Why do attorneys always say, "I'll have to check the statutes and get back to you"?

A I'm afraid this is a stall that most of us have used at times; there's not necessarily a statute involved at all. The trouble is that most clients expect attorneys to know all the law at that moment—except, for some unknown reason, it's okay not to know the statutes.

"I'll have to check the statutes" usually translates as "Give me a while to ponder this or confer with somebody who knows."

What is an attorney?

An attorney is always called an "officer of the court." As such, it is her duty to uphold the law and, among other things, never mislead a judge.

It is not mandatory for an attorney to be a member of the American Bar Association but, if she is, the association has a code of ethics which must be upheld.

Most states require every attorney to be a member of the state bar association but, more importantly, when sworn in after passing the bar examination, an attorney takes an oath promising to prosecute only suits of merit and to perform faithfully.

As part of the privilege of practicing law, an attorney also subjects herself to being disciplined for unethical conduct. This discipline can result in the attorney's disbarment, suspension, or other punitive measures.

Normally, an attorney keeps all funds belonging to—or that will belong to—a client in a trust account separate from any business or other accounts. Failure to be able to produce a client's money on request is usually an automatic suspension or disbarment.

Q I can't afford to pay a lawyer's fees since I was badly hurt in an accident and have gone into debt because of medical bills and lost wages. What's this "contingency fee" I hear about?

A When an attorney accepts a case "on contingency" that means you don't have to pay her unless she recovers money for you, either by settlement or trial. She will take a percentage which will be around 25 or 30% if settled, 40 to 50% if tried. Sometimes attorneys justify a higher percentage if the chances of winning are lower. On the other hand, sometimes one phone call will settle a case. (I call that the "bait and switch.") The problem is that even with a contingency case, many people are in a bind. This is because the majority of attorneys now demand "up-front money," an amount you must pay down toward expenses.

Most lawyers are not going to take a case unless they think they'll make money out of it. That means they won't accept your cause "for the principles involved." (They might if you're going to pay by the hour.)

By the way, only a tiny percentage of *all cases* in the U.S. bring in those huge awards, jury verdicts, that you see on the news. We're not paying substantially higher anything because of them—and that includes insurance—nor putting anyone out of work. Your insurance rates rise when the companies lose money on bad investments.

Q What's the difference between an attorney, a lawyer, a counselor, an attorney-at-law, and a counselor-at-law?

A None. In the most basic sense, an "attorney" is a person acting as an agent for another and has come to mean "advocate," while "lawyer" would be one learned in the law. One hopes that whatever he calls himself, he is both.

How to find an attorney

Q How do I find an attorney?

A That is one of the most difficult questions I am ever asked. In most places, the Bar offers an attorney referral service. However, this doesn't guarantee you any particular expertise because normally any attorney is allowed to sign up if he or she has the requisite amount of malpractice insurance and will agree to basic rules. A lawyer referral service usually gives you the three names that have reached the top of the list as it rotates.

It's best to check around with your friends to see if they have an attorney they can recommend. If you don't like that attorney, or if he or she doesn't deal with your particular kind of problem, most attorneys are very good about recommending you to someone else.

There is a multi-volume book, not known to most laypersons, *Martindale and Hubbell*. It can be found in most courthouse law libraries. It lists all of the attorneys in the United States by state and city, their reputation in the community, how much they're worth, representative clients, and even their promptness in paying their bills. They are graded.

Q Should I go to a big law firm or to somebody practicing on his own?

A It's mostly a matter of personal preference, though there are a couple of clear distinctions between the private practitioner and the large firm.

1. One difference is comparable to the distinction between a family doctor and a specialist in medicine: the large outfit can afford to have attorneys who concern themselves with one area of law, such as probate or products liability; the sole practitioner must have a general knowledge of just about everything that comes along, as does the medical family doctor.

2. "Bench strength." If your case is an involved one, and especially if going to court seems likely, you might consider that a large firm has more resources, more people to throw into the fray—from paralegals researching the law to lawyers who do nothing but trial work.

Advertising versus "solicitation"

Q I thought lawyers weren't allowed to advertise.

A Until the last couple of decades—and a Supreme Court decision— they weren't. Now they can, but in what manner varies with the states. For example, some states say a lawyer can advertise only three specialties and then is limited to practicing only those. One state I was in said an attorney could "advertise" but not "solicit"—ever! That's a thin line.

There is, of course, a great deal of advertising now. How aggressive varies with the Supreme Court or Bar Association of each state. I've seen some ads that tell you to get your file from your attorney and bring it in to the sponsor to see if your case is being handled properly.

Caveat: Look out for attorneys who promise too much.

Attorney-Client Relationship

General

The attorney-client relationship begins when a person asks the advice of an attorney and the attorney gives it. The time this occurs can be most important in situations involving the "privileged or confidential relationship" (discussed in detail below) and may also be involved in malpractice cases.

An attorney can't lie for a client and usually, in a criminal case, can't come right out and claim that the client is innocent. These factors often force an attorney into a "no comment" position. *Always* tell your lawyer the facts! I've had a number of clients who thought that if they could persuade me, they would win in court. If you twist the truth, you're setting your attorney up to be sand-bagged!

Q My brother-in-law says if I can con my attorney into believing me, I've got it made.

A Of all your brother-in-law's erroneous statements, that is the worst! Not telling the truth cripples your attorney and will be likely to lose you the suit. You must give it to your lawyer straight.

Fees, retainers, and liens

Q What's a retainer?

A An attorney can ask—or be offered—a retainer for many different reasons. Probably the most frequent retainer is what, in the trade, attorneys call "up front" money. This means that before she's willing to represent you, the attorney wants what amounts to a cash down payment. It may be small or large.

In a civil contingency case, the attorney may ask for a retainer to cover the initial expenses—"to get started," he may say. Or the lawyer may feel he should ask for a retainer as evidence of *your* good faith.

In a divorce or dissolution, most attorneys ask for a retainer of at least half the fee in advance.

On the criminal side, many attorneys demand—in advance—the whole amount of anticipated charges. This is because a criminal case is usually a one-shot deal, not to be repeated, one hopes. (One attorney I've heard of sets his retainer and fee in a murder case as "all you have"—house, car, jewelry, etc. He says, "If I win, it's worth it to you. If I lose, it won't matter to you anymore.")

Another type of retainer comes from a client who wants regular representation for a set amount. For instance, a corporation might have an attorney "on retainer" to handle whatever legal matters come up each month.

NOTE: A retainer is the consideration that binds the contract between you and your lawyer.

Q What do I get when I contract with an attorney and pay him a retainer?

A His services. An attorney contracts to represent you to the best of his abilities.

NOTE: He doesn't promise to get results.

The retainer part shouldn't make any difference as to the services you receive—unless, of course, you have been told that the attorney doesn't plan to do the work until he gets the retainer.

Q How much does it cost to hire an attorney to defend me?

A Often more than you'd expect. The big shocker for me in law school was to find out that if your attorney successfully defends a civil suit against you and wins, you—not the losing side—still have to pay your own attorney's fees in most cases.

NOTE: At least consult an attorney before you pay any sort of legal claim against you; the attorney fees may be much cheaper than paying off something you don't owe.

NOTE ALSO: Someone saying they'll sue does not necessarily mean that they will. A letter from your lawyer may be enough—or your lawyer may even say, "Ignore it."

Q Is my attorney ripping me off?

A I don't know. I do believe more people think the charges are unfair than is actually the case. However, since you're concerned, let's put your relationship with your attorney on a more businesslike basis from here on out. First, she's charging you either (1) on a flat-fee basis, or (2) hourly, or (3) on contingency.

1. *Flat fee.* Always adding a proviso or two, of course, many attorneys will quote you a flat fee for matters for which the amount of time spent is fairly standard. These often include: uncontested divorce or dissolution; bankruptcy; simple wills; adoption; name change. On this sort of case, ask your attorney what the fee will be, then check around and find out if that's the going rate (and I don't mean bargain basement). Attorneys don't like it, but you can "shop around"—especially on divorces.

My feelings on flat-fee cases are that most fees for divorce are too high; bankruptcy fees are too low because it's a time-consuming hassle; and there's no such thing as a "simple"—or "boiler plate"—will. (If it's cheap, it's suspect.)

2. *Hourly.* Here's where I think many lawyers cause bad feelings. You're likely to get a statement reading: "Services rendered—$999." Ideally, it should list what was done on your case on what date and then conclude with the number of hours @ price per hour for a total of ___.

If you're still not satisfied that your attorney could have fairly spent that time, you're certainly entitled to ask to see her "time sheets," which are the slips the attorney fills out with the time spent for each client, such as: "10/4—Ms. Jones—telephone call—.2 hrs." Also, if your attorney is charging you by the hour and you're conferring with him, find out if the meter's running when you're just chatting.

When you call to make your first appointment, ask if there's a charge for the initial conference and what the hourly rate is thereafter. Also, ask how the time is rounded off. It used to be to the quarter of an hour, now it's usually to the half hour.

3. *Contingency.* As discussed previously, if an attorney will take a case on a contingency it means that if he settles your case or wins and gets a money judgment for you, he'll receive a set percentage of that money; if he loses, you don't owe him anything except out-of-pocket expenses.

The percentages vary from place to place. The contingency fee probably gets its bad name from out-of-court settlements where the attorney collects the higher "if tried" fee because most attorneys consider filing the suit papers as "trial"—and clients don't. For this reason, you should talk over the contingency rules with your attorney at the outset. Also, you should find out how much effort he will put into settlement *before* filing suit and getting the higher fee.

Q Why am I being gouged by my attorney at that hourly rate?

A You're probably not; most attorneys are honest.

Much of the public has the notion of that meter ticking away eight hours a day at $100 or more an hour. Not so. It's difficult to get in as many as six hours "chargeable time" a day—and that's a long day. A lot of time is consumed on matters that can't be billed to clients and thus aren't those "chargeable hours."

Also, an attorney has overheads the client doesn't think about: secretaries and, perhaps, paralegals and/or legal assistants; office space and equipment, including dictator, transcriber, word processor, computer, business phone, fax machine, and copier—all expensive. In addition, most attorneys have at least the essentials of a library in books, CD-ROM or online service, which must be updated and for which they'll be paying during their entire career. Most will have some charity (pro bono) cases, along with the uncollectible cases that aren't even tax deductible. Remember, too, lawyers must pay for expensive malpractice insurance.

P.S. It is truly a fact that not all lawyers are rich.

Q I'm being sued, but I really think that I'm in the right. Will I get back my attorney's fees if I win?

A Usually not, though it doesn't seem fair. Normally, if you win, you'll be awarded "costs," court fees and the like, and expenses such as depositions, but you must pay your attorney's fees.

NOTE: Most credit agreements include a sneaky little clause that you will be responsible for costs of collection, including attorney's fees, *regardless* of who wins. I've been able to get some organizations to write in a change to the effect that the *losing* party will pay.

Q I thought you always collected if you got rear-ended in a car accident, but the attorney I went to said he'd take the case on a contingency of 40 percent if settled, 50 percent if tried. Is that fair?

A I need to know more about the extent of your injuries. They may be so slight that your attorney would have to take at least that percentage in order to break even. The other side is, he may expect to make one or two phone calls to an adjuster,* the insurance claims person handling the other side of the case, and have the matter settled. Two points:

1. It's a rare attorney who'll take a case on contingency who doesn't believe the odds are in his favor of winning. If it's a "matter of principle," you'll usually be told you'll have to pay for your principles.

2. If you'd prefer to take the risk and are unhappy with the contingency, tell your attorney you'd prefer to pay his hourly rate instead.

NOTE: With "whiplash" from "rear-enders" in particular, some insurance companies make it a policy *never* to settle and will always go to court, whatever the merits of the case.

NOTE ALSO: Although certain people joke about it, "whiplash," soft tissue injury, can be a serious and lasting condition. The vehicle may be minimally damaged but the force will have travelled to the body of the person injured. Also, the headrest may have acted as a fulcrum, adding to the severity of the injury.

Q Since my accident case is on contingency, will my lawyer settle it quickly for less than it's worth?

A Probably not, unless he's starving. The rules of ethics demand that your attorney either relay every offer from the other side to you with nothing more than a recommendation of whether you should accept or hold out for more, or he must have gotten "authority" from you as to the bottom amount you'd settle for. Either way, the final decision is yours.

NOTE: If you've hired a good lawyer, she'll tell you at the start what she thinks the case is worth and, if it's not cut and dried, how it's shaping up later after "discovery,"* the process of getting all the facts from the other side. She'll also tell you what she thinks your chances are if you go to court, as opposed to settling.

Q I never signed a contract with my ex-lawyer, but now that I've gone to someone else, he says I can't have my file back until I pay him. Can he do that to me?

A Yes. When you consulted that lawyer, you created an implied contract to pay for his services. The idea behind this rule of law is that you knew—or should have known—that an attorney charges for his services. You were therefore consenting to pay for them, even though it wasn't spelled out in a contract. By law, an attorney is allowed to retain a client's file until paid. This is a sort of lien.

NOTE: The charges for the services must be *reasonable*. If they're not, get your new lawyer to call the old and say, "Hey, Joe, let's get this little disagreement settled up . . ." NOTE ALSO: Many attorneys are too lax about giving the client a contract that sets out fees and anticipated expenses (though they'll usually be sure to sign up the client when it's a big one). On the other hand, you have a responsibility to check out the arrangement.

The client is boss

In the contract between attorney and client, the final decision remains with the client, unless the client has explicitly empowered the attorney to use his discretion to settle the matter. All offers of settlement from the other side—no matter how far below what the attorney thinks is a reasonable settlement—must be referred to the client. In fact, until the judge or jury gives a final verdict in a case, the client may demand settlement with the other side. Moreover, unless there's some emergency, any settlement the attorney makes is not binding on the client without the client's approval.

Sometimes the attorney will ask the client for prior authority to settle a case within a certain amount of money. When this happens, or when the client has approved an express settlement, then the client is "bound," whether or not it turns out that the attorney's advice is wrong.

If the attorney has settled the claim for too small an amount or has gone to court when he should have settled, the client has no recourse against his opponent and can only proceed against the attorney for this type of alleged malpractice.

Privilege and confidential communication

Once the attorney-client relationship is established, any statements made by the client to the attorney are "privileged."* This "privilege" belongs to the client, which means that only with the client's consent can the attorney divulge any information given to her.

The privilege applies only if the person invoking it is a client or has divulged the facts while seeking legal counsel before becoming a client. In addition, the person to whom the communication is made must be a licensed attorney or her employee. With some exceptions, the privilege does *not* apply if third parties are present.

The communication is *not* protected if the advice sought is for the purpose of committing a crime.

The client can waive the privilege if he or she chooses.

Crimes

The general rule is that even admission of a past crime is still privileged or confidential communication. However, legal ethics seminars continue to wrestle with individual fact situations as to what to do when one is confronted with knowledge of the commission of a serious crime. The problem is that if the attorney takes the step of withdrawing from the case, that withdrawal signifies to the judge that facts are known to the detriment of the client. On the other hand, the privilege exists because of the recognized necessity of a client being able to tell his or her attorney *all* the facts.

Case: A client told his attorney of his guilt in offering a bribe to have election returns tampered with. A grand jury wanted the name of this person and the attorney refused to supply it. The attorney was sentenced to jail on a contempt charge because of that action. The appellate court dismissed the contempt, holding that the attorney acted properly in refusing to identify the client.

Case: Here, one of four defendants admitted to his attorney that they had committed the crime with which they were charged. Unfortunately, the attorney broke faith and revealed the privileged communication and the defendants were convicted. This was reversed on appeal because the attorney had no right to so testify.

As to future crimes, I believe each attorney must decide how to handle the situation when he's given privileged information as to that. Obviously, the confidentiality cannot be carried to the point where an attorney does nothing while a crime is committed. On the other hand, the privilege is one of the most important that we possess.

I have seen legal ethics discussions where attorneys working for the IRS would strenuously argue that the privilege should remain sacrosanct even for murder, but had no problem finding that a plan to evade taxes should most definitely be reported.

Malpractice

General

When an attorney purchases a malpractice insurance policy, it's called an "errors and omissions policy." That sounds much better.

Malpractice can be defined as: a dereliction from professional duty or a failure of professional skill or learning that results in injury, loss, or damage.

The attorney's part of the contract with the client includes a duty to exercise reasonable care in using the skills for which she was hired. The standard is that of the other attorneys in the community.

An attorney must meet a standard that assumes he knows the basic law, as well as statutes and court rules. Where the law is uncertain, some courts have held that the attorney has the duty to research it.

Despite the above, it will remain difficult in many areas, such as giving advice or suggesting whether to settle a case or go to court, to show that the attorney dropped below the acceptable level of counseling his client. This is because, like a plastic surgeon, an attorney does not guarantee results.

Nevertheless, an attorney can be found guilty of malpractice in many areas. Some of the most common involve: defense of criminal cases; delays in filing suits and/or recording documents; estate planning; and poor advice as to how much a case is worth and whether it should be settled or tried.

A suit against an attorney for breach of contract or negligence is a peculiar creature because, most often, the plaintiff-client must prove he or she would have won "but for" the alleged wrongful actions of the attorney, i.e., re-try the case.

Is expert evidence necessary to prove legal malpractice? Here the law is changing. Expert evidence—testimony by other attorneys—is usually needed where the questions concern the conduct of a trial, lack of preparation, or bad advice.

The common sense of the jury is usually considered sufficient on such matters as an attorney allowing the time to run out on filing a case.

Case: This case seems close to what one of our most famous justices would have called "a derelict on the waters of the law." The attorney failed to tell the client about an offer from the other side that ended up being in excess of what the attorney got as a verdict in the trial of the case. The court said that although this was not proper practice, the plaintiff-client had not shown that the offer would have been accepted if communicated.

Q My attorney really screwed up my case, but my barber says I don't stand a chance of getting another attorney to sue for malpractice. Is that right?

A Well, actually, if your malpractice case really has merit, many attorneys will take it. However, there is a big "but." To win a malpractice case, you have in effect a play within a play: you must show that you would have won the original case and then show that the reason you didn't win was because of your attorney.

Q My attorney promised to get me all sorts of money for the car wreck I was in, but she lost the suit. My brother-in-law says that I should sue her for breach of contract. Can I do it?

A No—or at least it's very unlikely. Normally, an attorney losing a lawsuit is not liable for breach of contract or malpractice. An attorney can do a pretty crummy job and a court still won't hold that her representation of you has dropped so far down the scale as to be called malpractice. It must be below the standards set by attorneys of that area.

In your particular case, it would be very rare that a court would find that an attorney truly promised to win a lawsuit as part of the contract or bargain. (However, I have known some lawyers like that and they box themselves in by promising clients an unrealistic amount.)

Allowing time to run out

Probably the most obvious area of malpractice is when an attorney misses the deadline for filing suit, so that the client no longer has a right to go to court. This usually refers to the "statutes of limitation."* These are the old English common-law rules made specific by statutes: a person has a certain time to file suit in each of the areas of the law, such as contracts or torts. The length of time depends upon the kind of case involved. The idea behind this is that all litigation must eventually be laid to rest and that a potential defendant should not live his whole life wondering if suit is going to be brought over some matter.

NOTE: The plaintiff must always first show that the attorney-client relationship was created. This becomes quite involved if the client has hired a second attorney but is still trying to show that it was the first attorney's responsibility to get the matter on file before it was barred by the statute of limitations.

Settlement instead of suit

In this area of alleged malpractice, a client claims that the attorney advised him improperly to accept a settlement or that, when the suit was tried, the attorney had breached the contract by not learning enough facts and/or law.

Remember, however, that *seldom* is an attorney ever held liable because of results alone. In fact, surveys show that clients complain far more about a lack of communication and the fear that their case is being neglected.

Withdrawal

In many states an attorney must get the consent of the judge involved to withdraw from a case. Lack of payment is seldom an excuse for withdrawal.

The attorney must always have reasonable cause to withdraw because the implied contract is that when she takes on a case, she will continue with it until it is resolved.

Each state sets out how an attorney is supposed to go about withdrawing from a case. Even if a court finds that an attorney has a good reason for withdrawing, she may still be liable for any damage done to a client by her withdrawal.

Going to Court

Mechanics of suit

Q What actually happens if I decide to sue for *breach of contract*?

A First, you're unlikely to actually get to court as far as the percentages go: for example, approximately 98 percent of the cases are settled instead of going to trial in the federal courts. (More are tried in the state courts.) But, assuming your attorney has tried to settle the matter without result, here are the steps:

1. A petition* is drawn up. This is the paper which sets out the facts, the contract, and what the other fellow did that you claim is a breach of contract. You're called the plaintiff, and the other side is the defendant.

2. The sheriff's deputy or "process server" serves* (hands to the defendant or someone in the household over eighteen) the petition on the defendant.

3. The defendant has thirty days to file an answer.* This is what it sounds like: the other side denies everything you claim that's in dispute, paragraph by paragraph—or for some paragraphs he might say, in effect, that he doesn't know and, therefore, denies.

4. Probably before he gets around to filing that answer, the defense attorney, the lawyer for the defendant, will shoot off some motions.* These are papers filed in court. Some of the most common ask the judge for more time (to take more than thirty days, for instance) or claim your petition is so poorly worded the defendant just doesn't know what

you're even talking about ("Motion to Make More Definite and Certain").

5. Now, you think, comes the trial. Wrong. Even though settlement failed before, once the petition is filed, negotiations usually start up all over again. All the "discovery"* comes in this period, when each side finds out as much as possible about the other side's case, and also how good his witnesses appear. This discovery includes depositions* and interrogatories.* In a deposition a party (or certain others) is asked questions under oath and the whole proceeding is recorded by a court reporter. In contrast, interrogatories are written questions to which the person gives sworn written answers.

6. Trial—unless it's settled "on the courthouse steps." From the start all this would have taken place in either federal or state court, unless you had a small enough case for you to have gone to "small claims" or magistrate court. If so, forget all the above.

Q I've never been inside a courtroom. How does a trial work?

A It begins with the jury panel, the people who have been called to serve this term, usually by names picked from the voter lists, though this varies.

Next, again by something like a lottery, names are picked from that panel to be, tentatively, the actual jury—twelve plus one alternate or two in most cases, fewer in others. Now comes the "voir dire"* which consists of asking the jury members questions to decide who seem the best—and worst—for your side.

In some states, the voir dire consists of addressing questions to the whole jury panel en masse; in others, each attorney gets to ask questions of each jury member sitting in the jury box. When one is "struck," another takes his place. "Struck" means either side has said "No" to that juror. If you can convince the judge a juror has shown he will be biased or unfair, he will be excused "for cause." There is an unlimited number of these rejections. The other kind of "challenge"* doesn't require any reason—such as you don't like jurors with blue eyes—but these challenges are limited in number by state law.

Once a jury is chosen and sworn in, the judge reads some of the "instructions"* to the jury. These are just what they sound like: the rules the jury is to go by.

All this time you'll be sitting at a table with your lawyer, and the other side at another table with his lawyer. After the instructions, the plaintiff, the one doing the suing, puts on his witnesses first. The defense gets to cross-examine each of the plaintiff's witnesses. Then it's the defendant's turn to present his case and the plaintiff's attorney cross-examines.

The plaintiff goes first because he's the one who has to prove the defendant did something wrong.

At the end, the attorney for each side makes a speech to the jury, telling them why they should decide in favor of his client. The judge gives the jury much longer instructions than at the beginning and the jury "retire"; they go to the jury room and, after electing a foreman, decide the case.

In a civil case, the plaintiff must win by a preponderance of the evidence—has the "burden of proof."

Eventually the jury comes filing back in and announces the winner.

Q Is the law different in every state?

A Not very—except in Louisiana, where the law is based on Continental law. The law in all of the other states comes down to us from the English common law (with some Spanish thrown in in the West) and the basic principles of law are the same. Usually the biggest differences are in matters of "procedure," the technical rules.

Q I was in a really bad wreck that wasn't my fault. The trouble is, the man driving the other car was from a different state. Do I have to go there to bring suit?

A No. Most, if not all, of the states have what are called "long-arm statutes."* These are based on the legal fiction that, for the privilege of driving on the highway of another state, you have given your permission (even if you don't know it) to be sued in that state if you have an accident. Therefore, the other driver can be sued in your state and served in his state.

Q Can I get a lawyer who'll threaten to sue somebody but who won't make me actually go to court?

A I wouldn't, but some would. It would place me in an unethical position to tell an attorney for the other side that we were going to sue if necessary, while knowing my client wouldn't go to court. Also, as a practical matter, I wouldn't want to be placed out on a limb like that: never threaten what you can't produce.

I've known more than one attorney who we all knew wouldn't try a case. The insurance companies knew it, too, and their settlements with him were considerably lower.

Q If somebody sues me, but I win, can I make them pay my attorney's fees?

A Usually not. It seems wrong, but normally you're still out your attorney's fees—what you had to pay to have your suit defended. In most states you get "costs" back, but those are usually limited to what was paid into court and such things as "depositions."* The exception— rare—is if you can show "malicious prosecution," which means suit was brought against you groundlessly, with bad motive.

NOTE: In almost every credit arrangement, if you read the fine print, you'll find that you, as debtor, have agreed to pay attorney's fees—the cost of collecting—if you default.

Q How much does it cost to sue somebody?

A It's difficult to say. Whether you contract with your lawyer on a contingency or an hourly rate, there are some basic charges you'll be responsible for: filing fees, service, and, usually, depositions.

1. The filing fee (usually below $100) is paid into court when your lawyer files the petition, the suit papers.

2. The service fee (not expensive) is charged by the sheriff for "serving"*—handing a copy of the petition to—the defendant.

3. "Depositions"* are questions and answers under oath, taken down by a court reporter,* with the attorney on each side asking questions of the parties or witnesses or experts, such as doctors. The court reporter charges a per-page fee for this, so the amount depends on how long the deposition is. Depositions are usually expensive. If expert witnesses are used, such as accident investigators, they charge for their time—at rates of $100 an hour or more—whether they are doing on-site investigation, depositions, or testifying in court.

Next you'll have to pay court costs if you lose. If you've hired an attorney on an hourly basis, ask her to estimate how many hours she expects to put in. (She'll usually estimate at the top amount she anticipates, to avoid an angry client later.) Often the lawyer will charge a smaller amount per hour for office time than for time spent in court.

P.S. Do not expect to have a happy chat if you call your lawyer at home and say, "I didn't want to bother you at the office."

Q How long can I wait to sue somebody?
A That depends on what kind of suit it is and where you live.

First, in every state the time limits vary as to length of time in which you must bring suit (file a petition), according to the kind of action you're bringing. As an example, you might have only a year to sue a doctor for malpractice but five years to seek damages for personal injury in an auto accident. The amount of time after which suit can*not* be brought is called the "statute of limitations."

Second, the length of time always depends on the statutes (laws) in the state you're living in and where you're going to sue. These vary.

Third, there are some special exceptions that affect the time limit. They mainly have to do with minors and moving to another state.

The trial

Q I'm involved in a big dispute over a contract and what I want to know is: at the trial, what's to keep the other side from listening to each other's testimony and then lying to make theirs fit?

A Attorneys and judges call it "invoking the rule." That means either side can ask that all potential witnesses be kept out of the courtroom until they testify.

Q What does it mean when an attorney jumps up during a trial and says, "I object!"? Also, that string of words starting with "irrelevant"?

A The "string" is probably; "Irrelevant, incompetent, immaterial, and inadmissible." All sorts of rules have developed—actually based on common sense—as to what evidence can be brought in to help prove— or disprove—a case. When an attorney objects to testimony, he's saying it breaks one of these rules, and "irrelevant" is one of the reasons, meaning that testimony is not relevant to the point at issue.

The "hearsay objection" applies to the situation when the person isn't testifying as to his or her own knowledge but secondhand as to what someone else said to them. One of the main reasons hearsay is kept out is that the other side can't cross-examine to get at the truth because the person who counts is the one who isn't there.

Q How does a judge decide a case?

A At the trial level, the judge who hears the case for the first time goes by the "rules of law," the law which has been developed by decisions of higher courts (state and federal appellate and supreme courts) in the past. These are "precedents."*

If the particular point of law hasn't ever come up before, it's called "a case of first impression" and the judge is on his own.

There's an interesting difference between U.S. and European lawyers. The Europeans like going by statutes; the American lawyers don't feel safe until there's a court decision telling them what the statute means.

After judgment

Q I got a letter from a collection agency that said if they had to go to court, they would execute. Is that as bad as it sounds?

A   As far as the gas chamber, no. "Execution"* and "attachment"* go together. When a person wins a suit and gets a judgment against the other party, he or she can then "execute that judgment," which means to collect it. This is often by means of "attachment"—telling the sheriff what property of the losing party to go out and collect as worth the amount of the judgment. Therefore, a creditor could execute his judgment against you by attaching your car, for example.

NOTE: If you appeal the decision against you, the judgment creditor must hold off attaching your property *if* you post an appeal bond in at least the amount of the judgment.

Q   My barber says it's no use my going to small claims court because the judgment isn't worth much. Is that right?

A   Unfortunately, it often is, but the answer is not to give up on small claims courts. The judgment's all right; the trouble is with the collection. This is because you usually don't have an attorney in small claims and the sheriff isn't going to take the initiative to go out and collect your judgment for you. Find out your options, such as attaching a car or garnishing your opponent's wages, and then push the sheriff to do his job.

The appeal

Q   It always sounds so impressive on the news when they say, "The attorneys for Mr. Jones have announced they will appeal." Does this mean the verdict was wrong?

A   Not in the majority of cases. Whether it's a criminal or civil case and whether it's decided by a judge or jury, the loser (except usually not the state in a criminal case) can appeal to a higher court, i.e., a court of appeals or a supreme court, depending on the rules of that state.

The appeal sets out what the attorney for the loser claims were mistakes made in the trial, and that these were so bad the appellant (the one appealing) didn't have a fair trial. These are called the "grounds" for appeal, and there are usually several of them. An example would be if the judge went along with an objection and refused to let the jury hear certain testimony; the other side would claim this was wrong and made them lose the case.

NOTE: When I mentioned the state in a criminal case, I was referring to the rule in most states that the state isn't allowed to appeal if the defendant is found not guilty. That's why I'm amused when the news announces the prosecutor says he will not appeal—he can't.

Q How does an appeal work?

A The times may vary from one state to another or in federal court, but basically the mechanics are:

1. A party who loses in the trial court—the court where the matter first comes up before a judge or jury—sets out, for that judge, why he thinks he should have a new trial. This is so that the original judge has a chance to correct any mistakes he made in the conduct of the trial. This "Motion for a New Trial" is usually turned down.

2. The losing party, now called the "appellant," files a notice of appeal and requests the transcript, which is the record of every word said in the trial. This will be due in a certain number of days, for example, ninety days.

3. After receiving the transcript, the appellant has thirty days to file his or her brief with the next highest court (depending on what kind of case it is). The "brief"* is a written argument setting out, on the basis of prior cases, what the trial court did wrong and why it was so serious that the appellant should get another trial or have the whole thing thrown out.

4. The other side has thirty days to file its "answer,"* arguing why the judgment was proper.

5. The appellant gets to "reply,"* and then there's an oral argument before the appellate court,* and finally, based on all the above, the court makes its decision.

6. If the appellate court "affirms the judgment" of the trial court, the verdict or judgment stands and the defendant either is off the hook or the plaintiff can now execute on the judgment.

7. If the appellate court "reverses" the trial court, the reversal can be worded so that the suit is now dead for all practical purposes or the case can be tried all over again.

Q If I lose my case, can I take it to the Supreme Court?

A Probably not, if you're talking about the Supreme Court of the United States, although the media may make it sound as if the Supreme Court jumps in all over the place.

In only a few instances, such as disputes between states or a particular kind of case that raises a valid constitutional question, can a person appeal to the Supreme Court as "a matter of right." This means that the Supreme Court *has* to hear the case.

In cases decided by state courts, you can often appeal to the state supreme court, but to get heard in a federal court or the Supreme Court of the United States—except in those peculiar instances just mentioned—your attorney would first have to file a petition arguing why the Supreme Court of the United States should agree to hear the case. The Supreme Court would then have to decide that not only did your case meet all the qualifications, but also it involved a matter of national importance.

I guess this explains the line: "What are you trying to do? Make a federal case out of it?"

CHAPTER IX

Authors and Artists

Contracts and Copyright

INTRODUCTION/HISTORY

Authors and artists gained a place in history together tens of thousands of years ago. Pictographs evolved from the urge to communicate or record. Before there was a written language, drawings (petrograms) or carvings (petroglyphs) on the walls of one's home or nearby rocks told the story. Pictography was the first step toward writing. Symbols representing the spoken word (alphabets) began around 1700 B.C.E. (or earlier as new discoveries are made).

In a few millennia, this need to give permanence to expression developed into the idea that the created word, sound or picture was a kind of property which belonged to the creator.

Copyright law

From the beginning we told stories as we sat around the campfire. The talented storyteller could earn his keep by weaving tales of the tribe's history, the movements of peoples, feast and famine, drought and storm, rulers and their foibles. That was before agents and publishers and gallery owners.

You've learned the contract basics and how to read a contract. Having considered other specialized areas of the law, we turn to those of particular interest to authors and artists. These include the following:

1. Pre-representation agreement
2. Contracts with agents
3. Contracts with galleries
4. Contracts with publishers
5. Intellectual Property Law

Pre-representation agreement

Many agents have guidelines for submission. They range from allowing only an initial query letter to permitting the author to submit something on the order of 50 pages or three chapters and an outline. Some agents, however, demand the author first sign an acknowledgement like the following.

John Doe
Literary Agent Artist Representative
Request for Project Submission

Dear _____,

Your query has arrived at our office and we would be receptive to considering your project subject to your review and acceptance of the following information. We hope you understand that these are our submission policies and they are meant to help you in the most efficient way.

First peruse the General Agency Profile about The John Doe Literary Agency. Then if you feel your material would be appropriate for consideration by our Agency, do as follows. For fiction please send a ONE PAGE synopsis and the FIRST three chapters or a ONE PAGE synopsis and the FIRST fifty pages. (DO NOT SEND THE ENTIRE MANUSCRIPT.) If your project is nonfiction, send a proposal which must contain the Overview, Table of Contents (with brief chapter summaries), Author Biography and Credits (include other books published, by whom and when), Audience and Marketing information (including who will buy this book and what other comparable titles are currently in the bookstores) and finally include the first one, two, or three sample chapters. Should your project be a work for film (or television or cable), send a ONE-PAGE SYNOPSIS (NOT A TREATMENT) along with the entire screenplay. Whichever it is, be sure to send along a self addressed envelope with the correct postage to ensure the safe return of your work should it indeed fail to meet the criteria of The John Doe Literary Agency. (Note we do not return material without the proper sized return envelope and the correct postage.)

Please mark the outside of your mailing envelope addressed to us with a clearly visible REQUESTED, in the lower left-hand corner. If you wish to know immediately that your package arrived, we suggest you send — in addition to the above mentioned SASE — a self-addressed stamped post card that we can readily drop in the mail. Enclose a processing fee of $50.00 (not a reading fee) or send along a copy of your current WGA membership card and that processing fee will be waived. (If any of this you find unreasonable for any reason, we suggest you forego the opportunity of having your work reviewed by this Agency, and thank you very much for thinking of The John Doe Literary Agency. We wish you the best of luck with your writing and work.) Otherwise, The John Doe Literary Agency sincerely looks forward to seeing your writing project. Finally, make a copy of this letter, sign it and include it — along with your project, your processing fee, the SASE and so on — in your package, marked as specified above. (Note: If you fail to include any of the above, it may cause delay in processing your submission.)

I have read the above and understand your submission policies:
Signed: _____
Writer /Date

A Note about Response Time: It will take some time to get back to you, so please be patient. Sometimes we can get back to you right away, within two weeks or so. Sometimes it may take longer. It takes expertise, experience and time to properly evaluate manuscripts and proposals for books and projects to be considered by the Agency. The Agency must be very strong in its enthusiasm and commitment. The decision to take on a client requires serious thought. All aspects of a writer's work, background, and especially his or her professionalism are considered. It simply takes time.

P.S. You have deduced by now that this is a "form" letter. But do not for one moment think that it diminishes your work (or our response to it) in any way. As stated above we are trying to be efficient so that we can spend more time considering your material.

Q I wrote an agent asking about my writing project and he sent me back a form that set out his rules for submission. I was supposed to sign it, then send that paper along with my manuscript. Is this a contract?

A No. If it's like the one printed here, that agent isn't bound to anything. And if one party isn't bound, neither party is. In my opinion, your signing is nothing more than an acknowledgement.

Q I've read that I should submit my manuscript to several agents, but I signed a paper that one agent sent. Does that keep me from trying others at the same time?

A Technically no, so long as the "paper" isn't a contract and you're not promising her "an exclusive." I do think it would be best, though, to let each agent know you're making a multiple submission. If you don't, they'll be pretty ticked off at taking the time to consider your work, only to be told you already have an agent—you hope!

Q I've read that I shouldn't ask an agent to represent me if he charges a reading fee, or at least that reading fees be only a certain small percentage of the agency's income. Now I get this pre-representation thing asking for $50 but saying that's not a reading fee; it's a "processing fee." Is that okay?

A It's your call. I don't think there's a valid distinction. A rose by any other name is still a fee—except this lets the agent off the hook for even a pretense of reading. Hopeful authors are parting with their money with no promise of anything. Is it worth it to you? Apparently this agent won't consider you without cash up front. Others will.

Contracts with Agents

The author-agent relationship ranges from the equivalent of the old-fashioned handshake to a multi-page complex contract. If you're an experienced pro with the money trucks rolling up to your door, you already know the pitfalls. If you're just getting started don't, in your eagerness to find an agent, sell your soul. Read that contract carefully. Understand what the agent promises to do for you, what you must do, how much commission the agent will make, and when and in what manner either party can terminate.

Most agency contracts are fairly simple and end at the wish of either party, often with 30 days notice. This makes sense because the agent can't very well make you write. It's very important, however, that the details of dissolution be spelled out in the contract. What if the agent has sold first rights to your book but not the subsidiary rights when you part? What if the agent has not sold your manuscript but you find a chance to do so yourself? What if you just don't feel your agent is doing anything for you? Have it in writing!

The following sample agent contract is more favorable to the author and more demanding of the agent than the norm.

Author—Agent Contract

AGREEMENT, entered into as of this____ day of_____ , 19___ ,between (hereinafter referred to as the "Author"), located at

_____ ,and _____ (hereinafter referred to as the "Agent"), located at _____

_____WHEREAS, the Author is an established author of proven talents; and WHEREAS, the Author wishes to have an agent represent him or her in marketing certain rights enumerated herein; and WHEREAS, the Agent is capable of marketing the writing created by the Author; and WHEREAS, the Agent wishes to represent the Author; NOW, THEREFORE, in consideration of the foregoing premises and the mutual covenants hereinafter set forth and other valuable consideration, the parties hereto agree as follows:

1. Agency. The Author appoints the Agent to act as his or her representative:

(A) in the following geographical area _____

(B) for the following markets: ___ Book publishing ___ Magazines ___ Television ___ Motion Picture ___ Other, specified as

_____ _____

(C) to be the Author's __ exclusive __ nonexclusive agent in the area and markets indicated

Any rights not granted to the Agent are reserved to the Author.

2. Best Efforts. The Agent agrees to use his or her best efforts in submitting the Author's work for the purpose of securing assignments for the Author. The Agent shall negotiate the terms of any assignment that is offered, but the Author may reject any assignment if he or she finds the terms thereof unacceptable.

3. Samples. The Author shall provide the Agent with such samples of work as are from time to time necessary for the purpose of securing assignments. These samples shall remain the property of the Author and be returned on termination of this Agreement.

4. Term. This Agreement shall take effect as of the date first set forth above, and remain in full force and effect for a term of one year, unless terminated as provided in Paragraph 10.

5. Commissions. The Agent shall be entitled to a ___ percent commission for work obtained by the Agent during the term of this Agreement and a ___ percent commission for work obtained by the Author during the term of this Agreement, except that no commission shall be payable for the following types of work obtained by the Author. It is understood by both parties that no

commissions shall be paid on assignments rejected by the Author or for which the Author fails to receive payment, regardless of the reason payment is not made. Further, no commissions shall be payable for any part of the billing that is due to expenses incurred by the Author and reimbursed by the client. In the event that a flat fee is paid by the client, ___the Agent's commission shall be payable only on the fee as reduced for expenses ___ the Agent's commission shall be payable on the full fee.

6. Billing. The Agent shall be responsible for all billings.

7. Payments. The Agent shall make all payments due within ___ days of receipt of any fees covered by this Agreement. Such payments due shall be deemed trust funds and shall not be intermingled with funds belonging to the Agent. Late payments shall be accompanied by interest calculated at the rate of ___ percent per month thereafter.

8. Accountings. The Agent shall send copies of statements of account received by the Agent to the Author when rendered. If requested, the Agent shall also provide the Author with semiannual accountings showing all income for the period, the clients' names and addresses, the fees paid, the dates of payment, the amounts on which the Agent's commissions are to be calculated, and the sums due less those amounts already paid.

9. Inspection of the Books and Records. The Agent shall keep the books and records with respect to payments due each party at his or her place of business and permit the other party to inspect these books and records during normal business hours on the giving of reasonable notice.

10. Termination. This Agreement may be terminated by either party by giving thirty (30) days written notice to the other party. In the event of the bankruptcy or insolvency of the Agent, this Agreement shall also terminate. The rights and obligations under Paragraphs 3, 6, 7, 8, and 9 shall survive termination, provided that in the event of termination the Author shall have the right to have payments (less commissions) paid directly to the Author rather than to the Agent as set forth in Paragraph 7.

11. Assignment. This Agreement shall not be assigned by either of the parties hereto. It shall be binding on and inure to the benefit of the successors, administrators, executors, or heirs of the Agent and Author.

12. Arbitration. Any disputes arising under this Agreement shall be settled by arbitration before _____ under the rules of the American Arbitration Association in the City of _____ except that the parties shall have the right to go to court for claims of $_____ or less. Any award rendered by the arbitrator may be entered in any court having jurisdiction thereof.

13. Notices. All notices shall be given to the parties at their respective addresses set forth above.

14. Independent Contractor Status. Both parties agree that the Agent is acting as an independent contractor. This Agreement is not an employment

agreement, nor does it constitute a joint venture or partnership between the Author and Agent.

15. Amendments and Merger. All amendments to this Agreement must be written. This Agreement incorporates the entire understanding of the parties.

16. Governing Law. This Agreement shall be governed by the laws of the State of _____.

IN WITNESS WHEREOF, the parties have signed this Agreement as of the date set forth above.

Author_____

Agent _____

Q Why should I pay an agent ten or fifteen percent of my royalties? Why not just do without?

A First, if you're unknown, your unagented manuscript ends up in the publisher's "slush pile" which is a very precarious place to be. In fact, many publishers won't consider unagented material. Second, if you've been so lucky as to have your manuscript solicited by the publisher, a good agent would still be of help. This would be negotiating the best deal for you as well as navigating through the shoals of the contract between the publisher and you, handling subsidiary rights (book, film, foreign), and promoting your successful career.

On the other hand, some established authors have never had an agent and are doing quite well on their own, thank you.

Q My agent told me that she had sent my manuscript to certain publishers but I discovered that those publishers had not seen it at all! Now I've found a publisher for my novel but the agent claims that was one she had already contacted. Do I owe her the fifteen percent of everything?

A See a lawyer! This isn't a matter of contract law but investigation. You need to find out from the publisher if the agent's claims are true and get proof.

Q What does an agent owe me?

A The agent owes you the same sort of duties as are owed under most contracts: to submit your manuscript to a reasonable number of appropriate publishers in a timely fashion (and to continue submitting so long as is reasonable), to keep you informed of their responses, to inform you of any changes you might make based on those responses, to negotiate a sale for the best possible terms (not only price), and to use his or her expertise to promote your career.

Q What if the agent and I part company and then I—sell movie rights?—or am offered a contract to reprint the book?—or get selected by a book club? Do I still owe him a percentage? If so, for how long?

A Get it in writing! Be sure the contract covers all these questions that might arise after termination: under what circumstances and for how long you will owe the agent his or her fee, as well as how the contract can be ended and with how much notice.

Contracts with Galleries

Questions that are essentially the same as those of writers can arise between an artist and a gallery. When can the artist remove her paintings from the gallery? What if the artist subsequently sells a painting from his studio that the purchaser first saw in the gallery? What if the purchaser didn't see that particular painting but became acquainted with the artist's work because of the gallery exhibit? And, more particular to artists, who bears the cost of shipping and crating? To a purchaser? To a special exhibit? Who says if that exhibit is worth the cost of shipping? All of these questions must be specified in the contract as well as any others you can imagine.

Like beginning writers seeking an agent, artists who have *not* had extensive sales will often be too eager to be shown by a gallery. They accept an unfair division of the money upon the sale of a painting or sculpture. They fail to demand the specifics—or even to think of them.

Specify what terms you'll allow the gallery to accept from a purchaser, i.e., must the purchaser pay cash? If the purchaser can make installments, how many? How much down?

I've often had clients say, "Oh, we're such good friends we don't need a contract." If you're going to stay friends, get it in writing! Same thing: if you're going to get your career off to a clean start unmarred by later law suits, contract in detail and in writing.

Questions on gallery contracts

Q The gallery where I'm showing sold a painting of mine six months ago, but I haven't seen any money. Can I sue?

A Of course you can sue, but you need to check your contract to see what chance you'll have of winning. Does your contract specify how soon after a sale you must be paid? Is the time different for a cash sale or installment? If the contract doesn't mention time, what's customary in your community?

Q My contract says I'll be paid within 30 days of the sale, but the gallery owner says that my sculpture was bought on time payments so she doesn't owe me until she's paid in full. Is this right?

A Only if the contract says so. Otherwise I'd think you were entitled to your portion of each payment. Of course you might have gotten really lucky and have a contract that says you'll be paid the same as for a cash sale even if the gallery owner decides to wait on full payment.

Q The gallery owner has a chance to have prints of some of my work included in a very upscale magazine spread. He says I have to pay to get it camera ready. That's not fair, is it?

A Your contract should specify who pays for this sort of thing—and also for other costs such as shipping to an exhibit. If there's no mention, then I'd apply common sense. Does the write-up feature you or focus on the gallery? Will you benefit enough to make it worth your while to pay, fair or not?

Contracts with Publishers

Just as there is an endless variety of contracts between authors and agents, so too the contracts with publishers range widely. Much standard "boiler plate" is common to most contracts. The main variance is how much the contract is slanted toward the publisher or (much more rarely) the author. The contract that follows is one that takes a pretty fair middle ground. After we go over it, I'll give you some clauses from the more publisher-slanted contracts, including one that carries a big *caveat*!

Book Publishing Contract

AGREEMENT, entered into as of this _____ day of _____, 19 ___, between Mega Publishing Co. (hereinafter referred to as the "Publisher"), located at New York City, and Joe Author (hereinafter referred to as the "Author"), located at Any Town, USA

WITNESSETH:

1. Grant of Rights. The Author grants, conveys, and transfers to the Publisher in the literary Work *Joe's Book*, hereinafter referred to as "the Work," the exclusive right to publish, distribute, and sell the Work in book form, worldwide, in the English language, for a term of 5 years. Author also grants the Publisher the right to publish, distribute, and sell derivations of the Work in the form of booklets, Special Reports, and audio tapes on the same terms described throughout this document.

2. Delivery of Manuscript. On or before _____ (date), the Author shall deliver to the publisher the complete manuscript of the Work, approximately 100,000 words, which shall be reasonably satisfactory in form and content to the Publisher. If the Author fails to deliver the complete manuscript within ninety days after receiving notice from the Publisher of failure to deliver on time, the Publisher shall have the right to terminate this Agreement and receive back from the Author all monies advanced to the Author pursuant to Paragraph 8. If the Author delivers a manuscript which, after being given detailed instructions for revisions by the Publisher and 60 days to complete such revisions, is not reasonably acceptable to the Publisher, then monies advanced to the Author pursuant to Paragraph 8 shall be repaid to the Publisher.

3. Additional Materials. The following materials shall be provided by the Author: Author photo and publisher-supplied Author Questionnaire. The cost of providing these additional materials shall be borne by the Author.

4. Permissions. The Author agrees to obtain all permissions that are necessary for the use of materials copyrighted by others. Signed permission forms will be retained in the Author's files, with copies provided to the Publisher. The cost of obtaining these permissions will be borne by the Author.

5. Duty to Publish. The Publisher shall publish the Work within 24 months of the delivery of the complete manuscript. Failure to so publish shall give the Author the right to terminate this Agreement ninety days after giving written notice to the Publisher of the failure to make timely publication. In the event of such termination, the Author shall have no obligation to return monies received pursuant to Paragraph 8.

6. Royalties. The Publisher shall pay the Author the following royalties: 15% of the wholesale price on the first 10,000 copies distributed, 17% of the wholesale price on the next 5,000 copies distributed; and 19% of the wholesale price on all copies distributed thereafter. Royalties are not payable on author copies sold pursuant to Paragraph 16 of this Agreement. These royalty rates shall be discounted only in the following circumstances: copies sold as remainders at a higher than 55% discount.

All copies sold shall be cumulated for purposes of escalations in the royalty rates, including revised editions, except for editions in a different form (such as a paperback reprint of a hardcover original) which shall be cumulated separately. Copies sold shall be reduced by copies returned in the same royalty category in which the copies were originally reported as sold.

7. Subsidiary Rights. The publisher shall have the right to license subsidiary rights in the Work, with the proceeds divided as specified herein:

Right	% to Author	% to Publisher
Reprint edition through another publisher	50	50
Book Club	50	50
Digest, abridgment or condensation, second serial	50	50
Syndication, Anthology or Quotation	50	50
First Serial (U.S.)	50	50
Motion Picture, Dramatic, Radio or Television	50	50
Foreign Language	50	50
Commercial & Merchandising	50	50
Audio-Visual	50	50

In conjunction with any sale or license of motion picture, dramatic, radio or television rights in the work, the parties agree that the purchaser or licensee may be granted the non-exclusive right to publish or cause to be published summaries, synopses, or extracts of or from the Work, up to a maximum of five percent (5%) of the total text of the Work, or thirty-five hundred (3,500) words, whichever is less, provided that such summaries, synopses or extracts: (i) are used only for advertising or promoting the derivative work produced pursuant to such sale or license; (ii) are not published in book form or in the form of partial serializations, and (iii) are not represented as having been written by the Author unless (s)he is the actual writer thereof. The parties further agree that any purchaser or licensee of such rights shall be required to take such steps as may be necessary to protect the copyright in the Work.

8. Advances. Upon delivery of the manuscript, the Publisher shall pay to the Author a nonrefundable advance of $_____, which advance shall be recouped by the Publisher from payments due to the Author pursuant to Paragraph 6 of this Agreement.

9. Accountings. Commencing as of the date of publication the Publisher shall report every 6 months (in July for the sales period January through June; in January for the sales period July through December) to the Author, showing for that period and cumulatively to date the number of copies printed and bound, the number of copies sold and returned for each royalty rate, the number of copies distributed free for publicity purposes, the number of copies remaindered, destroyed, or lost, the royalties paid to and owed to the Author. If the Publisher sets up a reserve against returns of books, the reserve may only be set up for the four accounting periods following the first publication of the Work and shall in no event exceed 15 percent of royalties due to the Author in any period. Any overpayments made by the Publisher to the author or amounts for which the Author is indebted to the Publisher may be deducted from any sums due the Author from the Publisher, on this work.

10. Payments. The Publisher shall pay the Author all monies due Author pursuant to Paragraph 9 within thirty days of the close of each accounting period.

11. Right of Inspection. The Author shall, upon the giving of written notice, have the right to inspect the publisher's books of account to verify the accountings insofar as the Work is concerned, during normal business hours, at his sole expense, provided that no more than one such examination may be held for any royalty period.

12. Copyright and Authorship Credit. The Publisher shall, as an express condition of receiving the grant of rights specified in Paragraph 1, take the necessary steps to register the copyright on behalf of the Author and in the Author's name(s) and shall place copyright notice in the Author's name(s) on all copies of the Work. The Author shall receive authorship credit as follows:

Copyright c (date) Joe Author

13. Warranty and Indemnity. The Author warrants and represents that he or she is the sole creator of the Work and owns all rights granted under this Agreement, that the Work is an original creation (except for those materials for which permissions have been obtained pursuant to Paragraph 4), that the Work does not infringe any other person's copyrights or right of literary property, nor, to his or her knowledge, does it violate the rights of privacy of, or libel, other persons. The Author agrees to provide the Publisher with a letter reverting all rights back to the Author from her previous publisher. The Author agrees to indemnify the Publisher against any final judgment for damages (after all appeals have been exhausted) in any lawsuit based on an actual breach of the foregoing warranties. In addition, the Author shall pay the publisher's reasonable costs and attorney's fees incurred in defending such a lawsuit, unless the Author chooses to retain his or her own attorney to defend such lawsuit. The Author makes no warranties and shall have no obligation to indemnify the publisher with respect to materials inserted in the Work at the Publisher's request. In the event a lawsuit is brought which may result in the Author having breached his or her warranties under this Paragraph, the Publisher shall have the right to withhold and place in an escrow account 50 percent of sums payable to the Author pursuant to Paragraph 9, but in no event may said withholding exceed the Author's liability as defined above.

14. Artistic Control. The Author and Publisher shall consult with one another with respect to the title of the Work, the method and means of advertising and selling the Work, the number and destination of free copies, the number of copies to be printed, the method of printing and other publishing processes, the exact date of publication, the form, style, size, type, paper to be used, and like details, how long the plates or film shall be preserved and when they shall be destroyed, and when new printings of the Work shall be made. In the event of disagreement after consultation, the Publisher shall have final power of decision over all the foregoing matters. No changes shall be made in the complete manuscript of the Work by persons other than the Author, except for reasonable copy editing, unless the Author consents to such changes. Publisher shall provide the Author with galleys and proofs which the Author shall review and return to the Publisher within thirty (30) days of receipt. If the cost of the Author's alterations (other than for typesetting errors or unavoidable updating) exceeds 20 percent of the cost of the typography, the Publisher shall have the right to deduct such excess from royalties due Author hereunder.

15. Author's Property. The Publisher shall not be responsible for loss of or damage to any manuscript, illustrations, or other property of the Author except loss or damage due to the Publisher's gross negligence. The Author shall retain one copy of the manuscript and any other materials submitted to the Publisher hereunder.

16. Free Copies. The Author shall receive 30 free copies of the Work as published after which the Author shall have the right to purchase additional copies at a 40 percent discount from the retail price.

17. Revisions. The Author agrees to revise the Work on request by the Publisher. If the Author cannot revise the Work or refuses to do so absent good cause, the Publisher shall have the right to have the Work revised by a person competent to do so and shall charge the costs of said revision against payments due the Author under Paragraph 6 for such revised edition. In no event shall such revision costs exceed $500.

18. Successors and Assigns. This Agreement may not be assigned by either party without the written consent of the other party hereto. The Author, however, shall retain the right to assign payments due hereunder without obtaining the Publisher's consent. This Agreement shall be binding on the parties and their respective heirs, administrators, successors, and assigns.

19. Infringement. In the event of an infringement of the rights granted under this Agreement to the Publisher, the Publisher and the Author shall have the right to sue jointly for the infringement and, after deducting the expenses of bringing suit, to share equally in any recovery. If either party chooses not to join in the suit, the other party may proceed and, after deducting all the expenses of bringing the suit, any recovery shall be shared equally between the parties.

20. Termination. The Author shall have the right to terminate this Agreement by written notice if: (i) the Work goes out-of-print and the Publisher, within six months of receiving notice from the Author that the Work is out-of-print, does not place the Work in print again. The Work shall be considered to be in print if it is available in any edition in the United States or is under contract thereof. (ii) if the Publisher fails to provide statements of account pursuant to Paragraph 9; (iii) if the Publisher fails to make payments pursuant to Paragraphs 6, 8, or 10; or (iv) if the Publisher fails to publish in a timely manner pursuant to Paragraph 5. The Publisher shall have the right to terminate this Agreement as provided in Paragraph 2. This Agreement shall automatically terminate in the event of the Publisher's insolvency, bankruptcy, or assignment of assets for the benefit of creditors. In the event of termination of the Agreement, the Publisher shall grant, convey, and transfer all rights in the Work back to the Author.

Termination of this Agreement or reversion of rights to the Author shall be without prejudice to any licenses of rights in the Work previously made by the Publisher, and the Publisher shall continue to receive its share, as specified herein, of all proceeds derived from such licenses.

Upon termination the Publisher shall pay royalties on those copies represented by the reserve for returns.

21. Force Majeure. The failure of the Publisher to publish or republish the Work, or otherwise to perform its obligations hereunder, shall not be a violation of this Agreement if such failure is caused by strikes, wars, natural disasters, acts of God or other circumstances beyond the Publisher's reasonable control.

22. Production Materials and Unbound Copies. Upon any termination, the Author may, within sixty days of notification of such termination, purchase the plates, offset negatives, or computer drive tapes (if any) at their scrap value and any remaining copies at the lesser of cost or remainder value.

23. Non-Competition. The Author agrees that (i) the Work shall be his/her next book-length work; (ii) during the term of this Agreement, (s)he will not publish or cause to be published any book or article on the same or similar subject matter as the work which would tend to interfere with or diminish its sale; (iii) that (s)he will give the Publisher the right to review and make a publication offer on his/her next book-length work before it is offered to any other publisher.

24. Promotion. The Author consents to the use of his or her name, portrait, or picture for promotion and advertising of the Work, provided such use is dignified and consistent with the Author's reputation.

25. Miscellaneous. This Agreement (i) constitutes the entire agreement of the parties and supersedes any and all prior agreements and understandings between the Publisher and the Author with respect to the Work; (ii) may be executed simultaneously in counterparts, each of which shall be deemed an original, but all of which together shall constitute one and the same instrument; (iii) shall be construed and enforced in accordance with the laws of the State of _____; (iv) may be modified only by an instrument in writing signed by both parties; and (v) shall be binding upon, and inure to the benefit of, the Author's heirs, executors, administrators, and assigns and the Publisher's successors and assigns, provided that no assignment shall be made except in conformity with the provisions of Paragraph 18. Any reference herein to the singular shall include the plural and the masculine gender shall include the feminine where the context so requires. No waiver of any provision of this Agreement, or the breach thereof, shall be deemed a waiver of any other provision or breach. The caption headings contained in this Agreement are inserted for convenience only and shall not control or effect its interpretation in any respect.

IN WITNESS WHEREOF, the parties have signed this Agreement as of the date first set forth above.

Author: Joe Author   Publisher: Mega Publishing Co.

By:_____   _____
Authorized Signature   Authorized Signature

The numbered comments below correspond to the numbered paragraphs in the contract.

Comments

1. Later on the contract says the publisher will be copyrighting the book in *your* name; this paragraph is where you license the publisher to publish, distribute and sell your copyrighted material worldwide. And note: it's in *book* form, not other media.

a. These rights are to publish in English. Foreign language translations are *not* covered here.

b. The publisher lists its additional rights but this list is *not* all-inclusive as is an example given below. Be sure you know what rights you're selling—and what money you might be losing!

c. The term is 5 years. The contract does *not* say if the rights then revert to you or if the publisher has a right to renew the agreement.

2. You have to return the advance if you don't deliver or revise as set out here.

3. Okay.

4. Okay.

5. If it's *the publisher* who fails to publish within the time stated, the author can keep the advance and cancel the contract.

6. Royalties vary. This paragraph sets out your percentage of the *wholesale* price (the price the bookstore pays) under varying conditions. This is different than the more common royalties on the *list* price, the retail amount. It does *not* say if the book will be hardcover, trade or paper back.

7. Distinguish from 6 above. This lists the author/publisher percentages for a flat sale of different rights. It also picks up that foreign language right not covered above and goes into other miscellany.

8. The all-important *advance*! This is how much you'll get a) here when you deliver the manuscript; or b) under many contracts when you sign, though the manuscript is not completed. Question the word "completed." At what point is your manuscript "completed"?

1) You have to "make back the advance," i.e., the moneys advanced you are subtracted from the royalties owed you.

2) Many believe that the size of the advance demonstrates what effort the publisher plans to make to promote the book.

9. Accounting. Contracts vary and this is essential, so find a lawyer to translate the often creative accounting used by your publisher.

10. Payments. Good.

11. Okay.

12. Copyright. Very important. The publisher has agreed to preserve your exclusive rights as creator of the book by means of copyrighting it for you. (Up until publication you have a common law copyright.) You want to be sure the book (or other work) is copyrighted in *your* name *not* the publishers.

13. Warranty and Indemnity. This paragraph is going to be filled with legalese in just about any publisher's contract, so we'll sort out the clauses one by one.

a. Warrants and represents—means you promise and hold forth the following:

b. Sole creator—no plagiarism and no co-author. If there is, you need a signed agreement that the co-creator relinquishes all rights and acknowledges you as "sole" creator (or that this contract encompasses all creators of the work). You are also promising you haven't stolen this work from someone else.

c. Owns all rights—you haven't already sold, assigned or given away any rights such as to another publisher or that, for one reason or another, the rights belong to someone else.

d. Original creation except where you've needed to and have obtained permission from another—again relates to plagiarism. You have not in any way taken or reworked the work of a third party. You're also saying that this book of yours hasn't already been published.

e. Infringe copyrights, violate rights of privacy or libel—isn't necessarily as clear-cut as it seems. The infringement wouldn't necessarily mean plagiarism but could be inadvertent. This slides right into two biggies: the right of privacy and libel. (Note: this contract is pro-author in using "intentional." Check yours.) The publication of a letter from someone else to you would be considered violation of their right of privacy, for instance. Libel is writing which falsely damages a person's reputation, personal or business, or holds the person up to shame or ridicule. It can be negligent or intentional. Some statements are considered so damaging that they are "libel per se"* and damages are assumed and need not be proved. Don't do it.

f. Indemnify—the clause basically says that if, after the case goes to court is lost and appealed, you have breached these promises and the publisher has had to pay damages on account of that breach, you must pay out enough to cover all it has cost that publisher. You also agree to pay reasonable costs and attorney's fees. However, since this sentence relates back, I would say that in this particular contract you must pay these only if you did indeed breach a warranty. In many publishing contracts, you agree to the payment even without a breach on your part.

Note: if suit is brought—and before it's determined if it *is* your fault—the publisher can put half of what it owes you in escrow pending the outcome.

14. Artistic control is shared unless you can't agree. Then the publisher has the final say.

15. Okay.

16. Okay.

17. Revisions. This is clear English, but read carefully.

18. Okay.

19. If someone infringes on *your* copyright, you and the publisher can sue together and split any damages. Either of you can choose to go it alone.

20. Termination is as important as anything else. Each contract varies as to when each party shall have a right to terminate. This contract clearly recites the circumstances wherein the author shall have such a right and how it shall be enforced and what happens to the money.

21-23. Cover other contingencies with the most important being that you agree not to compete with your own work.

Caveat: And talk about compete! Some publishers are putting in a clause that you will work on nothing else until your work for the publisher is complete.

a. NOTE: the above contract did *not* have a section that is becoming increasingly popular with publishers. If you see it in your contract, beware! You are giving away all rights that might exist in the future but which no one can imagine now. In essence that clause is: "Seller grants to the Publisher English rights . . . (to) *all media now in existence or hereafter known or devised.*" Right now this phrase is usually in reference to electronic or cyberspace rights, but the wording is so broad you don't know what you're giving away or what it might be worth if it ever came into existence—and neither does the publisher! Strike this out of the contract.

Another publisher's clause floating around has you contract to sell the *idea* itself. This is particularly bad for those writing for periodicals and newspapers who frequently re-work an idea for different markets.

Q In my contract with the publisher, do I give up all my rights to my work?

A If you're submitting a piece of short fiction or nonfiction, mark it "First Rights Only" so that you have control over reprints, for instance. And see above where some publishers are demanding you give up rights to the *idea*. Look out!

If you're signing a contract on a book, check carefully as to what rights you're agreeing to give the publisher. Some do a blanket "all rights" or "primary and secondary rights." That means reprints, condensations, magazine excerpts and the biggies like paperback and book clubs. Try to negotiate *each* right. I say "try" because some publishers believe every word is writ in stone and won't want to change even if it's uninterested in some of those rights.

NOTE: in this contract, first rights to a *book* are in paragraph 1 and other rights are in paragraph 7 with different royalties.

NOTE ALSO: this contract grants the publisher the "exclusive right to publish, distribute, and sell the Work." Some publishing contracts throw in "license" which means you're granting the original publisher the right to license to another publisher. This could be interpreted as the right to sell another publisher mass market or paperback rights! Read carefully!

Q I wouldn't *really* have to give back my advance, would I?

A Yep. You agree that if your work isn't "reasonably" satisfactory, on time, or revised as directed, the publisher can—and usually will—demand a return of that advance. This is a business and you'd better abide by the terms of the contract.

Q I just quote a few lines from a song in my story. I don't have to go to the hassle of finding out who can give permission and then contacting the person and all that, do I?

A Yes.

Q The corporation closed down the division or imprint that was going to publish my book. Now what can I do?

A Write the legal department asking for a letter re-assigning all rights to you and canceling your licensing agreement.

a. If your book goes out of print, do the same thing and also ask for the plates.

b. If a periodical doesn't get around to publishing your work for an unreasonable time, write withdrawing any rights given them to your material.

c. Under the contract here, a "Duty to Publish" is set out along with what you can do if it's breached. Some publishers include a clause that all rights revert to the writer in case of bankruptcy, going out of business, or allowing the book to go out of print.

Q The way I read this contract, I'm not promising anything I don't do on purpose. Right?

A Right.

a. You promise the work is solely your original creation. You know that. (Side issues have already been discussed.)

b. Infringing on copyright is "iffy" in that you might unknowingly do that, but this is a remote scenario.

c. *To your knowledge* you don't violate the rights of privacy or libel another. This is an important phrase. If you're signing a contract that doesn't contain it, negotiate its insertion. What constitutes the "right of privacy" is difficult to pin down and might be inadvertently violated, so that you and your publisher were hauled into court—at your expense.

d. *Caveat*: many contracts make you responsible for costs and attorney fees even if the suit is groundless and you are not in breach of these warranties. Often you even agree to indemnify the publisher if it makes a settlement for an unjustified claim. Some of that language is:

Seller agrees to hold harmless and indemnify Publisher from any claims or suits (including costs, expenses, and reasonable attorneys' fees) arising out of a breach or *alleged* breach . . .

NOTE: even a "claim" without suit is a "gotcha" here. Often you're on the hook for those expenses, too, although your team wins in court.

Be sure this paragraph is worded so that you're only responsible for an actual breach—that "upon a finding in a court of law that the liability was incurred because of a breach of warranty by Author, Author will indemnify and hold harmless Publisher . . ."

Q If I change a person's name in my book, she can't sue me for libel can she?

A Yep. If the person could be identified in a reasonable fashion and you hold that person up to ridicule, scorn or accusation, that name change and other attempts to disguise, will not protect you from a libel suit—and its loss. Truth is a complete defense, but . . .

Q My contract doesn't say anything about travel expenses for when I hit the road to promote my book. How much is the publisher obliged to pay?

A Nothing. If your contract promises no travel reimbursement, you're out of luck. Today's custom is for the author to foot the bill.

Q How much publicity will the publisher provide?

A That depends on the publisher and on what you can get included in the contract. Payments for promotional tours, displays in book stores, ads in the New York Times? Get it spelled out.

Q Is it okay for me to try to sell a chapter of my book to a magazine?

A No. Unless you have an exceedingly liberal contract with your publisher, your contract would prohibit that. On the other hand, your publisher might *want* a chapter sold as part of the promotion.

Intellectual Property Law

The history of protecting intellectual properties goes back to the 15th century. Gutenberg had invented printing and shortly thereafter not only Bibles but also secular books were available to the people. The City of Venice, followed by others, began granting the privilege to print a book. Copyright.

In 1886 the Berne Convention was held for the Protection of Literary and Artistic Works. It adopted the European view that copyrights exist to protect the author. The opposite view is taken by others including England and the United States. This view is that the public interest is paramount and that the author should have no more protection than is needed to induce him or her to create—a position codified in the Copyright Convention in Geneva in 1952.

From the early days of this country, the U.S. has held that a creation carries a kind of property right. Between 1783 and 1789, all but one of the new 13 states passed some form of copyright law. It took until 1909 to enact the all-encompassing one we had until 1978. That law changed a number of things, the most important of which was to extend the life of copyrighted material so that the protection lasts until 50 years after the death of the author.

Although the publisher normally does it for you, it is your responsibility to copyright your material. To do this you must send to the Copyright Office in Washington, D.C. (see phone number at the end of this chapter) an application for registration, two copies of your work, and a fee. It is very important to note that you have copyright protection by giving notice of your copyright. This is done by displaying "on the title page or the page immediately following" the word Copyright, the abbreviation Copr., or the symbol © (c in a circle), accompanied by the year, and your name.

As cyberspace and other forms of "publication" develop, the copyright laws will require revision. Presently, material in permanent form can be protected: tape recordings, computer discs, film and so on. Paintings and other works of art are included in copyright protection. When you create any artistic work *in fixed form*, it immediately becomes your property. You have the *exclusive right* to distribution and display, and also to make derivative works such as prints.

No action is necessary to secure this common law copyright, no publication or registration. Included are written, dramatic, musical, and artistic creations. However, registration may be required for protection, e.g., bringing action for copyright infringement. The future holds an array of possibilities for the display of original work and a creator who will need protection.

Q I worry about sending my manuscript to all these places. Can someone just steal my idea?

A Well, you get a "Yes and No" answer. Ideas cannot be copyrighted.
On the other hand, your work has what's called a "common law copyright" until it's published—your words become your property as soon as you create them, whether they flow from your pen tip, your typewriter, or keyboard. Once a work is published, the law requires you to have that statutory copyright described above. The common law copyright is cancelled out by the statutory.

I advise clients to give notice of their common law copyright by putting the "c in a circle" (©), date and name. In England and other countries they assert "a moral right."

Q Just what is plagiarism anyway?

A The word "plagiarism " comes from the Latin word "plagiarius" meaning kidnapper or abductor. It was used by a writer in ancient times, Marcus Valerius Martial, a Roman born in 38 AD. He said that a fellow poet who had claimed to be the author of Martial's poems was a plagiarius, an abductor of his poems, which were like freed slaves.

Plagiarism means about the same thing these days, stealing the work of someone else. And when the work is protected, that's copyright infringement.

Q What's the point if I can't copyright my ideas?

A Well, one point is that there are said to be a very limited number of plots in the world and if they could have been copyrighted, you would be out in the cold. What you copyright is the (one hopes) unique way you put words together—or paint on a canvas—or make music—and more. Even that speech you make *about* those ideas can be copyrighted if you're speaking from notes or recording it.

Q What's this public domain I hear about? Like some golden oldies are in the public domain?

A If a work has fallen into "public domain" that means anyone can use it without infringing a copyright or owing a royalty. A creation can be in the public domain as the result of a number of happenings: the copyright ran out; the work was never copyrighted; those steps the Copyright Act requires were not followed.

Q I put two chapters of my novel on the Internet for criticism by a writing group. Have I lost my right to copyright?

A I don't think so. There's not enough case law for a definitive answer, but going by copyright law I'd say you retain your common law copyright and that upon "publication" you can register your statutory copyright. This is where the law needs updating. It is illogical that a work could be exposed to millions and not be "published" but a booklet handed out to a few friends would be. I'm also including intent in my answer. You did not "intend" to "publish" your book on the Internet but were simply soliciting criticism, much the same as if you took the pages to your writer's group and asked for input.

Q A man flat out stole whole pages of my novel and published them as part of his. I have a copyright. If this is copyright infringement, what happens next?

A You sue. Your right will get all messed up if you let your material float around out there without doing anything. You need to bring an injunction to prevent further sales of the plagiarist's book and a suit for damages.

Copyright office phone number with a menu as to information, registration and forms: 202-707-3000. For fax-on-demand of brochures and such: 202-707-2600. The Copyright Office homepage with links from there is www.loc.gov/copyright.

CHAPTER X

When All Is Said and Done

When human beings come together in tribes and form a social contract, humanity has laws. These laws may be decrees of a witch doctor as to what is taboo; they may be dictated by custom; they may be established by democratic legislation; but laws they are. That we agree together to abide by the rule of law is the social contract.

In the early development of English common law, on which our jurisprudence is based, suits could be brought only if the facts came within a limited number of petitions called the "King's Writs."

The next development was to create Courts of Chancery, which were for all of those cases that could not be squashed and shaped into one of the King's Writs. The Chancellor of the court sat on a wool sack and sniffed a posy to protect him from the smell of the people. Today the law is for your use and you are constitutionally guaranteed "due process of law."

The most popular misconceptions of law that I've seen in thirty years' practice are:

1. "If you pay your creditors one dollar a month, they can't touch you." Wrong.

2. "If you disinherit someone, you must leave that person one dollar in your will." Wrong.

3. "I'll garnishee him!" "Garnishee" is not a verb, but means the person who is in debt to your debtor. Also, your debtor can only be garnished after a judgment has been secured.

4. "I had it notarized!" Not magic.

5. One of the most popular misconceptions is also the most dangerous: "legal technicality." Usually when this expression is used, the

"legal technicality" in question is a violation of an important constitutional guarantee. It protects you from the rack and thumb-screw, from the midnight knock, and from being convicted by an ex-post facto law for having been a Girl Scout at age twelve or a Democrat at age twenty-two.

6. Your barber and brother-in-law *always* know better than your attorney and *always* "have a friend who . . ." *Don't* believe them!

I hear you muttering it's easy for me to say, "Read that contract." Just try doing it when some man is drumming his fingers on the desk or some woman is tapping her nails! Well, I hope I've made it possible for you to stick to your guns. A bargain that's so great it must be agreed to *now* is usually no bargain at all. After reading *Sign Here* you know your rights. You know something about the law. You know enough to tell that drummer or tapper, "Hey, wait a minute. I want to read this" or "I'll take this contract home to go over it."

You understand now that contract shoved at you isn't in secret code. You *can* understand it. Put down that pen. Pick up the contract to read it. Make me proud of you! Only then will you *sign there*!

Finally, one other statement I've been hearing for three decades.

Q There ought to be a law.
A There probably is.

Glossary

A

abstract—history of title of land; every recorded conveyance or encumbrance that might possibly affect purchase

accelerate—to speed up the due date of an installment loan; to demand the balance paid in full

adjuster—one who estimates or figures the amount of damage done to a person or thing for an insurance company

adverse possession—rights acquired by a person or persons illegally on or in possession of property without the permission of the owner

annul—to void or cancel out

annulment—the voiding of a marriage; differs from divorce or dissolution in that a marriage that is annulled becomes as if it had never been

answer—response filed by the defendant in a lawsuit to the charges or allegations in the complaint or petition filed by the plaintiff

antenuptial agreement—a contract prior to marriage to establish each party's rights pertaining to assets and debts

anticipatory breach—an act done before performance due on a contract, which has the effect of nonperformance or breach of contract

apparent authority—allowing an agent to perform such acts—hold himself out in such a manner—that the principal is bound as if the agent had real authority

appeal—asking a higher court to change or reverse what a lower court has done or ordered

appellant—the one doing the appealing

appellate court—a court with jurisdiction to review a lower or trial court

attachment or attach—taking property into custody by legal means; this can be before suit to force a person into court, or after suit to satisfy a judgment

attorney in fact—one who has power of attorney for another, is *not* necessarily an attorney

avoidance—defense of insurer that it needn't pay because of acts of the insured

B

barrister—in England, an attorney qualified to try cases, as opposed to a "solicitor," who does not

bilateral—both sides; a "bilateral" mistake means a mistake by both parties

binder—temporary verbal or written insurance coverage prior to issuance of the policy

breach—break

breach of contract—failure, without legal excuse, by one party to a contract to carry out or fulfill the terms of the agreement

brief—a written document, usually arguing the law to a court, as an appellant's brief or a trial brief

Bulk Sales Act—requirements having to do with a business that intends to sell or transfer its entire inventory

C

calendar—court's list of when case is to be tried, or a motion heard, etc.; docket

capacity—see "legal capacity"

caveat—warning

caveat emptor—Latin for "let the buyer beware"

cf.—a Latin term meaning "compare"; directs the reader to another part of the book or to an explanatory or contrasting view or case

chain of title—the record of the transfers of the title to a certain piece of property and the names of those involved, the grantors and grantees

challenge—removal of a juror from deliberating on a case. Can be "preemptory" (without legal cause) or "for cause" (juror cannot fairly judge the case)

charitable immunity—doctrine that a nonprofit organization, such as a hospital, cannot be sued

chattel—a thing; personal property as contrasted to real property

civil—relating to rights, duties, and legal actions that do not fall into the "criminal" category

cloud on the title—a claim that could be a defect in the title, such as a mortgage not marked as paid

collateral—property put up to secure a loan, which can be taken if borrower defaults in payment

color of title—such things, as paying taxes, associated with ownership of property, demanded by some states if one is to acquire adverse possession

common law—from England, the great body of principles recognized as the civil law in most of the United States—distinct from statutory law

community property—property held by spouses in a marriage in a community property state

competent—legally able to contract or testify in court

condition precedent—a condition that must be fulfilled before a contract will exist or come into being

condition subsequent—a condition to be performed after a contract is in effect which is required by the terms, such as notifying the insurer of an accident claim within a certain number of days

consideration—that which binds a bargain, such as money or an exchange of promises consortium—the right of each spouse to the affection and services of the other

consortium—right to spouse's company and support

constructive eviction—acts or conditions such that a person is legally considered to be evicted

contempt of court—any act in defiance of a rule or order of a court, or which hinders justice, or causes loss of dignity to the court

contested—fought against, as in "contested divorce"; the opposing side will make an appearance and not let the matter go by default

contingency fee—an attorney's fee based on a percentage of the money recovered, as in a damage suit

costs—here pertaining to the expenses of a lawsuit, such as filing fee and service

court reporter—person qualified to record every word of testimony in court, hearings, depositions, etc.

coverage—what is covered, i.e., insured, by your insurance policy

cross-examine—to question the witness appearing and testifying for the opposing party

D

damages—that sum of money which will compensate the injured party for his loss

deductible—amount of money insured must pay before the insurance company owes anything

default—to fail to do what one is obliged to do; to default on a note is to fail to pay when due; when a case "goes by default," the losing party has failed either to appear or to answer the complaint

deposition—answers to verbal questions under oath before a court reporter

detrimental reliance—being put in a worse position because of relying on another's statements or promises

devise (noun or verb)—to leave, or what is left, by a will (technically refers only to real property)

disability—see "legal disability"

discovery—the process before trial to enable each party to a lawsuit to determine as much as possible about the other's suit or defense, as by interrogatories (written questions that must be answered) and depositions

dissolution (divorce)—the severance of marriage without fault—with petitioner and respondent instead of plaintiff and defendent

docket—the court calendar setting times for hearings, trials, etc.

double indemnity—provision in a life insurance policy paying twice the face amount under the circumstance of death by accident

dower rights—rights to property acquired by virtue of marriage—historically, widow only

durable power of attorney—see power of attorney

E

easement—a right to pass over or take from the land, but not an interest in the land itself; an incorporeal hereditament

easement of necessity—a right to pass over the property of another (as the original owner of the whole parcel) when that is the only means of ingress and egress (travel in and out)

eminent domain—right of a public body to take private land for public use, but still with due process of law

encumbrance—any charge, lien, or liability against a piece of property

endorsement—see "rider"

entirety—term used to indicate married persons' joint ownership of property, if not "community property"

escheat—forfeiture of lands back to the state

estate—(1) the extent of a person's interest in real property, as an "estate for years" or a "fee simple estate"; (2) all of one's assets of every kind, as in "I give, devise, and bequeath all of my estate," although disapproved by some courts as having no legal meaning

et seq.—Latin abbreviation meaning "and following"; for example, a reference to "page 8 et seq"

exclusions—here used to mean what an insurance policy does *not* cover

execute—(1) to sign a document, making it effective; (2) to put into effect a judgment; for example, one can execute on a judgment by attaching property

exposure—amount of damages one might be forced to pay; extent of liability

express—the terms of a contract that are spelled out (opposite of implied)

F

fault—refers to the one (the party at fault) upon whom legal responsibility for a wrong may be placed

fee simple—the largest estate in real property, the closest one can come to owning real estate outright

fixture—something by usage or so attached to real property that it cannot be removed without damage, or contracted to be treated as a "fixture," such as wall-to-wall carpeting

fraud—an intentional misrepresentation of a fact that another individual will act upon to his detriment and is meant to do so

G

garnish (verb), garnishment (noun)—to withhold, or the withholding of, wages or moneys due, to apply to a debt owed a third party, the judgment creditor

give notice—often used in a context denoting "required," as when furnishing another party with information about the occurrence of an event or an intention to take certain action; for example, to give notice of eviction, give notice of a loss and insurance claim. Recording a mortgage "gives notice" to all of that encumbrance

grace period—the additional time an insurance policy remains in force after a premium is due; can apply to other debts

grantor, grantee—the one transferring title and the one to whom it's being transferred, as in seller and buyer

grounds—legal reasons

guarantee—promise to make good, see warranty

guardian ad litem—Latin for "guardian for purpose of suit," one whom the court appoints to protect a minor's interests

H

higher court—a court further up the hierarchy with jurisdiction to review and change the actions of a lower court; when a case is appealed from a trial court to a court of appeals, the latter is the "higher court"

I

implied contract—an agreement "implied" or invented by a court when fairness demands it

implied warranty—a legal addition to the terms of a contract that certain unexpressed promises or "warranties"—such as safety, fitness for use—are part of the terms of a sale

incompetent—legally impaired and thus not able to contract (a variety of degrees not used here)

incorporeal hereditaments—inheritable interests that are "without body" (incorporeal); for example, an easement is an interest pertaining to land but *not* an interest *in* the land

injunction—a prohibition; a court order to refrain from a particular course of conduct

in re—Latin, meaning "in the matter of, in regards to, as to"

instructions—rules of how and what to consider, read or given by a judge to a jury prior to its deliberation

insurable interest—sufficient interest in the object of the insurance as to prevent it from being a mere wager

insured—person covered by insurance

insurer—the company doing the insuring

intentional tort—a wrong (tort) done on purpose, for example, battery, as contrasted to "negligence," which is a "tort" but not an intentional one

interrogatories—written questions to other side in a law suit

J

joint tenant—holding an undivided interest in the whole, with another person, with right of survivorship

judgment—the decision of a court as to the merits of the claims of the parties (here)

jurisdiction—a court's power over the parties and subject matter of a suit

jurisprudence—the philosophy of the laws that bind society

jury panel—the group called to jury duty from which the actual jury is picked to hear a case

L

legal capacity—the legal capacity to contract required of the contracting parties, who must not be laboring under a disability such as being an unemancipated minor

legal description—the exact boundaries of a piece of property, measured in "metes and bounds" or "degrees and minutes"

legal disability—lack of the capacity to contract

lemon law—rule that after a set number of attempts to repair, a vehicle must be replaced or reimbursement made

lessor, lessee—one giving the lease, other renting

liable, liability—subject to being held responsible for, or the responsibility for, a wrong, as for breach of contract or damage to a person or thing

lien—a hold on property (real or personal) for a debt due

life estate—comparable to ownership of property but limited to the lifetime of the person being given a life estate

limits of liability—when used as an insurance term, the extent, the dollar figure, for which the insurer will be responsible upon the happening of the risk insured against

local counsel—an attorney authorized to practice law in the jurisdiction where the case is being tried

long-arm statutes—laws pertaining to particular situations wherein a person outside the state can be made to appear there, for example, a resident of New York having an auto accident in Missouri can be sued in Missouri through its "long arm" statute

M

material fact—effecting the outcome

matter of record—anything filed or held in the records of a court or body such as a county. The complaint filed in a lawsuit becomes a "matter of record"; a deed filed with the county clerk is a "matter of record," and as such, provides notice

mechanic's lien—a statutory lien on a building for work or material furnished in the erection or repair of the structure

medical or med. pay—medical expense coverage without regard to fault

merchantable—saleable and fit for the intended use

merchantable title—good or clear title with no defects not bargained for

minor—under age, generally not able to contract

motion—a request, usually in writing, in the course of a lawsuit asking the court to take or allow a certain action; for example, a "Motion to Dismiss" asks the judge to throw out a case; a "Motion for Extension of Time" asks a judge for more time in which to file, say, an answer

N

negligence—falling below the standard of care exercised by a reasonable person

next friend—one who brings suit on behalf of a minor

notice—often used in a formal sense of communicating information by a required means (as in "notice in writing") when one party has a right to receive it and the other a duty to convey it

nuisance—can be "public" or "private"; a public nuisance affects an indefinite number of persons, such as those living within range of noxious fumes; a private nuisance endangers or interferes with the enjoyment of one's property

O

option—a right to buy a piece of property in the future

oral contract—a contract not in writing and, therefore, not enforced under certain conditions; for example, a contract for the sale of land

P

parol—in relation to contracts, extraneous, outside the written terms, verbal

partition—division by a court of jointly held property

party in interest—one with a legally recognized interest in the outcome of a lawsuit

petition—or "complaint"; the document that begins a lawsuit, setting out what wrongs the plaintiff claims were done to him by the defendant

pleadings—the various documents filed in court that make up the written body of a lawsuit

power of attorney (durable)—the right given another to act on behalf of the donor of the power—lasting

precedent—a case setting forth the law on a particular legal point, which other courts will follow in deciding the same or a similar legal issue—an important concept in our law

privilege—here, as in "privileged communications," disclosure of which cannot be demanded

privity of contract—concept comparable to tracing blood lines in a family tree, the idea being that a manufacturer or producer cannot be sued for a defect in goods unless the person damaged by the defect has a contractual relationship with him. This concept is fast becoming history because the courts no longer hold that there must be "privity of contract" between the plaintiff and defendant where previously there had to be this contractual link

proofs of loss—evidence, such as original purchase receipts, that must be furnished an insurance company to prove the extent of the loss claimed

publication—the publishing of certain required notice to a party in an approved manner, such as notice of probate in an approved newspaper a certain number of times

Q

quitclaim deed—a deed that conveys only what interests a person actually has, with no promises or warranties as to the extent of that interest

R

real property—the land and what is attached thereto; real estate

record (noun)—the body of proceedings, e.g., the trial record

record (verb)—to place on file with the proper governmental unit; for example, to "record" a deed with the county clerk

release (noun or verb)—the agreement that, or to agree that, a person or legal entity shall be liable no longer and for which agreement consideration is received, as when signing a "release" in exchange for reimbursement for a loss

reply (noun or verb)—in a lawsuit, the response to, or to respond to, the "answer"—the petition is followed by the answer, which is, sometimes, then responded to by means of a "reply." Also, in the appeal process, the appellant's last written word is a reply.

retainer—a fee requested by an attorney, usually prior to his undertaking to represent the client

rider or endorsement—a specially designed addition to a standard insurance policy. Can be additions or subtractions; i.e., a "fine arts rider" adds to your coverage; a title insurance endorsement subtracts

S

secured or unsecured debt—a debt with or without collateral

seisin—ancient concept of title plus possession plus something more (real property law)

service, serving—most often means handing a summons to the person being "served"; "service by publication" is by means of a newspaper and other statutory ways of giving notice allowable in certain defined cases

settlement, settle—often means the agreement between the parties to a lawsuit, making trial (or continuance of a trial) unnecessary

solicitor—English attorney who does not make court appearances

specific performance—making one do exactly what has been contracted for, as, for example, conveying the land specified in a real estate contract, because monetary damages are considered to be an unacceptable substitute where the object contracted for is unique

statute—a law enacted by a legislature as opposed to common law. Technically means a state law as contrasted to ordinance (city) and act (federal)

Statute of Frauds—the name of an old English law that certain contracts had to be in writing and signed by the party against whom they were to be enforced

statute of limitations, limitation of actions—specifies the amount of time, with certain exceptions, within which a lawsuit must be brought; for example, a state statute may declare that a negligence action must be filed within five years

strict liability—a doctrine wherein proof of injury or damage is enough to make a case without proof of negligence

substantial performance—enough work performed (though not complete) that a court will enforce at least partial payment or that action which takes a contract out of Statute of Frauds

T

tenant in common—co-owner of a piece of property but one whose interest(s) may be in different amounts and who, as distinguished from a "joint tenant," can separate out his piece and does not have right of survivorship

terms—rights and duties of each party to a contract

tort—a legally recognized wrong

U

undivided interest—an interest in the whole piece while not owning it all

undue influence—a wrongful psychological advantage; the wrongful substitution of the will of another so that a party is not acting freely of his own accord

underinsured—insured but insufficiently—same rules as for uninsured motorist coverage

unemancipated minor—a minor unable to contract and for whom a parent or parents is (are) still responsible; not married or working independently

uniform—used herein as pertaining to "uniform" laws which each state may adopt or not, as its legislature determines, but which make the law on a certain issue "uniform" in the states adopting it

Uniform Commercial Code (UCC)—a body of provisions dealing with and regulating commercial transactions

Uniform Consumer Credit Code—a body of provisions designed to protect consumers in their credit transactions, including borrowing money

unilateral—on one side only

unjust enrichment—unfair benefiting of one side of a transaction

V

void—of no legal effect

voidable—a contract or transaction that can be set aside or "voided," but is in force until a court sets it aside

voir dire—Latin, meaning literally "to see, to speak," but used to mean the qualifying questions asked of prospective jurors

W

waiver—knowing relinquishment of a right; for example, "waiver of default" is not holding one party to the provisions of a contract regarding default

warranty—a promise or guarantee

warranty deed—a deed that "warrants" or guarantees a set of conditions; one such is a "warranty of title" that the grantor (seller) is conveying good title without defects

word of art—a word having a particular legal meaning

wrongful death—a statute allowing beneficiaries to sue for damages from the one causing the death of, for instance, their father

Index

A

abstract 71, 172, 176
  defined 71
abuse in collecting debt 218
acceleration of debt 208-209, 223
acceptance
  definition of 3, 10
  on trial basis 11
accident
  in parking lot 85
  insurance definition 69
accident insurance 78-79
  advertising of 46
admission of a past crime 267
adoption 124
  consent of parent 125
  open 125
  process 125
advance
  to author 295, 298
adverse possession 72, 177
advertising
  accident insurance 46
  by attorneys 260
  deceptive 147-148
  free gift with purchase 6, 147
age
  lying about 78, 89
age of majority
  by state 20
agent, literary
  duty to author 287
  percentage of royalties 286
  reading fees 283
  submission guidelines 281-282
alimony 135, 139
"All Sales Final" 148

Alzheimer's disease
  and competency 21
American Bar Association 258
annual percentage rate 212, 223
annulment 112, 117
  grounds for 118
antenuptial (prenuptial) agreements
  114-115
appeal 277
appraisal 84
arbitration 23
architect
  performance of contract 29
  plans approved by client 19
artist
  contract with gallery 287
"As is" 155
attorney 255
  advertising 260
  as officer of the court 258
  bad debt turned over to 232
  confidential communication 267
  contingency fee 265
  contract with 266, 268
  definition of 259
  duty to client 257
  fees 263-264
  finding 259-260
  lying to 261
  malpractice against 268-270
  withdrawal from case 271
attorney-client relationship 261, 267,
  270
auction
  with reserve 7
auto insurance 55, 73, 85
  collision coverage 58-59
  liability coverage 57-58
  medical pay 59
  risk 72
  theft 60
  uninsured and underinsured 59
automobile warranties 151

Order Form

Order additional copies of *Sign Here* for your friends, colleagues, and relatives, or for classroom use.

Call 1-800-996-9783 to order by credit card.

Or copy and mail this form to: Columbine Books, P.O. Box 456, Angel Fire, NM 87710

Name _____

Company _____

Address _____

City, ST, Zip _____

Daytime phone _____

_____ copies of *Sign Here* at $18.95 each _____
Shipping $3.00 for first book, $1.00 each additional _____
NM residents add $1.18 tax per book _____
Total _____

Payment: _____ Check _____ MasterCard or Visa

Card # _____

Exp Date _____ Signature _____

Or call 1-800-996-9783 to order now by credit card.
Ask about our quantity discounts on orders of 5 copies or more
Visit our web site at: www.intriguepress.com/signhere